The Effect

– where science meets spirituality

Linda Hoy

...concerning the disappearing rabbit, the vanishing cat, the dimension-hopping goldfish and the groundmuts who found they had legs.

The Effect

– where science meets spirituality

Linda Hoy

...concerning the disappearing rabbit, the vanishing cat, the dimension-hopping goldfish and the groundmuts who found they had legs.

BOOKS

Winchester, UK
Washington, USA

First published by O-Books, 2012
O-Books is an imprint of John Hunt Publishing Ltd., Laurel House, Station Approach,
Alresford, Hants, SO24 9JH, UK
office1@o-books.net
www.o-books.com

For distributor details and how to order please visit the 'Ordering' section on our website.

Text copyright: Linda Hoy 2011

ISBN: 978 1 84694 906 7

A CIP catalogue record for this book is available from the British Library.

Design: Stuart Davies

Printed and bound by CPI Group (UK) Ltd, Croydon, CR0 4YY

We operate a distinctive and ethical publishing philosophy in all
areas of our business, from our global network of authors to
production and worldwide distribution.

CONTENTS

"How do you know I'm mad?" said Alice.
"You must be, said the cat, "or you wouldn't have come here."

Introduction: Chasing the white rabbit: *Adventures first....*   1

Chapter 1: Plato's cave and puppets: *You are old, Father William...*   6

Chapter 2: Quakers and the ministry of silence: *They all thought in chorus*   19

Chapter 3: Inside the looking-glass *Let's pretend there's a way of getting through...*   27

Chapter 4: Near-death experience: *The flame of a candle after the flame is blown out*   35

Chapter 5: The search for dark matter: *Down the rabbit hole.*   55

Chapter 6: Creativity *It Writes all manner of things that I don't intend.*   65

Chapter 7: Precognitive Dreams *The effect of living backwards.*   82

Chapter 8: Time and The Dark Arts: *The Mad Hatter's tea party*   98

Chapter 9: DreamTime: *Finding the key*   121

Chapter 10: Entanglement: *Tweedledum and Tweedledee*   135

Chapter 11: Love: the double doorway. *Joining on Again.*   148

Chapter 12: Multiple universe theory. *Believing six impossible things before breakfast*   165

Chapter 13: Groundhog Days: *More like a corkscrew than a path*   179

Chapter 14: The Control Centre: *To be a queen!*   197

Chapter 15: Momento Mori: *Always Teatime*   221

Chapter 16: End-of-Life: *The Cheshire Cat*   229

Chapter 17: Conclusion: *Fan her head*   242

Acknowledgements

I would like to thank everyone who's supported this project. In particular, Steve Cook from the Royal Literary Fund who had the foresight to place me as a writing fellow in a science department, without which this book would never have been written. Thanks also to Tim Birkhead and others in Sheffield University's Department of Animal and Plant Science who welcomed me into their midst. I am also grateful to Sheffield University's Physics Department and particularly to Sean Paling and to Bernard McLuskey who opened my eyes to the wonders of dark matter.

I am indebted to other writers involved in the Royal Literary Fund's fellowship scheme, in particular, Briane Keane and Anne Rooney who shared their writing experience with me.

For my spiritual grounding and guidance, I owe an enormous debt of gratitude to the Sheffield Quaker Meeting and sincerely hope its many Friends will be tolerant of the liberties I've taken with describing their activities. I'm particularly grateful to Philip Hunt for the account he dictated to me of the last moments of Eleanor's life.

I must also thank Harold Mitchell for introducing me to the Scientific and Medical Network and providing me with all the right books just when I needed them and to Max Payne and his wife, Mary, for hosting our discussions; also Elizabeth and Peter Fenwick for allowing me so much use of their material.

Thanks to Bevan Hoy for all his helpful advice, to Liz Hoy for providing the account of her daughter's illness and my daughter, Mikita Brottman for sharing her manuscript: Phantoms of the Clinic. Special thanks to my agent, Robert Dudley for having faith in such an outlandish project. And most of all, to my son, Marcus, for devoting so much time to the text and having faith in its possibilities.

Linda Hoy, Sheffield 2011

Adventures first. Explanations take such a dreadful time...
Alice in Wonderland: Chapter Ten.

When Alice was sitting on a grassy bank one day, wondering whether to thread a daisy chain, she saw a white rabbit with a waistcoat and a pocket watch, mumbling to himself that he was late. She could have decided that, as a talking white rabbit with a pocket watch had no place in the normal scientific order, she must have been mistaken. But she didn't. She stood up. The white rabbit disappeared. And there are those who say that when something cannot be seen and touched and heard, it ceases to exist.

But Alice didn't think like that. She did something courageous and adventurous and scary and followed the white rabbit. When he disappeared inside a rabbit hole, Alice took a gigantic leap into the darkness and went with him. Tumbling down the rabbit hole, she encountered a whole new level of existence where the laws of physics were turned upside down, shaken inside out and taken to the cleaners.

In order to take this flying leap inside the rabbit hole, we first have to wipe the screen. We have to open our minds to the prospect that the impossible might be possible; that weird and wonderful things can happen but only to those who have the courage to explore. We have to accept that there might be more to life than our parents and teachers ever taught us; that what we've been told were answers were really no more than strands of barbed wire stretched across the openings they didn't want us to explore.

So, welcome to the journey that will turn your view of life on its head, shred it through the blender and spit it out like magic beans. Welcome to The Effect, the journey of a lifetime.

Or two.

Introduction

Chasing the White Rabbit

There are some subjects I've been advised to avoid like the plague:

- Plague
- Cancer
- Death
- Angels

And if I ever want anyone to read a book about popular science:

- Quantum physics.

So, I've just erased the section explaining how, as my mother died from cancer over thirty years ago, I found myself accosted by twenty seven angels and began searching for an explanation in the realms of quantum physics. .

In those days I wasn't just an atheist, but a fundamentalist, evangelical born-again atheist with no intention of changing my philosophy to incorporate a platoon of flying phantoms. Angels were not for the sussed and skeptical like me; but the woolly-minded, gullible and those two strings short of the full harp.

However...

Such weird events continued. I'd recently launched a career as an author of books for young people and each new piece of fiction became surrounded by coincidence, a strange sense that the words were already written and my task was simply that of brushing the dust from the surface. It became quite normal to know exactly when a friend would phone or even what they were about to say. Episodes of déjà vu occurred several times a week or even daily and events I'd witnessed in my dreams the night before had a way of turning up the following day.

I knew time only flowed one way; I knew my books weren't cobbled together from stuff I'd read before, yet I also knew that these events were the most important thing, maybe the only thing that had ever really happened to me. I felt as though I were being led. Being led to where, of course, I didn't have a clue. I felt increasingly that I was chasing after a white rabbit and tumbling down a rabbit hole where the laws of physics had been swallowed by a large black hole. The events appeared to answer the question most frequently asked by children on my author visits into schools: *Where do your ideas come from?* I never had a clue where ideas came from but began to suspect that they came out of a rabbit hole as well. And yet, throughout all this, I clung on to my skepticism like a drowning angel grasping a straw boater, believing that, unlikely as it seemed, there had to be some sensible explanation.

To my credit, lessons in school science had drizzled by me like a Pennine fog. I was the one on the back row, painting my nails and leafing through rock magazines as the teacher struggled to explain Newtonian physics. I say *to my credit*, because I never paid enough attention to learn that all these strange events simply weren't allowed to happen. Instead, I simply began to think: *What if?*

- *What if...* ours is not the only universe..? What if other dimensions exist around us? Other worlds of which we can only catch the occasional glimpse
- *What if...* we're not all as separate as we look, but what if our minds or souls are linked together on some strange invisible level..?
- *What if...* time is not a straight line but a spiral? Or what if it's a double helix? What if the future in some strange way,

has already happened? And what if it's possible for us to transcend time and space so we can glimpse our possible futures and select the ones we want?

My friends with science degrees rolled their eyes and scoffed. They were the ones who'd not only been paying attention but taking notes and drawing diagrams in Physics. It didn't occur to them to think, as we say nowadays, "outside the box" – or, as I've come to call it, outside the boxing ring – because what "the box" means all too often is a couple of scientific contenders fighting for their corner.

And then the great day dawned when I discovered the new physics which not only accepts the existence of all these weird phenomena, but sees them as the gateway to the theory of everything – of finally piecing our knowledge of the universe together. I discovered that Einstein himself formulated the concept that time is not a straight line but curved, the leading scientist, Bohm, deduced that all of us are connected like the sea inside a wave and Everett's multiple universe theory suggests a multitude of dimensions existing alongside ours.

So although all I knew at the time about science could have been written on the back of a postage stamp and still left room for the glue, I began reading books on physics. I immersed myself in a multiverse of universes, strings, super-symmetry, dark matter and black holes. I studied textbooks covered with equations, graphs and formulae and yet, though intrigued, kept thinking all these scientists had somehow missed a trick. Without recourse to calculations or teams of workers in labs, I'd reached the same conclusions. Not only that, but I'd embarked upon a whole new level of existence – I'd seen the future, hopped inside other people's minds and found ways of escaping what scientists call our time-space continuum. Like reaching some new level in a computer game and finding that I'd grown wings, I felt uplifted.

So, if we really are surrounded by a multiverse of universes, why should science and the spiritual always live light years apart?

One of the most important recent scientific breakthroughs has resulted from the integration of cosmology and quantum physics: Stephen Hawking, among others, has used our understanding of how tiny particles work to unravel the mystery of black holes and shed light upon the origins of the universe.

The time has come to make similar links between science and the spiritual. At the moment there is plenty of stuff we simply do not understand. Yet not knowing can be a strength. Admitting that we do not know is like a plain white sheet of paper waiting for a story or the relationship between two people who've yet to take each other by the hand. The first title that I gave my book was Groping in the Dark, assuming I was hacking a path through undergrowth, exploring virgin territory.

But I was wrong.

As I began more reading, I found that other minds, far greater than mine, had hacked this path before me. Plato in Ancient Greece, for starters. The Nobel-prizewinning physicist, Wolfgang Pauli, disturbed by the way in which his presence in a lab would cause glass apparatus to explode, consulted Carl Jung, the great psychiatrist and the two of them went on to discuss the strange relationship between mind and matter. The Yorkshire novelist and playwright, J.B.Priestley, author of An Inspector Calls, became obsessed with time flowing backwards. And the most unlikely candidate I encountered, John Dunne, an aeronautical engineer writing in the nineteen twenties spent much of his life trying to discover why time, as he put it, *got mixed up.*

Dunne, a down-to-earth, practical man who experienced vivid dreams with a habit of coming true, became obsessed with trying to work out mathematically how this could come about. And might it be possible, he thought, to see into the future at times other than when we're asleep? And was this just his own idiosyncratic talent or could he teach it to anyone else?

He found the answer was Yes. And Yes. The books Dunne wrote in the nineteen twenties and thirties describing his time-travel techniques also suggested that it's possible for us to live our lives again in a series of Groundhog Days. His books sold in their tens of thousands. People enthused about his theories until after the second-world war when, for those who'd survived its horrors, the excitement of living one's life again took something of a nosedive; Dunne's *Experiment with Time* went out of fashion like a gas mask. However, his basic theories were sound. And I've filched my title from his description of how all of us can position ourselves to explore the other dimensions he claimed existed all around us.

He called it The Effect.

Chapter 1

Plato and puppets

"You are old, Father William," the young man said
"And your hair has become very white
And yet you incessantly stand on your head.
Do you think at your age it is right?"
Alice's Adventures in Wonderland, Chapter Five

My mother, Dorothy, was obsessed with puppets. I never found out why. First there were finger puppets, sewn from scraps of felt with cotton-thread noses and tiny pearl buttons for eyes; then there were old shoe boxes, painted and decorated with slits in the sides for cardboard characters to be threaded through and bounced about on strips of card. Later, there was a makeshift puppet theatre and two marionettes; but, as a six-year-old, having quite a few years to go before discovering *Waiting for Godot* and other plays by Samuel Becket, I have to confess, I found the crossed wires, endless entanglements and repetitive movements no inspiration at all for making up a story.

Many years later, my mother read in the local newspaper about a team of puppeteers wanting a helping hand. I remember her description of her first encounter with the shock-headed puppet-master, Father William, who opened the door to a rambling, Gothic mansion, led her inside and then, somewhat unexpectedly, showed her an altar and shrine. The puppets were, he explained, managed by an arm of the Theosophical Society and their productions were related to religious themes and German folklore. My mum knew nothing about either but, with ambitions of starring in a professional puppet show, busied herself with sewing miniature pairs of lederhosen and embroidering tiny laced, Fraülein bodices whilst humming tunes by Engelbert Hümperdink.

Mum's debut was a disappointment. Her only role was the tediously slow rising and setting of a yellow cardboard sun-on-a-stick to denote the passage of time while other characters gathered apples to place on their children's heads and gathered in circles to tap-tap-tap and clap-clap-clap. When I demanded to know why, after sewing all those lederhosen she wasn't even offered a speaking part, she seemed a tad unsure. And I was much too polite to suggest that her pronounced Yorkshire accent and the snobbery of the puppeteers might have anything to do with it.

My mum was not the only one to feel strung along. There were never enough speaking parts to fill the hungry egos of the puppeteers and even less when they stopped talking to each other. Their only drama was played out in the courtroom as one of the cast, hand-in-glove with a local solicitor, sued for rightful ownership of the German folktales he'd set appallingly to verse. Gloves came off, fists started flying and… my mum gave up her ambitions and went home.

A few years later, my mum was taken ill. She was in hospital, after a minor operation, surrounded by a wardful of well-wishers and work colleagues for her sixtieth birthday, marking her retirement from work. Noting the oversized,

---

No more than four visitors per bed

---

placard, I sidled into the ward sister's office to check how long it would be before she could come home so I could plan the date for her big party.

Are you the next of kin?

7

Words to reduce a giant to a jelly.

I was told that the operation had unearthed a terminal cancer and that nothing could be done to save my mother and after scraping myself off the floor, had to walk back inside the ward abloom with celebration bouquets and beaming visitors with a smile as firmly frozen as a fishcake.

And then began a strange clutch of coincidence. My mum had cancer and would never see the longed-for years of her retirement and yet there was something strangely beautiful about her last few months of life.

She had the chance to take her first-ever holiday abroad and was well enough to enjoy it. On her return, we seemed to share a strange charmed life together. On days when she was well enough to go outdoors, the sun shone, brass bands played, Morris dancers appeared, she found a ten pound note on the floor and encountered long-lost friends. If I believed in angels – which of course, I certainly did not – I would say there was one watching over us every step of the way.

And speaking of angels...

I discover that a work colleague is a die-hard Christian and feel – not just sorry for her – but quite cheated; she seemed such a sane, nice person. So when I start to write a book about an angel, it's not, of course, because I believe in angels any more than I believe in Santa Claus or fairies at the bottom of the garden. If anything, I'm taking the rise out of my colleague to whom – with her fresh, rosy cheeks, rimless glasses and sensible all-weather shoes – my fictional angel bears more than a slight resemblance.

Lurking at the back of my mind is a quotation that I've heard somewhere about angels being in charge of us, *bearing us up* in case at any time we *dash our foot against a stone.*

I've no idea where the quote comes from but fancy the words as an intro to my soon-to-be-completed, hopefully-best-selling children's novel. I just don't know where to find them.

Over the next few months, my story continues apace. My angel uses her halo to electrify her harp and form a celestial rock band and the half-remembered lines keep on nagging. I look them up in poetry books and dictionaries of quotations. While I wait for Google to be invented, I try the local library.

Nothing. It occurs to me that the quote could come from the Bible. I do have a copy somewhere although it takes a bit of finding. Even longer to dust. My first mistake is when I turn to the back to look up "angels" and find that God has neglected to include an index in His Word. Then I try the front for chapters about angels. No better. I sigh and as the book falls open on my lap, glance down at the page before me. Staring up at me, I see:

he shall give his angels charge over thee, to keep thee:
And in their hands they shall bear thee up,
lest at any time thou dash thy foot against a stone...[1]

I blink.

Apparently these are the words of Satan during Christ's temptation in the wilderness.

I note down the chapter and verse and tell myself that, of course, coincidences happen: given the number of events that take place in a lifetime, it would be even more of a coincidence if they didn't. And thank the God I don't believe in that I'm not one of those two-pages-short-of-the-authorized-version no-hopers who would mistake this common coincidence for some kind of heavenly miracle.

I reflect smugly on this later as I switch on the car radio and hear Abba singing, *I believe in Angels,* walk into the pub to hear Gram Parsons singing *The Grievous Angel...* watch a Dennis Potter play about an angel on TV and read Charles Causley's, *I Saw a Shot-down Angel in the Park...* As I walk along the High Street, someone pushes a flier into my hand with a quotation about... yes, you guessed. And I'm standing in the kitchen when

I hear the letter box rattle and turn to see a disembodied hand thrust a piece of paper through. With a bit of a shiver down my spine, *I just know* what this will be. And of course, I'm right. I copy down the quotations in my notebook and find that each one, quite coincidentally, provides a complete summary of each chapter of my near-completed novel. Twenty seven chapters altogether and, I note reluctantly, grudgingly... twenty seven formation-flying angels parachuting down to their respective page.

You might imagine that I'm about to tell you how this encounter with twenty seven angels saved my mother's life, transformed my novel into a number-one best-seller and me into a born-again Christian. But you'd be wrong. I was a woman with an edge you could drive a car over, an attitude it had taken me a lifetime to fix in place. And anyway, the market for children's fiction in the early eighties was on the look-out for drugs, crime and teenage parents; angels were for Big Girls' Blouses.

But yet these strange new episodes of synchronicity kept popping up like white rabbits out of a hat and, as rabbits do, they multiplied. I began attending Quaker Meeting and found that, in the company of others, seated in silence, my clusters of coincidence became stronger. When I told my mum about the Quakers, she said that an hour's peace and quiet sounded just the thing for her. I looked forward to the day when she might feel well enough to sit still for an hour beside me, but sadly, that was not to be.

However, I was troubled by another major problem: my father had insisted that neither of us should let mum know about her diagnosis. I had no option but to go along with his cheery: *We'll soon have you up about again...* But inwardly, I winced.

Would I have had more courage if it had just been up to me? I can't say. But the situation continued until my mum lay in a state of limbo, as weak as it's possible to be whilst clinging on to life. Like many people, I knew nothing at all about death. We'd agreed that mum should end her days at home but had no idea what would actually happen. My father and I found ourselves listening for each and every breath, checking each frail heartbeat. What if she died without our noticing?

I had the overwhelming sense that this was not the best way for us all. It was ridiculous to assume my mother would simply not notice she was dying. She'd fallen out with religion many years ago, yet I'd never asked her why.. What if she wanted to make peace with whatever it was that she'd fallen out with? Religious people wrap the event in ritual, a rite of passage; a Catholic, even one who never went to Mass, would expect a priest to perform last rites. The Anglican church might offer a final Communion. But I could hardly imagine my mother's reaction to opening her eyes and finding an unknown priest hovering by her bedside.

I became increasingly distressed, overwhelmed by the sense that things weren't right, and yet unable to think of an alternative. I still had no personal belief. so when I sat in Quaker meeting and mouthed my request, it was not to God or Jesus or the Holy Spirit, but an anonymous Something Out There. It wasn't a prayer because it didn't last long enough; as communications go, it was a post-it note, a brief text, an aside; a whisper from the corner of my mouth: *Help!*

Later that day, there was a phone call. The last thing I wanted was to hear from someone who'd had no contact with my mum for the last three years, let alone, Father William, the Episcopal puppeteer. "I just wondered how Dorothy was."

Gulp.

My mother was doubly incontinent, barely breathing, looked like a skeleton and was much further from life than death. I replied with typically-Yorkshire understatement. "Erm... she's not very well."

Pause.

"I thought about coming to see her."

What?! The two hadn't spoken for years. The idea of my

mother being expected to sit up and make polite conversation with the shock-headed priest when she had all on to keep breathing had me, for once, lost for words. "She's... she's... she's not very well *at all*."

But Father William refused to be deterred. "That's just what I thought. I was standing at the bus stop, waiting for a 52 when Dorothy suddenly came into my head. I think I need to see her. Would you mind driving over to collect me?"

In spite of all my protests that my mother would fail to recognize Father Christmas if he walked inside her bedroom, Father William refused to be deterred. Something about the certainty in his voice had me reaching for my car keys. As I drove to collect him, cursing beneath my breath, it never occurred to me that he could be the answer to my post-it-note prayer; I just saw him as a bloody nuisance.

In the car, I struggled to outline the state of my mother's health, or lack of it, but Father William simply nodded. "That's exactly what I thought," he offered. "That's why I needed to come."

I ushered him into my mother's room with no lack of trepidation. But as he walked in with a cheery, "Hello, there, Dorothy," my mother opened her eyes and turned to face him. "Do you remember me?" he asked.

She nodded.

There was a pause as he stepped across and held her hand. His voice softened. "I think you've been waiting for me."

She slowly nodded.

"You do know what I've come for?"

Mum nodded again and offered a brief smile.

As Father William began to unpack his bagful of accoutrements, I did have a few misgivings, but the smile on my mother's face convinced me that my father and I should take a back seat and allow him to go ahead. The service turned out to be a bizarre mix of scented candles, wafting incense and Father

William, wearing his flowing robes, striding around the room chanting *Let it be! Let it be!* There were moments when my father and myself found it best not to meet each other's gaze as Father William persuaded us to join in with the chanting. My mother however, remained completely conscious, totally aware of what was going on and looked more peaceful than I'd seen her for a long, long time.

Afterwards, as mum fell asleep, I felt the urge to go back home. The odor of the sickroom had seeped inside my clothes, the sickly smell was in my hair, even it seemed, my skin. I only lived ten minutes drive away and felt a desperate need to wash and change my clothes.

Back home, I collapsed into a chair, slept heavily for a while, then took a shower. I remember shampooing my hair, delighting in the clean suds, and then strangely, looking through my wardrobe and choosing something colorful to wear. A summer dress.

I said goodbye to my family, then walked out to my car and, as soon as I stepped outside, felt conscious of a change. My feet were light. I felt buoyant. I had a sense of vigor. As I turned on the car ignition, the radio burst into life: *Bright eyes...*

My children had loved the Watership Down story about a colony of rabbits and as a family, we'd been to see the film. The song about the death of one of the rabbits sounded upbeat and positive:

Bright eyes, burning like fire...

To my embarrassment, I found myself joining in.
Linda!

Here I was going to see my mother on her deathbed, the worst day of my life, yet there was this inexplicable energy and joy welling up inside. The words had a life of their own, springing from my throat, singing along with gusto:

Bright eyes how can you close and fail?

It made no sense that a day of such trauma should have me feeling so elated. Thank the god I didn't believe in there was no one there to see me, or even worse, to hear.

How can the light that burned so brightly
Suddenly turn so pale?[2]

I arrived at the house to find my father pacing up and down the landing.

Why had he left mum on her own?

"Thank God you've come," he stuttered.

I paused at the bedroom door, expecting him to follow, but he was already heading off downstairs.

I waited.

Dad glanced away from me. "I'm sorry," he mumbled. "I just can't...."

I walked into the bedroom.

Everything had changed. No longer sleeping peacefully, Mum was struggling to breathe. I spoke but she seemed not to hear. I sat down at her bedside and squeezed her hand. Then several things happened; the order is etched on my brain. First, Mum opened her eyes and looked, not at me, but directly over my shoulder. "Oh, hello," she said cheerily, as though greeting a long-lost friend.

Foolishly, I turned.

Nobody there.

Secondly, she turned and looked towards me. As I squeezed her hand, she smiled. A weak smile but a smile of recognition.

And then, her eyes grew dim. They clouded over, lost their sparkle and grew pale.

Just like in the song.

* * * *

Over the next few months, the events I've just described kept swirling through my mind.

I was, of course, bereaved, and that involves a huge adjustment. I was concerned about my father; but at the same time, my belief system, my sense of who I was as a person, had been blown away like a dandelion clock.

People speak dismissively of those who espouse atheism whilst life is passing smoothly but, at the first sign of a crisis, turn to god or religion for support. But this was not support. More like being overwhelmed by a tsunami. And the kind of person I was just couldn't carry on regardless: I had to find some rational explanation, not only for my twenty seven angels, but now also for the weird events surrounding my mother's death.

I'd always assumed that when we died, that was it. Notions of heaven or an afterlife were a sop for those afraid of coming to terms with mortality. Yet I was convinced my mother had seen someone familiar seconds before she died. Someone invisible to me. And in fact I later went on to discover overwhelming scientific evidence that frequently, at the point of death, a long-lost friend or relative appears as though to guide people through the transition.

For the first time in our history, it's now become a regular event for people to be brought back from the brink and talk about their experience. Advances in technology mean that those who at one time would have died, are likely to recover on a life-support machine or after resuscitation. Their accounts, described in Chapter Four, reveal some amazing similarities and the strongest evidence we have that other dimensions exist beside our own.

It would be easy to attribute the elation I experienced setting off in my car to a sense of relief that the arduous months of my mother's illness were drawing to a close. Or a sense of reassurance with our bedside service, pleased with a job well done. However, I know when I'm satisfied that things have been done properly and when I'm in the grip of something over and beyond myself. I went on to read of studies which record time and time again that, although dying can be painful and traumatic, death itself is joyful. I felt certain that, although my mother had been suffering, once she turned the corner and eased forward, she left behind her discomfort and began to sense light and elation. Her experience was so powerful that, as I set out to see her, a portion of this joy and light was projected in my direction.

Many of us have had the experience of simply *knowing* what's happening to someone close to us, even when geographically, we're a long way apart. The scientist, Rupert Sheldrake, has investigated how people often know when a close friend is about to phone and how some dogs sense when their owners are returning home; he's even conducted experiments with a Manhattan parrot who appears to read its owner's mind. Physicists call this *entanglement* and relate it to the way that quantum particles appear to show an awareness of what is happening to their "other half" anywhere in the universe. We'll look at this in greater depth in Chapter Ten

I was only 99% convinced about my Quaker Meeting post-it prayer. It could, of course, have simply been coincidence: Father William, waiting for his bus, may have had a sudden out-of-the-blue thought about my mother, decided to leave the bus stop and find the nearest phone. And anyway, he didn't fulfill my job description of a divine messenger. Look at the tangle his puppet group was in. Could he not have asked the powers-that-be to pull a few strings to pacify the puppeteers?

Scientific studies of prayer have always aroused controversy although they've pointed to its effectiveness in areas such as healing and in doubling the rate of pregnancy in IVF treatment.[3] William Tiller, Professor Emeritus of Materials Science and

Engineering at Stanford University has shown the results of channeling attention towards easily-measurable areas such as increasing the acidity of a solution or increasing the activity of enzymes. We'll examine this, with relation to remote healing, in Chapter Eleven.

The notion of Father William and the 52 bus at first seemed relatively simple: there he was minding his own business when an ethereal bleeper tweaked his ear and told him to phone my mum. But what if he were already on the bus? Would he have got off? And what if the bus was just rolling into view? Might something have delayed it? What if a child had run across the road?

If it really is possible, as Tiller suggests, to affect what occurs by focusing our minds, how can we influence only one event? Everything has repercussions, what scientists call *the butterfly effect*.[4] In Chapter Twelve we'll examine some of the amazing theories put forward by scientists to demonstrate how one event can change without altering everything round it, including the notion that there are parallel existences running beside our own – entire worlds in which Father William catches his bus and never gives a thought about my mother.

Many years ago, I was intrigued to find that, like my mum, people had been enthralled by puppets for at least two and a half thousand years when I read of Plato's reference to a puppet show in his *Allegory of the Cave*:

Imagine prisoners who have been chained since their childhood deep inside a cave: not only are their arms and legs immovable because of chains; their heads are chained in one direction as well so that their gaze is fixed on a wall.

Behind the prisoners is an enormous fire, and between the fire and the prisoners is a raised walkway, along which puppets of various animals, plants, and other things are moved. The puppets cast shadows on the wall, and the prisoners watch these shadows. Behind this cave there is a well-used road, and upon this road people are walking and talking and generally making noise. The prisoners, then, believe that these noises are coming directly from the shadows they are watching pass by on the cave wall.

The prisoners engage in what appears to us to be a game: naming the shapes as they come by. This, however, is the only reality that they know, even though they are seeing merely shadows of objects. They are thus conditioned to judge the quality of one another by their skill in quickly naming the shapes and dislike those who play poorly.

Suppose a prisoner's chains break, and he is able to get up and walk about (a process which takes some time, as he has never done it before). Eventually he will be compelled to explore; he walks up and out of the cave, whereby he is instantly blinded by the sun...[5]

I still find this account the most astute description of our human state. Our view of the world is just as limited as that of Plato's prisoners who think the shadows before them are all that can exist. Rather than breaking through our chains and beginning to explore the world outside, we congratulate ourselves on performing the most trivial of tasks. The shapes that we're so proud to name are more likely nowadays to be images on a screen than shadows on a wall, but we still delude ourselves that naming shapes is what gives life its meaning. As we move about and dance and sing, we think we act independently, but fail to see the puppet master hidden from our view; we fail to see the hidden strings that link us all together and when we gaze out to what we see as the bright lights of our horizon, we are really only gazing at the footlights of our tiny stage.

Chapter 2

Quakers and the Ministry of Silence

To her great surprise, they all thought in chorus...
"...Better say nothing at all. Language is worth a thousand
pounds a word."
Alice through the Looking Glass, chapter three.

My first stopping point, as I tumbled down the rabbit hole, was not a shelf of vials labeled **eat me** or **drink me** nor a magic mushroom that made me grow or shrink; it was something even more bizarre: a group of people seated in a circle thinking the same thoughts.

The persistence of my twenty seven angels, their sheer bloody-mindedness and their ridiculous number gave me a sense of being haunted - like having a poltergeist in the house, watching the plates whizzing across the settee, muttering: *Here we go again...*, picking up all the pieces whilst clinging to the notion that there's no such thing as ghosts.

I knew there was something there. Something that defied reason. I'm not one to frighten easily; in fact to be honest, I consider myself the most open-minded, willing-to-give-it-a-go, adventurous soul that I know; yet here I was gripped by that spine-tingling, cold-sweating, insomniac state that people call blind panic. I was reminded of the story of the wolf who gobbles up the baby goats. The tiniest kid, sneaking from his hiding place inside the grandfather clock, takes a sharp knife, cuts open the stomach of the sleeping wolf, lets out his brothers and sisters and fills the gap with rocks. I was that wolf: dragged down, hauling a great weight – filled with something foreign and foreboding. So much for angels as airy messengers of peace. More like a delivery of hard-core rubble and concrete.

On the rare occasions when I faced up to my fear, the rocks' sharp edges pierced my heart. Although I called myself a non-believer, my non-belief was a stronger faith than that of anyone I knew. It determined who I was. I was Linda – dyed-in the wool atheist, outspoken, spiky, sussed and radical. My concept of who I was had taken a lifetime to assemble – who would I be without it? What would I be? What if people thought I was a Christian? I hated Christians. But what else can you call someone who allows a troupe of angels to order her about?

In the end, one fearful night, in the early hours, unable yet again to sleep, I tiptoed downstairs. I had a husband and three young children fast asleep and the last thing I wanted was for them to ask what I was up to. And anyway, I'd no idea. I had the notion that I would initiate something of a parley. *What, Linda? Are you mad? Talk to a load of angels?*

I poured myself a stiff vodka which seemed the only start. Pity I couldn't offer the bottle round. And how do you address a host of angels anyway? Do you begin by saying *Oh, holy ones...* I was at the time a teacher in a large secondary school and as I took a deep breath and another glug of vodka, focused my thoughts in the way that seemed most natural... as though my angels were a rowdy, misbehaving class. I glowered at any that might be hiding behind the bookcase and adopted a Paddington Stare: *Now, look here...*

I paused. Whatever was I doing? I didn't believe in angels It was like having a chat with the Wicked Witch of the East. *I'm sorry.* Sigh. *I don't believe in you... I don't believe in anything...* I didn't speak out loud, but that's how I started off. Long pause. Another drink. *OK. I realize that you're trying to get in touch with me.* Another pause. *I am willing to give it a go......I've just got no idea what to do.*

At this point, I should have heard - if the angels had been given a half-decent script - a fanfare of trumpets, an opening harp arpeggio, heavenly voices rising in sweet harmony and a chorus line of feet can-canning across the settee.

I didn't. What actually happened was entirely unexpected and even more bizarre: a strange and overwhelming sense that whatever I'd said was OK. It was perfectly all right. It was fine for me to be just who I was. It was as though I were being enfolded. Enfolded in what... I'd no idea. White, gossamer wings, presumably. I simply had an overwhelming sense of peace. Peace and love and reassurance that everything would be all right. So much love and reassurance, I simply broke down in tears.

The next thing was a message, not out loud, but as loud as possible whilst hearing it inside my head. The message made no sense – which was why I knew for certain that it came from outside rather than simply a thought. It seemed a second-hand, garbled, Chinese whisper of a message, like one of those jokes you get in cheap Christmas crackers, written in pidgin English in a factory in Laos and received with all the excitement of a row of vacant stares at a Christmas party. The message only had nine words and took much of my life to decipher. I'll come back to them in a later chapter.

The following day, I'd planned to go into town. My mum had broken the Pyrex jug of the coffee machine I'd bought her and wasn't well enough to go out and search for a replacement.

First I called in the library to look for Books-about- Religion-for-People-Who-Don't-Believe-in-Religion-God-or-Angels but, amazingly, couldn't even find the appropriate section let alone such a book. Which is why I'm writing this one now. Then I called in a department store on the High Street to enquire about the coffee jug. The assistant shook her head. "You could try Cockaynes," she offered.

Cockaynes was a very posh department store - well out of my price-range - specializing, so I thought, in jewelry and fur coats. I looked confused.

"They do have a kitchen department," she explained.

I assumed that if they did, they'd have just sold the very best porcelain tea sets for tiny sachets of best Assam. I was not impressed.

"You know where I mean..? On Angel Street..?"

Silence.

"Are you all right?"

I swallowed hard, nodded and set off.

I can't remember whether I found a replacement jug or not. What I do remember is that Cockaynes' kitchen department was towards the rear of their store on Sheffield's Angel Street. I walked out through the back into Hartshead Square then paused. The building opposite caught my eye. The Quaker Meeting House.

All I knew about Quakers could have been written on the back of a postcard and still left room for the picture. In my teenage years I'd been a member of the youth campaign for nuclear disarmament and we'd met at the home of some Quakers. Of course, I'd been much too preoccupied with trying to look supercool and impress the boys than ask anybody's parents about their religious faith. They just let us have a room. Oh, and when I asked for the bathroom they showed me upstairs into a huge room packed with crates of books and bicycles and I was about to turn and leave when I spotted a toilet and sink buried somewhere in the corner.

Dare I walk inside the Meeting House?

What if the Quakers asked me what I wanted? Whatever would I say?

I turned and tried to walk away, then found my legs had swizzled back. Before I knew it, my feet were striding stoutly over Hartshead Square, dragging me behind them.

Someone had left the door open and, after a furtive glance across my shoulder, I found myself inside the Meeting House. As luck would have it, there was Something Going On. A clattering of tea trolleys, an industrial-sized tea urn, plateloads of distressingly-plain biscuits and enough small chat to drown out the local radio station. I tried to blend in the background as I browsed the leaflet rack and checked out the notice board with advertisements for Amnesty and the Campaign Against the Arms Trade. Leaflets explained that Quakers met in silence - something I'd never have guessed from the hubbub in the hallway - and if anyone felt moved to speak, they did so. With a life made hectic by three noisy kids and a secondary school rabble, an hour of silence sounded like heaven on earth. But what if I was overcome with giggles? What if my tummy rumbled? What if I farted? What would I do? Apart from looking round and pretending it was someone else, of course. And what if I needed the bathroom? Could I actually sit still for a whole hour? And what if anyone asked me whether I believed in God or Jesus or the virgin birth? What would I do when they found out I was only an impostor?

My misgivings quickly melted. I fell into the Quaker silence like a landlocked fish in water. I wallowed and floated in peace. No one asked what I believed or what I didn't, but as others expressed their reservations about church ritual, the literal truth of the Bible and other Christian teachings, I breathed out a long, long sigh of relief. Here was a place for those who weren't too sure about priests or hymns and prayers and not always sure about God. Other churches, I supposed, were for people who'd already found God and were looking for a place to worship, Quakers seemed to be offering a haven for those searching who weren't sure what they would find. The Quaker Meeting went on to become the mainstay of my life. And it all began the night I picked up the courage to walk downstairs with the intention of giving twenty seven angels a good talking to.

When I did this, I never thought of myself as stepping outside my time-space continuum. I wouldn't have known a time-space continuum if it had leapt on me with a sharp knife from out of the grandfather clock. And yet this is what many cutting-edge scientists call it when we project our consciousness to Something Out There. We'll address this concept later in Chapter Fourteen.

To my great relief, I had no problems with tummy rumbling or breaking wind in Quaker meeting, but at first found it difficult to empty my head of thoughts. I'd find broad boulevards of calm and then start whittling about my lesson plans for Monday. One Sunday, I found my thoughts returning to my latest idea for another teenage novel. My book about the angel had been scooped up by a London agent who encouraged me to come straight back and start the next. I had a plot brewing about a girl acting in a play which mirrored her own life. I was writing about the girl's relationship with her father but couldn't think of a play that involved a father and his daughter.

I tried to wipe the embryonic story from my mind, but still the thoughts kept nagging until a young man, Derek Guyton, struggled to his feet: *I shall do such things, I know not..."* he intoned ... *but they shall be the terrors of the earth...*

I sat and stroked where my beard would be if I had one. The words meant nothing, but then Derek went on to talk about Shakespeare's play King Lear, and Lear's troubled relationship with his daughter, Cordelia.

My ears pricked up.

All I knew about King Lear could have been written inside a coronation mug while still leaving room for the tea, but a few days later my attention was grabbed by a poster outside The Anvil, Sheffield's socialist council-run cinema.

The only showing was a matinee when I was supposed to be teaching Year Nine. There was no way any self-respecting school-teacher would throw a sickie and sneak into the cinema when they were supposed to be teaching the most disruptive class in school. So there I sat one freezing winter afternoon in an unheated cinema, with my notebook and pencil and the whole of 9G continually asking why, if this was supposed to be a cinema, there was no popcorn, no cartoons and no adverts and why the film was in black and white (it was the 1971, Peter Brook version). Thankfully however, they were so exuberant at our day out from school they forgave me for the fact that I never even explained what all of us were doing there.

And so began another weird procession of coincidence, this time based on Shakespearean quotes, fathers and daughters. And it was not my story about the angel – although I used that later as a successful TV play – but *Your Friend, Rebecca*, a modernized version of *King Lear* which established my writing career. Carl Gustav Jung, the famous psychiatrist, has written much about the nature of coincidence – or as he calls it, synchronicity[1]. Julia Cameron, in her book, *The Artist's Way*[2] writes about the link between synchronicity and creativity. Other writers and artists throughout the centuries have written of similar links which we'll go on to examine in Chapter Six.

But back to the Quaker Meeting. Time after time, as I wallowed in the silence, I found words and images occurring only to have them picked up by others in the room. On one occasion, conscious of my frustration at waiting to start my next project, I half-remembered a quotation from the Bible: something that started out *Those that wait upon the Lord...* I was tempted to stand and quote the measly section I could remember, but felt daunted by one of the Elders, Vere Rodgers, a formidable woman with an eccentricity I hope to emulate in old age. Apart from her dress sense, that is. Whereas other Quakers go for a bit of tasteful simplicity, Vere would slink to Meeting swaddled in furs, gold jewelry, make-up skimmed with Carlite Browning and an unfailing recall of verses from the Bible. I could imagine, if I misquoted the Old Testament, her fur hat would bristle up in horror and terminally moult. Yet as I sat with lips squeezed firmly closed, Vere tapped her silver cane on the parquet flooring and tottered to her feet. *"Those that wait upon the Lord..."* she declaimed, *"will renew their strength; they shall mount up with wings as eagles; they shall run, and not be weary; and they shall walk, and not faint.*[3]

We're all aware of how this telepathic skill has been mimicked by centuries of charlatans, claiming to read our palms and tealeaves. So-called psychics and numerologists use all manner of clues to tell our fortunes and always, of course, for a price. Nonetheless, modern scientists such as Rupert Sheldrake and Elizabeth Targ have brushed the charlatans aside and found that yes, it is sometimes possible to know what someone else is thinking. And once quantum particles are linked, they seem able to communicate no matter how far apart they travel. We'll examine this concept of entanglement later in Chapter Ten.

David Bohm, the American-born British quantum physicist, has suggested that this extra-sensory perception occurs because of another level of existence through which we're all connected. Other scientists are also searching for other invisible dimensions; in struggling to understand the action of gravitons and why they seem so much less powerful than other forces in our universe, Stephen Hawking, Research Director at Cambridge University and holder of the Presidential Medal of Freedom has reached the conclusion that they are slowed down by travelling through a fifth dimension.[4]

I don't know how long it took Professor Hawking to work this out and I suspect it involved a few research teams and a little bit of cash, but I came to a similar conclusion in less than five minutes – for free - in a dream about a looking glass.

Chapter 3

Inside the Looking Glass

Let's pretend there's a way of getting through into it, somehow, Kitty.

Let's pretend the glass has got all soft like gauze, so that we can get through.

Why, it's turning into a sort of mist now...

Alice through the Looking Glass, chapter one

My looking-glass dream occurred some time after the death of my mother. Once I realized just how little I knew about the meaning of life, death and the universe, I began exploring new ideas, reading everything I could get my hands on from Plato and Socrates onwards, devouring stone circles and Goddess theories, Jung's Reflections and dipping my toes into quantum physics.

Yet none of these new ideas would blend together. I wanted a theory of everything; I wanted all the separate concepts to weave into one grand tapestry; I wanted to grasp the spiritual the way I'd learned to speak French – some basic vocabulary and a background of verbs, before making polite conversation, ordering snails-on-the-side and booking myself a room with a view in a chateau.

My spiritual life refused to work like that. I remember a Quaker Friend, David Brayshaw - the wisest, kindest man I knew. David stood one day at a Quaker funeral and stated that he knew – absolutely knew, that all of us emanate from the same great river; after breaking off to form our own individual drops, we all return to be part of the great stream once again.

A lovely picture which I yearned to share. David was intelligent; he was on the same spiritual quest that I was, and yet he'd reached a completely different conclusion. Was there a great river or wasn't there? And if there was, why hadn't I discovered it? And why should it run underground most of the time, hidden away?

I knew I'd had spiritual experience: I had insights; I had revelations; I had barrage after barrage of amazingly weird coincidence; I had loud thoughts in my head which I took to be spiritual promptings; I just didn't know where I was going. I didn't have a roadmap or a structure; I didn't have a decent dictionary or a map of France or a picture of the Eiffel Tower.

Later that evening, sitting by the fireside, I struggled to assimilate where I'd got so far with my spiritual quest and felt more and more frustrated. Why should we as a species be born with such insatiable curiosity if everything we want to know is always beyond our grasp?

Before I went to bed, I gave it one last rant: *Why? If I've been given such a huge dollop of determination to discover the great mysteries of Life, the Universe and Everything and a brain to think things out, do I always finish up feeling as though I'm living at the bottom of a treacle well?"*

Of course, I wouldn't have called it a prayer. More of a howl; a teenage sulk; an Alice standing up in court and tipping the jury box over. But what followed only a few moments later, just as I settled to sleep, was a remarkable series of dreams, each very short, but giving me time to wake and consider the implications before dropping back to sleep to pick up the next installment. It was the method I'd learned as a teacher for explaining complex ideas to children - not sending them to bed – but using lots of familiar pictures and breaking down the complexity into simple, baby steps.

These were my baby steps…

In the first dream I was walking along an embankment with my mother. By this time, as I mentioned, my mum had been gone for some time, but in my dream she was in her prime. As we walked along I noticed a reflection of the moon in the river. Then I stopped and realized there was another moon in the water. Did the place where we were walking have two moons? Or was the first moon simply a reflection of the first? I remarked on this to my mother, comparing the moon with the reflections I'd seen of rainbows – a double rainbow in the sky.

At this point I woke briefly and tried to summarize what I'd seen: the place where I'd walked with my mother was a place where she still seemed young and healthy and where the moon had more than one reflection.

I went straight back to sleep. The next dream involved something similar but my memory of it now is more hazy. It involved sailing on a boat and again, watching a reflection of something else reflected in the water. I woke again, compared this to my first dream and then went back to sleep.

There was a third dream about which I now remember nothing, but it was the fourth which held the key – the roadmap, the lid of the jigsaw with the picture of the Eiffel Tower. In order to describe it, I have to fill you in on my Gothic taste in bedroom furnishings.

My room has a Victorian four-poster surrounded by lace curtains and heavy drapes. At the foot of the bed is an old-fashioned dressing table with three mirrors – a large round one in the centre and two adjustable side mirrors for checking whether the back of your head's still there. As I sit on the stool facing the mirror, with the bed behind me, there's a door on my right leading to the landing and, on my left another door which leads into the bathroom.

In the dream I'm sitting on my stool, looking in the side mirror, when I suddenly notice that – by glimpsing in the large mirror – I can see myself asleep in bed. The notion that I can see myself as a separate person fills me with elation. It's as though this is the pinnacle of life – something I've been longing for. I'm overwhelmed with an orgasmic sense of joy and exuberance, so strong that I begin to wake but before I fully do so, someone walks behind me. I see his reflection in the mirror as he walks behind my back. I don't turn. By the time I've registered there's someone there, he's gone through the door on my left that leads into the bathroom.

The most significant part of the dream seemed to be this final figure. As I woke, I knew I had to keep that shot in mind as a loud voice in my head talked me through what I'd just seen:

This figure would have had an existence before he stepped into my room and would continue to exist after he had left; the fact that I couldn't see him any longer meant that he'd moved elsewhere – not that he ceased to be. We see people for the first time when they're born and we stop seeing them when they die; but that doesn't mean that they haven't existed before or that they cease to exist when they leave us.

Beyond our own concepts of time and space are other dimensions. When we try to glimpse them, it's like viewing the world through a looking glass. The glass has only two dimensions – length and breadth – but these other worlds out there have more. What we see of them is pared down to the dimensions that exist inside our world – like trying to see the whole of our lives reflected in a small mirror. The fact that we cannot see something in our limited view doesn't mean that it cannot exist.

Although these other dimensions are beyond our understanding, there are points of intersection – *There are cracks*, as the great singer, Leonard Cohen tells us, *and that's where the light gets in* [1] A dream can be such a point. At some time in the future, we'll rise above all this. We'll be able to look back and see our present selves and that will be like gazing at our reflection in a two-dimensional glass. This experience won't be scary, but joyful and exuberant.

The idea that death is not the end and that our souls might carry on elsewhere is a notion I'd always thought of as a woolly-brained fear of coming to terms with mortality. My looking glass dream, however, encouraged me to investigate. I was staggered to find that the world's foremost expert in near-death experience, Dr. Elizabeth Kübler-Ross, had assimilated the findings of over twenty thousand people who claimed to have had near-death experience and also said in one of her final lectures:

> We can ask... questions before we are asleep... Those who have been tuned in to their sleep states, to their dreams, become aware that many of our questions are answered in this state. As we get more tuned in to our own inner entity, to our own inner spiritual part, it is very understandable that we can get help and guidance from our own all-knowing self, that immortal part we call the butterfly.[2]

We'll have more to say about her research in Chapter Four, but first some scientists who've also experienced revelation through their dreams.

The Danish Physicist, Niels Bohr had been struggling to understand the structure of the atom. He'd tried all kinds of designs - he had all the pieces of his jigsaw but no picture to help him fit them all together. And then one night, in his dream, he saw the nucleus of the atom, with the electrons spinning around, just like our planets round the sun. He knew that this was it. He just needed a few more experiments to prove it to the world. In 1922 he was awarded the Nobel Prize for physics as a result.

Another Nobel prizewinner was the neurophysiologist, Otto Loewi. Following a period of fruitless research, he had a dream and recorded the details in his autobiography. It was 1923, the night before Easter Sunday, when he dreamed of an experiment that would prove once and for all that transmission of nerve impulses was chemical, not electrical. He says:

I woke, turned on the light and jotted down a few notes on a tiny slip of thin paper. Then I fell asleep again. It occurred to me at six o'clock in the morning that during the night I had written down something most important, but I was unable to decipher the scrawl.[3]

He tried unsuccessfully to recall the dream or interpret his note. On the Sunday night he went to bed and read for a time before turning out the light. He then awoke between two and three in the morning, which was unusual for him and knew what the nature of his dream had been that night and the previous night. He got out of bed and immediately went to the laboratory to put his new idea into action.

In the final chapter of Alice in Wonderland, Alice rises to her full height in the courtroom and begins to upbraid the Queen, the court and their ridiculous goings on. Scorning the Queen's *Off with her head!* she suddenly sees the characters for what they really are – not only faulted and foolish adults - but figures on a pack of playing cards.

It's a moment of epiphany; an awakening; a realization that there's more to life. There's more to Alice. She's a three-dimensional person whereas the characters are nothing more than marks on pieces of cardboard. And this is the point where Alice literally wakes up and the story reaches its conclusion.

And of course to us Alice herself is only two-dimensional - only a series of marks on paper. If you visit the British Library on Euston Road in London you can view, with their beautifully-crafted illustrations, the Reverend Dodgson's original notebooks which he donated to his real young friend, Alice Liddell. The stories may conjure an entire make-believe world, but at the end of the day consist of no more than lines going up and down and lines going side to side. As we stand and study them, we're drawn for a moment into Wonderland, imagining the make-believe world which the Reverend Dodgson invented for Alice but, as we turn away, that world is gone; we have a broader existence. We have trains to catch and missions to pursue. We have dimensions of depth and time. We can learn all we will about Alice but Alice knows nothing of us. She may affect our lives but no matter how we shout, like children at a puppet show, we can never make her notice us. The room in the British Library is a point of intersection, but we can never go through into Alice's world – the most we can do is bring her into ours.

The concept of interconnected worlds-within-worlds is explained by the Californian theoretical physicist, Michio Kaku who, as a child, used to enjoy watching goldfish in the Japanese Tea Gardens in San Francisco. What intrigued him was the notion that the fish have no concept at all of themselves as creatures living in a pond and even less concept of the existence of another world out there. For them, the pond is all there is.

In his book, *Hyperspace*, [4] Kaku describes how a fish might react if it were pulled out of the water and introduced to creatures without fins, to a world of blinding light and the realization that all its laws of fishy physics simply don't apply any more.

Kaku realized how frustrating it would be for this dimension-hopping goldfish to try and explain to its piscine pals where it had been and what it had experienced. How could it describe a waterless world? A world beyond the pond? How others would dismiss its claims of an extra-dimensional existence as the ramblings of a crazy, attention-seeking goldfish with an overactive brain?

Like goldfish in a pond, we find it difficult to imagine that other dimensions exist; if our known world is the only realm, it confirms us as the most intelligent, perceptive beings in the universe. We take for granted that the cells inside our big toe are unaware of their connections with all the rest of our body, that the germs inside our drains know nothing of an afterlife inside the sewer, that wildlife on an offshore island is ignorant of all that exists on the mainland... we know that the entire world is a cascade of Lilliputian colonies oblivious to their true place in the great scale of things…

But what about us… ?!

Like our many ancestors who ignorantly saw themselves as the only truly intelligent race, many of us cling to the crazed idea that life more intelligent than us must be a contradiction in terms. Others, like well-schooled fish, might contemplate the place where the water meets the sky or choose to question the dimension-hopping fish when he returns from his near-death experience and reflect upon his story; we may note that other fish have taken this course before and carped on about a similar world of blinding light; we can ponder the origins of the hand that feeds us and entertain the notion that when goldfish are cast from the pond they do not disappear forever. We can meditate on the sound of one fin flapping and a fish's weightless weight and wonder why, no matter how far we travel, we always seem to return to the point of our departure as we duck beneath the familiar bridge that welcomes us back home.

Chapter 4

Near-Death Experience

It might end, you know,' said Alice to herself, `in my going out altogether, like a candle. I wonder what I should be like then?' And she tried to fancy what the flame of a candle is like after the candle is blown out, for she could not remember ever having seen such a thing.

Alice in Wonderland, chapter one

This is the account of a twenty-eight-year old woman who nearly died during an emergency caesarean:

I was in excruciating pain, physically exhausted, and in labor for fifteen hours. Dr R. said, "I'm sorry, M, I'm going to have to put you to sleep." The next thing I remember was being above the room. I looked down and could see everything and everyone including my body with Dr R. and two nurses standing over it. I felt terrified and panic-stricken at first, but then the feeling passed. I realized I was very big. I was taking up the whole room. I also felt very, very good. Better than I've ever felt before or since. The feeling was extreme, extreme exhilaration. I felt brilliantly, totally alive – like all my senses were tuned to maximum awareness. I was very interested in what was going on. Dr R. yelled: "Her pressure is still dropping!" The anesthetist started squeezing a black rubber ball that was connected to an apparatus over my face. Dr R. said some numbers I can't remember, and then, "OK, she's stable." My husband was sitting in the corner. He looked scared and had a sad look on his face and tears in his eyes. A nurse was wheeling in a bassinet that squeaked a little... The next thing I can remember was being awakened by the nurses washing me. They said, "You had a girl." [1]

The writer of this account went on to reassure the researcher, Michael Grosso, that her husband and hospital staff were able to confirm everything she saw and heard. Although her body appeared lifeless – her eyes were closed and she seemed completely beyond hearing – she was actually able to see and hear and not only experience emotion but experience it with heightened awareness. This ability to use our senses at a time when we are – to all intents and purposes, dead – is one of the main characteristics of the increasingly-common phenomenon known as near-death experience.

If you'd been living more than fifty or sixty years ago, the chances are that, when you died, little would be done to try and bring you back to life. Not because no one loved you but because present-day technology hadn't been invented. Your friends and family would assume very sadly that your time had come and would make a start on planning for your funeral.

Nowadays there's a good chance that, when you begin to complain of sudden chest pain, someone will call an ambulance. If you're involved in an accident, someone passing with a mobile phone won't just remark sadly that your time is up, but will call the emergency services. Sirens wailing, you'll be wired up to all the latest high-tech equipment as you're sped to the nearest casualty department and wheeled into the operating theatre. In other words, if and when you stop breathing, there's a good chance this will occur within reach of the technology and expertise to jumpstart you back to life. Over and over again, we hear reports of people who have been clinically dead and are, shortly afterwards, sitting up in bed with a cup of tea, describing their experience to incredulous friends and relatives.

The last twenty or thirty years, in particular, have seen a real sea change in our chances of surviving a heart attack, stroke or accident. Most of the towns we inhabit are in reach of the ambulance service; the majority of us carry mobile phones. Many places where people congregate, especially in the US, have well-displayed defibrillators and staff trained how to use them. But of those who do remember the time they spent during their clinical death – and in one study after another – the figures hover round the thirteen-to-eighteen per cent mark - their accounts tear through the shredder any certainty that our consciousness - whatever it is that makes us human - depends solely on the workings of our brain.

The best-known writer on near-death experience is the pioneer of the hospice movement, Dr Elisabeth Kübler-Ross. Ross studied the experience of twenty thousand people right across the world who had returned to life. This is how she describes their experience:

> You register everything with this new awareness, even during the time your body has no blood pressure, no pulse, no breathing and in some cases, no measureable brain waves. You realize exactly what everyone says, what they think and how they act. You will later be able to tell in minute detail, for example, that three blow torches were used to cut your body out of the crashed car. It has even occurred that people could recall the exact license plate number of the car that ran into them and the driver who decided to take off.[2]

Ross's findings have been ratified by one researcher after another. One is the American cardiologist, Michael B. Sabom who took the opportunity to study patients he encountered in his work:

> I had known from the beginning of my study that the majority of the patients I would be interviewing regarding their near-death experience would have been resuscitated

from cardiac arrests…I had personally directed and participated in well over a hundred such procedures. I knew what a
resuscitation consisted of and how it would appear to an
onlooker. I had been eagerly awaiting the moment when a
patient would claim to have "seen" what had taken place
during his resuscitation. Upon such an encounter, I had
intended to probe meticulously for details which could not
ordinarily be known to nonmedical personnel. In essence, I
would pit both my experience as a trained cardiologist and the
description of the resuscitation in the medical chart against
the professed visual recollections of a lay individual.[3]

Sabom was astonished to find several patients whose reports of
events while they were unconscious or "dead" held up to his
scrutiny. One such patient, described in his book, Light and
Death, was a young musician called Pam Reynolds who
underwent a rare operation to remove a life-threatening, giant
basilar artery aneurysm in her brain. So vivid was her awareness
of events taking place during her operation that, with her musical
ability, she could even name the note made by the sound of the
surgeon's drill:

It was a natural D… I remember seeing several things in the
operating room when I was looking down. It was the most
aware that I think that I have ever been in my entire life …I
was metaphorically sitting on [the doctor's] shoulder. It was
not like normal vision. It was brighter and more focused and
clearer than normal vision … There was so much in the
operating room that I didn't recognize, and so many people…I
thought the way they had my head shaved was very peculiar.
I expected them to take all of the hair, but they did not …The
saw-thing that I hated the sound of looked like an electric
toothbrush and it had a dent in it, a groove at the top where
the saw appeared to go into the handle, but it didn't … And the

saw had interchangeable blades, too, but these blades were in what looked like a socket wrench case ... I heard the saw crank up. I didn't see them use it on my head, but I think I heard it being used on something. It was humming at a relatively high pitch and then all of a sudden it went Brrrrrrrrr! like that.

Someone said something about my veins and arteries being very small. I believe it was a female voice and that it was Dr. Murray, but I'm not sure. She was the cardiologist. I remember thinking that I should have told her about that ... I remember the heart-lung machine. I didn't like the respirator ... I remember a lot of tools and instruments that I did not readily recognize.[4]

During the "standstill" period of Pam's operation, her brain was found "dead" by all three of the normal clinical tests - her electroencephalogram was silent, her brain-stem response was absent, and no blood flowed through her brain.

Much research on the subject of Near-Death Experience has been carried out by Peter and Elizabeth Fenwick whose book, The Truth in the Light,[5] examined over three hundred such accounts. Peter is an internationally-renowned neuropsychiatrist and a Fellow of the Royal College of Psychiatrists and his wife, Elizabeth, has written a number of books on health and family issues. Dr. Peter Fenwick describes the state of the brain during a near-death experience:

The brain isn't functioning. It's not there.... But, yet, it can produce these very clear experiences ... an unconscious state is when the brain ceases to function. For example, if you faint, you fall to the floor, you don't know what's happening and the brain isn't working. The memory systems are particularly sensitive to unconsciousness. So, you won't remember anything. But, yet, after one of these near-death experiences, you come out with clear, lucid memories ... This is a real puzzle for science. I have not yet seen any good scientific explanation which can explain that fact. [6]

In their 1994 study, Elizabeth and Peter Fenwick found that 77% of those patients having near-death experience reported feelings of deep peace or euphoria. In one study after another, these findings are repeated. In Carol Zaleski's "Otherworld Journeys", for instance, she quotes the account of P.M.H. Atwater, an American woman who had a near-death experience following an attack of thrombosis:

When I was satisfied that I was dead, there came a joyous euphoria, like a prisoner being released from a long jail sentence... It was finally over. I was free! [7]

A study by researchers, Bruce Greyson and Nancy Evans Bush concentrated on patients whose accounts were more distressing. In quite a few of these however, once the patient stopped struggling against the experience, their feelings became more positive. One example came from a nurse who had been in a postoperative fever following a hysterectomy:

Suddenly I was overcome by a feeling of complete peace. My feelings were that I was safe and it was beautiful, weightless. I loved it. I felt at one with all, a great joy and ultimate peace of mind and body. I knew no harm in any way would come to me. All was peaceful and profound love surrounded me. There is no description on earth that can compare with this place and feeling. I felt something was saying, "You're safe now; don't be afraid; this peace will help you."

The beauty of the feeling overwhelms me even now, and sometimes I try to recreate it in my mind. I cannot. The depth of this experience cannot be understood by a person who has not had it happen to themselves. Anyone who has felt this peace would never want to leave or have it leave them. [8]

We might assume that anyone who's been through the trauma of a heart attack or accident would feel nothing but joy and relief when their pain is finally over. And yet accounts suggest that this euphoria is not produced by events; it just arrives. It reminds me of my dressing-table-mirror revelation. I was in perfect health – so can't pass it off as a near-death experience – but the whole event was accompanied by a deep sense of exhilaration and orgasmic joy that didn't make any sense. I wasn't joyful *about* anything. I saw a reflection of myself in bed which was interesting in an abstract *Oh, I didn't know I could do that* sort of way like suddenly realizing how easy it is to whistle. And similarly, in these post-mortem-ecstasy accounts, people don't sound elated *because* they've died; they're simply overcome with joy.

Since near-death experience began to be reported on a large scale from the nineteen-seventies onward, scientists have been searching long and hard for a rational explanation.

One possibility seemed to be that many of the symptoms were brought on by the generous cocktail of drugs frequently administered to the terminally ill. There have been huge advances in palliative care in recent years and we no longer expect patients to spend their last few weeks in agonizing pain. Heroin and morphine – drugs frequently prescribed for the terminally-ill - are well-known for causing euphoria and triggering hallucinations. Surely all these visions of ecstasy could simply be explained as one wild, smack-saturated trip?

The first objection to this argument is that scientists have actually found a negative correlation between the use of palliative drugs and near-death experience: feelings of joy and euphoria are more frequent in patients who have not been prescribed a heavy dose of opiates. As Carol Zaleski explains:

Recollection, if not experience, of near-death visions seems to be hindered rather than promoted by the deranging or dampening effects of alcohol, anesthetics and drugs. Survivors who report the most vivid, coherent and purposeful visions... are precisely those whose faculties were clearest. [9]

These findings are confirmed by Osis and Haroldsson who suggest:

Medical factors which cripple communication with the external world also cut down phenomena related to an afterlife. [10]

Elizabeth Kübler-Ross in fact, has argued against the overprescribing of palliative drugs which, she claims, *Rob terminal patients of the glimpse of heaven that is their deathright.*[11]

In order to answer the criticisms of those who refused to believe in her findings, Elizabeth Kübler-Ross organized a project involving people who had been blind for at least ten years. She relates:

Those who had an out-of-body experience and came back can tell you in detail what colors and jewelry you were wearing if you were present. Furthermore, they can tell you the color and pattern of your sweater, or of your tie and so on. You understand that these statements refer to facts which one cannot invent. You can recheck the facts providing you are not afraid of the answers. However, if you are afraid of them, then you may come to me like some of those skeptics and tell me that those out-of-body experiences are the result of lack of oxygen. Of course, if it were only a matter of lack of oxygen, I would prescribe it for all my blind patients. [12.]

Another two-year study was carried out by researchers Ring and

Cooper on over 30 blind patients of whom 80% of their sample claimed some kind of visual perception. With people who had been blind from birth, there was some uncertainty about what they were actually seeing - for example, knowing which color was which – but one woman was able to accurately describe the appearance of rings on her fingers as she looked down on her body lying in the operating theatre. [13]

This amazing incident reminds me of an event involving Vic, the father of my ex-partner, Karl. I always regretted that I'd only come to know the much esteemed Victor Ofaradei Tchum-Ampofo towards the latter part of his life after he'd been debilitated by a couple of strokes. Karl and I used to collect Vic each week and wheel him up to the local pub, the Hanover, for the weekly quiz where Vic never failed to astound me with his comprehensive general knowledge. As one side of his body was paralyzed, I would act as his scribe, always making sure I was sitting on his good side so he could lean across and whisper me the answers.

When Vic was suddenly taken ill, Karl and I rushed to the emergency ward and found Vic thrashing around, flailing his arms with such force that it took two of us to restrain him. It wasn't long before he became weaker. Quite suddenly, Vic raised his head, opened his eyes and glanced across my shoulder. "Oh, hello," he exclaimed, as though greeting some old friend who'd suddenly appeared.

I turned. The same way I'd turned when my mum had done exactly the same thing twenty years before. But the curtains were drawn around the bed; there was no one there. Karl and I both kept our hands wrapped around Vic's wrists as he became weaker and weaker and drew a few last peaceful breaths.

It wasn't until he'd passed away that I realized what Karl and I had been doing: we'd been holding both Vic's arms. We'd both been in such a state of panic that we'd failed to note the fact that during the last few minutes, Vic's paralysis had gone: he'd rolled and flailed on one side, then the other. It seemed so unlikely that I kept mulling it over – yes, Karl was standing there and I was at the other side and I could no longer remember which was Vic's good side and his bad but it had certainly taken the strength of two of us to hold him down.

I described this afterwards to my medical friends, but as no-one could offer any explanation, the event was pushed into the background. And there it stayed until a few years later when I chanced across the writing of Elizabeth Kübler-Ross who describes the different stages all of us go through at death. The first one, mentioned earlier, is that of increased perception, when our senses seem to be heightened; the second is that our bodies become whole: those who've been blind suddenly find they can see and those who've been deaf suddenly find they can hear and those who could not walk suddenly find themselves dancing. As Ross explains:

> Those of my patients suffering from multiple sclerosis, being able to move only in a wheelchair and having trouble uttering a sentence, tell me full of joy after they return from a near-death experience: "Doctor Ross, I could dance again." And there are thousands who during this second stage could finally dance again. [14]

So, this second stage is characterized by wholeness: our bodily imperfections disappear and we are suddenly fit, strong and in our prime. The third stage is that we never die alone. Someone arrives to collect us. As Ross says:

> In general, the people who are waiting for us on the other side are the ones who loved us the most. You always meet those people first. [15]

Such an experience quoted by Peter and Elizabeth Fenwick

concerns a woman called Gillian McKenzie who, during her near-death experience, encountered her much-loved grandfather:

> A voice at the end said, "Gill, you know who I am," and I thought, "Heavens, this is God and He knows my name." Then the voice chuckled and said, "Gill, there is someone here you do know." It was my grandfather, who'd died two years before. "Grandfather," I said, "I'm not staying here. Hamish can't cope, I've left a pile of shirts to be ironed and he doesn't know how to do them." [16]

In another example collected by the same authors, the writer recognizes her deceased mother:

> I saw my deceased mother – not the mother I had known, but I knew she was my mother, a young mother. She was smiling at me and had her hands stretched out to me. I was so happy. I was desperate to reach her. I had nearly got to her hands when I felt myself being pulled away from her. I got angry. I felt I had a long, long, long nightdress and I was being pulled downwards. I was desolate as the people and my mum disappeared. They had looked so happy and contented. I find it hard to describe the happiness on their faces. I wanted to be with them. It was no hallucination. How can you hallucinate a mother whom you knew and loved and remembered when she died, and see an entirely young beautiful girl, and each know who the other is? I do not grieve for my mother, I know she is happy. [17]

So, the third stage is the recognition of a much-loved, deceased friend or relative and the next stage is that something strange happens to time. One such time warp occurred in the case just reported when the writer saw her mother – not as she remembered her – but as a much younger woman. As Kübler-Ross points out, people undergoing near-death experience find themselves miraculously well with all physical disabilities cured, and often appear to lose the effects of ageing. They may go back to being young and fit and healthy or it may be that the people they encounter may be much younger than they remember them; it's just as though on this so-called "other side", people live forever in their prime.

The most vivid account of this process is provided by Carl Gustav Jung who had a heart attack in 1944. He became unconscious and left hanging to life by a thread but, during that time, experienced an amazing range of visions. He foresaw the death of his doctor who, on the exact day – April 4, 1944 – that Jung was well enough to sit up for the first time – took to his bed and died shortly afterwards of septicemia.

During the next few weeks, Jung was fragile and depressed but his visions continued. He describes the reality and timelessness of them:

I would never have imagined that any such experience was possible. It was not a product of imagination. The visions and experiences were utterly real; there was nothing subjective about them; they all had a quality of absolute objectivity.

We shy away from the word "eternal", but I can describe the experience only as the ecstasy of a non-temporal state in which present, past and future are one. Everything that happens in time had been brought together into a concrete whole... The experience might best be defined as a state of feeling but one which cannot be produced by imagination. How can I imagine that I exist simultaneously the day before yesterday, today and the day after tomorrow? There would be things which would not yet have begun, other things which would be indubitably present, and others again which would already be finished – and yet all this would be one. [18]

I encountered one of the finest and most moving portrayals of this in Figueres, home of the Salvador Dali foundation in Spain.[19]

Dali is famous for his melting clocks. You see the motif building up in his early paintings, slithering into the background of all kinds of weird canvasses but the main place they make their appearance – a room in which I just had to sit down and marvel for so long I suspect the staff were starting to think of me as an exhibit – lies upstairs - an entire ceiling painted with a glorious depiction of the heavens.

Around the walls is a frieze showing people's day-to-day existence – drawing water from the well, working in the fields, fighting in a battle or lying in bed. Above them are figures similarly engaged but at the moment of their death – someone falls into the well, a soldier is killed on the battlefield, somebody dies in bed. Around and above these figures, celestial hands reach down and draw them through the scene of their trauma and into paradisiacal splendor. Appearing around the edge – where earth blends into heaven and life segues into death - are one example after another of Dali's melting clocks. All my life I'd been intrigued by these clocks: Why was Dali so obsessed with them? What did they symbolize? And now they suddenly made sense. Death is the end of time as we know it – not because it means our time is up, but because it presages a dimension in which time exists no longer. It melts away. Opening up before us is a whole new level of existence in which, as Jung describes it, past, present and future all merge into one.

Shortly after my trip to Catalonia, I visited the Museum of Religious Art in Glasgow with its artifacts from all kinds of faiths relating to birth, marriage and death. And dead was how I stopped in my tracks as I rounded a corner and came face-to-face with Dali's Crucifixion. I'd seen the painting in print and been intrigued: what had happened to the great surrealist? Where were his visual jokes? Where were the ants and melting clocks?

Could it be the fact that it hardly seemed surreal at all that made it even more surreal?

Most paintings of the crucifixion depict Christ's suffering. That seems to be the point. Yet here Dali painted a man who – as in the accounts of so many who have survived near-death experience – rose above pain, a man whose wounds are healed, a man with power and strength, rising with his arms outstretched in a state of sublime transcendence. He looks like someone flying, just like those who describe their near-death experience as a return to life in its prime. (*If I tried to describe all the weird episodes of synchronicity that occurred whilst writing this book, I would never get it finished. But this one is worth noting: after writing the paragraph above, I decided to take a break, make a coffee and pick up my current reading, "The Conscious Universe" by Dean Radin.[21] My bookmark had rested on the account of an experiment to transfer images by thought between distant subjects. The image the experimenter was asking subjects to transfer..? Dali's crucifixion*)

But might all these accounts of rejuvenation simply be hallucinations? Might they have been induced by factors which often accompany trauma – endorphins and lack of oxygen to the brain, for instance? Or the hallucinatory impact of opiates and anesthetics?

Many of us experience hallucinations at one time or another. Maybe as a result of high temperature and fever or even a dose of magic mushrooms. Or a mild recreational helping of the kind of opiates used in palliative care of the terminally ill. But these hallucinations – like our dreams – take many and varied forms. One person sets off on a trip to the woods with the fairies and another goes out to lunch with a twelve-foot spider. Some hallucinators do appear to fly but this might be followed by beaming off on the Starship Enterprise, meeting Marilyn Monroe and making passionate love to her. In a near-death experience, it's your granny that you meet – not fairies or celebrities – unless you had a famous granny, of course. Opiates and other drugs can induce a "rush" and, in many people, that might involve a sense of rushing towards a light. However, in the same way that all of us during our sleeping hours, have different dreams, so those under the influence of drugs have different hallucinations. With near-death experience, people's accounts are very similar. They float along a long dark tunnel where they see a speck of light in the distance. The light becomes closer until it expands into a glowing brightness of extraordinary beauty and splendor. They become enfolded by this light which emanates love and peace. They're met by dead friends and relatives before progressing to a review of their time spent here on earth; some remember that they have family to care for and unfinished business to attend to. Some have left a pile of ironing behind. Whatever... this is the stage at which people find themselves quite suddenly back inside their bodies. We know no more because this, it would seem, is the point of no return.

Another explanation put forward by skeptics is that patients have heard about near-death experience and already know what symptoms to expect and such expectations have an effect on what they see and hear as their own life slips away.

And yet the study by Peter and Elizabeth Fenwick found that only 2% of their subjects had any previous idea of what a near-death experience was. The other 98% had never heard of such a thing. Never read about it and had no concept at all of the various stages they might go through. Other studies disclosed patients with a similar naivety. A small number held strong religious faith which gave them belief in an afterlife but the vast majority of patients had no expectations at all: there seemed no favoring those of one religious faith against another; and no exclusion of atheists or agnostics. Out of the 350 people in the 1994 Fenwick survey, 39% said that religion was important to them; 41% that it wasn't and 20% weren't sure. We do know however, that there appears to be no relationship whatsoever between near-death experience and religious belief.

As Carol Zaleski explains:

Age, sex, race, geographic location, education, occupation, religious upbringing, church attendance, prior knowledge of near-death studies, all have negligible effect on the likelihood of near-death visions. Suicide victims seeking annihilation, fundamentalists who expect to see God on the operating table, atheists, agnostics and "carpe diem" advocates find equal representation in the ranks of near-death experiencers. And their answers to survey questions show that, for all the religious implications of near-death experience, a person's beliefs about God, life after death, and heaven and hell do not determine the content of his vision. [22]

Not only have researchers had to face a barrage of criticism from skeptics and scientists but also from religious groups complaining that people who weren't Christian had apparently been admitted into heaven. Their orthodox religious view insisted that yes, there is an afterlife, but we secure a place there only by religious faith. As one Lutheran pastor complained: *If life after death could be empirically verified "beyond a shadow of a doubt", then there would seem to be little need for faith.* [23]

A similar reservation was raised by Stephen Vicchio who complained: *the empty tomb for Kübler-Ross and Moody is superfluous if not redundant. There is no need for Easter if we are immortal.*[24]

A number of different studies into near-death experience all show that somewhere between 13 and 18% of patients report some kind of afterlife experience which raises the question: are these the only ones who have such an experience? Or does everyone have the experience but only 13-18% remember it? We know, for example, that – in spite of so many people's insistence that they never dream - everybody does. Scientists have studied brain patterns and eye movements during sleep and when those who claim never to dream are woken suddenly from a state of rapid eye movement, then yes, they remember their dream. It seems as though for the vast majority of dreams, we forget about them within only a few seconds of awakening.

Might this be the same with near-death experience?

In December 2001, the medical journal, *The Lancet*, published a 13-year study of near-death experience observed in ten different Dutch hospitals, one of the few studies in which a large group of people were actually interviewed immediately after their resuscitation. The chief investigator, cardiologist Pim van Lommel, MD reported that:

Our results show that medical factors cannot account for the occurrence of near-death experience. All patients had a cardiac arrest, and were clinically dead with unconsciousness resulting from insufficient blood supply to the brain. [25]

Of the 344 patients investigated by the Dutch study, 18% had some memory of their experience. As Dr van Lommel reports:

In our prospective study of patients that were clinically dead (flat EEG, showing no electrical activity in the cortex, and loss of brain stem function evidenced by dilated pupils and absence of the gag reflex), the patients report a clear consciousness, in which cognitive functioning, emotion, sense of identity, or memory from early childhood occurred, as well as perceptions from a position out and above their "dead" body.

Near-death experience pushes at the limits of medical ideas about the range of human consciousness and the mind-brain relation. There is a theory that consciousness can be experienced independently from the normal body-linked waking consciousness. The current concept in medical science, however, states that consciousness is the product of the brain. Could the brain be a kind of receiver for consciousness and memories, functioning like a TV, radio or a mobile telephone? What you receive is not generated by the receiver, but rather electromagnetic information waves (photons) that are always around you and are made visible or audible by the brain and your sense organs? [25]

When we come across events which fly in the face of conventional scientific belief, we can either deny their existence (*it **has** to be the effect of drugs or endomorphins, in spite of what they say*) or we can open our minds to the possibility that modern science still has a lot to learn. As van Lommel explains, the traditional view is that consciousness is the product of our brains, but if consciousness continues after our brains are dead, then we need to do some rethinking.

The majority of the world's population – both now and in the past - take for granted the existence of the soul, a consciousness that exists over and beyond the body. Western science tends to afford this notion the same respect as belief in unicorns and tooth fairies and, of course, you can't experiment on souls. You can't put the soul in a test tube, shake it about and examine it under a microscope. The soul doesn't lend itself to mathematical formulae, probability tests or genetic engineering. You can't put the soul on an overhead projector or test for it in exams. Your CV has no section for a soul; it will not get you funding; it's no use at all for citations or getting a space in the staff car park. It will not obtain you membership of the Royal Society nor get you published in a scientific journal. For a scientist, in other words, it appears to be a steep skateboard-run on the long, winding slope to ignominy and failure.

And yet...a frequently-reported phenomenon amongst those who attend the dying is a visible movement in the air hovering above the body. It's been described as a will-of-the-wisp or like the shimmering air we sometimes see above the tarmac of a road on a hot sunny day. One such example was reported to Peter Fenwick at a conference in New Zealand:

I met a GP who told me the following story. He had been playing golf, when another player on the course had a heart attack. He went over to see if he could help, and as he approached he saw what he described as a white form which seemed to rise and separate from the body. He had seen many people die before, he told me, but this was the first time he had ever witnessed anything like this. [26]

From the time when near-death experience first began to clash with the views of modern science, such accounts tended to be written-off or belittled by contemptuous scientists. In 1892 for example, the Swiss geologist and alpinist, Albert Heim, published accounts from mountain climbers who had survived near-fatal falls. Part of his aim was "to reassure bereaved families that death by falling is a more dreadful experience for onlookers and relatives than for the victim." The thirty survivors he interviewed reported feeling calm, detached from the scene of danger, and joyful. *They had, so to speak, fallen into heaven.* [27]

Oskar Pfister, a Swiss minister, lay psychoanalyst and friend of Freud, published an interpretation of Heim's findings in 1930, theorizing that *the victims were evoking infantile fantasies in order to evade the unacceptable prospect of death.* [28] A similar argument was used to explain away their miraculous experience in 1967 by R.C.A. Hunter in his article, *On the Experience of Nearly Dying.*[29]

In a series of final lectures just prior to her own demise in 2004, Elisabeth Kübler-Ross described the suspicion that greeted much of her early work:

The opinion which other people have of you is their problem, not yours... If you have a clear conscience and are doing your work with love, others will spit on you and try to make your life miserable. Then ten years later, you are honored with eighteen doctorates for the same work. This is the situation in which I find myself. [30]

But Kübler-Ross, thankfully, shrugged off the disdain and disbelief of many of her colleagues, and persevered with what very few doctors have done – sitting with patient after patient through their dying moments, noting and recording what they saw and described. Ross lived long enough to witness a sea-change in public attitudes towards our treatment of the terminally ill and, as she described above, received the great accolade of being honored with doctorates from eighteen different universities.

Chapter 5

Dark Matter

*Alice had not a moment to think about stopping herself before she
found herself falling down what seemed to be a very deep well.*

*Either the well was very deep or she fell very slowly, for she had
plenty of time as she went down to look about her and to wonder
what was going to happen next...*

Alice in Wonderland, chapter one, p.26

The fishing village of Staithes perches on a North Yorkshire
clifftop and teeters towards the bay. The village is a labyrinth of
tiny cobbled alleyways surrounding higgledy-piggledy cottages,
many of which have coffin windows let into the gable ends, as
the stairs are too steep and twisting for the dead to leave by the
doors. Standing sentinel are vertiginous cliffs, housing hordes of
seabirds whose nests are perched even more precariously than
the cottages they overlook.

To the south lies the Cleveland Way and the grandeur of
Yorkshire's heritage coast with Whitby Abbey and the cliffs of
Flamborough Head; for those unfamiliar with this coastline, I'll
just add that it's no surprise that this is where Bram Stoker's
Dracula chose to disembark. And to the north... well... what at
first appears to be a factory, spewing out dust and smoke, a huge
blot on the landscape... and you might be forgiven for
wondering what on earth that's doing in the North York Moors
National Park.

Yet it's not inside North Yorkshire, but just over the border in
Cleveland. And you're not looking at a factory but a potash mine,
the deepest mine in Europe. Eleven hundred meters below
ground are over a thousand kilometers of tunnels, extending five

kilometers out below the sea; inside this mine, suspended inside a huge chamber dug into the salt, is a laboratory full of scientists searching for dark matter.[1]

The notion of dark matter began in the nineteen thirties when the Swiss astronomer, Fritz Wacky, suggested that a distant cluster of galaxies would fall apart were it not for the gravitational pull of some unknown substance holding them in place. The name "dark matter" arose because this mysterious substance appeared to neither reflect nor absorb light, making it impossible to observe even with the strongest telescope.

Later, in the nineteen seventies, the American astronomer, Vera Rubin studied the rotation rates of distant spiral galaxies. Their speed appeared to defy all we know about velocity and mass. Basically, the further things are from the centre of the galaxy, the slower they should be travelling. As this was not the case, Rubin concluded that some mysterious force was slowing down the galaxies, pulling them together.

In 2007, a group of scientists led by the British astronomer Richard Massey, at the California Institute of Technology, published the first three-dimensional dark-matter map, demonstrating how this mysterious substance could coalesce around galaxies, pulling them together. And in 2008, the Hubble telescope was able to take a photograph of an ethereal halo cradling a distant galaxy. Might this ghostly halo have been caused by clumps of dark matter bending light from distant stars?

As evidence increased for the likelihood of dark matter, scientists raced to be the first to discover proof of its existence. Our solar system is orbiting the galaxy at (hold on to your hats) over two hundred kilometers a second, and so they assumed that every now and then, a dark matter particle would interact with an atomic nucleus here on earth and leave some kind of trace. And as we know the kind of traces that other – earthly – substances will leave – we simply have to wait for the appearance of a ghostly signature, a trace which forms the shape of something that we've never seen before. And what better place to look for it – away from houses, traffic, cosmic rays and background radiation - than at the bottom of a mine.

Were you to take part in this quest, you would first have to don a miner's uniform of boots, helmet, light and emergency air supply. Accustomed to smooth, modern lifts with swishing doors, you may feel a little wary of entering what appears to be a makeshift lion cage. You may feel even more fearful as the doors clang shut and you drop for six or seven minutes through pitch blackness, conscious of the lengthening void between your body and the world you've left behind.

As the lift arrives at its destination beneath 1,100 meters of solid rock and as the doors clank open, you find yourself in a hot, cavernous chamber with the constant breeze necessary to keep air circulating underground. You stagger through the blackness for six hundred meters or so to the chamber in which a laboratory, shifting disturbingly with the movement of the salt, is suspended from the ceiling. Here, you encounter scientists whose quest is to search for weakly-interacting massive particles – or WIMPS - by means of a time-projection chamber, a piece of equipment about the size of four large chest freezers, in which they hope to track the course of the dark matter as it scurries along in the dark.

In the same laboratory at Boulby are other members of the United Kingdom Dark Matter Collaboration as well as overseas researchers. And meanwhile, other scientists are investigating different corners of the globe – below the Mediterranean, in Illinois and at various other locations in the USA including President Obama's old college, Occidental, just outside Los Angeles. Elsewhere, other explorations are taking place under mountains and even inside the Antarctic ice as well as, the most expensive project of all, the Large Hadron Collider at CERN in Switzerland. Teams of top scientists... millions spent on research… Nobel prizes at stake… and the possibility of finding some of the 96% of the universe that's missing… You might imagine all this is something of a long shot, but in 2009 there was a sighting of something that could well turn out to be the elusive substance in the Soudan iron ore mine in Minnesota.

So the days are gone when the existence of dark matter was considered some kind of flaky pie-in-the-sky. But why is it so important?

As Gerry Gilmore of Cambridge University's Institute of Astronomy explains:

Dark matter is what created the structure of the universe and is essentially what holds it together. When ordinary matter falls into lumps of dark matter, it turns into galaxies, stars, planets and people. Without it we wouldn't be here.[2]

The discovery of dark matter is potentially something that can turn science as we know it on its head. One of its possible implications is that of supersymmetry – the theory which suggests that every particle in the universe has a doppelgänger – a replica – like some kind of heavier twin. Again, this may sound unlikely but its potential discovery is one of the reasons for building CERN's Large Hadron Collider in Switzerland.

Many people assume that dark matter is the substance of black holes and therefore exists only out in space; however, what scientists are searching for at Boulby and elsewhere are weakly-interacting massive particles that may well be in existence all around us. The concept of "weakly-interacting" means that – when these massive particles encounter mundane particles of matter like a cup of tea or a slice of cheesecake or even me or you – they mostly pass straight through as if we don't exist.

There are implications in all this. The word "quantum" simply means "package" and quantum physics refers to the building blocks that make up atoms; instead of being solid lumps like most of the stuff we build with, these sub-atomic building blocks are tiny packages of energy.

We tend to take it for granted that stuff is fixed and separate – this is a table; this is a cup of tea and that thing over there is a slice of cheesecake. But quantum science suggests that everything is made from quivering waves of energy, waves which move and vibrate; these quivering waves pass through each other but then turn into particles when they're being observed. When we consider that everything we know is made of these quivering waves of energy, then the strange apparition hovering above a dying man on the golf course - seen by the doctor mentioned earlier – makes a bit more sense.

These quantum packages refuse to obey the normal rules of science. Physics dictates that they can only be in one place at any one time and... well no; to everyone's amazement, these tiny particles can be here... ☺

and they can be here... ☺

both at the very same instant.

They can disappear from here: ☹

and turn up here: ☹

without travelling though any of the space in between.

When photons of light are fired at a wall through two vertical slits, they start out as tiny particles, turn into waves, waft through both slits at once and then, when they reach the other side, turn back to particles again. And the reason that they change from waves back into particles seems to be that they know they're being watched.

Just imagine, as an illustration, my fish tank where the large blue crab has a tendency to devour baby fish. Let's say that, in order to protect them, I stretch a screen across the tank and place my spawning fish behind it away from the crab's large jaws. Let's say I then erect another screen with even smaller holes that only the tiniest fish can swim through. I place lots of plants and tiny crumbs of fish food there to make an ideal nursery. The following morning I switch on the tank light expecting to see the baby fish swimming around in their new enclosure and what do I find? The big blue crab sitting inside the new nursery there licking its lips without a single hole in either screen. And not only that but the blue crab also sits grinning at me, back in his old corner. (*Actually anyone who's ever kept crabs in their fish tank will know this is not so unusual as crabs do appear to duplicate when they shed their shells, but the shells don't count as real crabs – they just look like them - and that's enough of crab husbandry for a chapter on quantum physics*).

While we're on the subject of tiny, weenie stuff, scientists have also suggested the likelihood of strings so small that a hundred billion billion loops could stretch across a single photon. If you find this scale difficult to visualize, just remember that an atom is a hundred thousand times bigger than a photon.

Hope this helps.

It certainly didn't help me.

Don't ask how small an atom is and don't ask how they measure all these tiny bits and bobs or even who has time to sit and count them. The important thing is the discovery that, for strings to behave in the way they apparently do, they would have to resonate in ten dimensions. If we think of our dimensions as being four – three of space and one of time – then not only much of the missing universe but also six extra dimensions are in existence all round us.

Physicists have also been baffled by the behavior of these quantum particles. How can they know whether anyone's watching? And how can it be possible for them to be the sound waves of a wailing cat one minute and then turn into the kind of particles that constitute a slice of cheesecake the next?

Scientists are obsessed with rules. They observe how stuff behaves and then make laws to predict what it will do in future.

If they decide the earth is round, they want it to be round all the time; not just at weekends. If an apple falls on someone's head, then if somebody else sits under the same tree, they want the apple to hit them on the head as well, or at the very least, travel downwards. They don't want the apple to fly off into space, start crying or read out the shipping forecast. They don't want the apple's behavior to depend on whether anyone's watching or not. Scientists don't like anarchy. They whittle away until they've made up a law and without any laws, there can't be any science.

So, they say.

However, no matter how many rules scientists have tried to make, quantum particles simply take no notice. If it's a day for being a wave, one of them will be a wave; if it's a particle-kind-of-a-day, one of them will be a particle. Creatures after my own heart, but not too popular with reductionist physicists who like to have everything tied up, neatly bound, pigeon-holed and doing as it's told.

This conundrum has achieved notoriety in the story of Schrödinger's Cat. When Marcus, my elder son went to live in Copenhagen, he would phone home regularly on a Saturday to check out the fortunes of his local football team. As time went on, he would find out the score on the internet but I remember him saying that he feared his team, Sheffield United had neither won nor lost until he made the crucial phone call. "It's like the Copenhagen scientists," he explained. "And Schrödinger's cat."

I never liked to show my ignorance. But why were so many Danish scientists supporters of Sheffield United? And what did it matter whether one of them had a cat? Then I discovered that the famous Schrödinger didn't own a real cat but, like the Cheshire strain which Alice encountered, an imaginary disappearing cat. You may be relieved to read therefore, that no actual cats were harmed or injured during the formulation of this theory.

Schrödinger, the famous Copenhagen scientist, said, *What if there were a box? And what if there were a cat inside the box? And what if there were some poison that could kill the cat and some radioactive stuff that may or may not have decayed and caused the can of poison to open. But because it's one of those quantum kind of things that won't behave a certain way until it knows whether anyone's looking, this won't happen unless somebody actually opens the box and peers inside. So, while the cat is inside the box and no-one has looked at it yet, at what stage is it dead and when is it still alive?*

You may think this question has all the practical applications of a Mad Hatter's tea party and that scientists would be better employed working out ways of putting an end to famine, war, pestilence and babies that cry on planes but, needless to say – like some piddling item of trivia in a pub quiz – they've been taxing their brains about it ever since.

And one possible solution has been produced by multiple universe theory. In this explanation, the cat both lives and dies because the universe splits in two: one world in which the poison is opened and the cat dies a prolonged and painful death and another in which the radioactive stuff refuses to decay and the cat lives on. That's probably the same world in which Sheffield United win every match, get promoted, fly to the top of the premier division and also win the Cup.

Which brings us round nicely to DreamTime.

This is the Aboriginal name for what others have called the Great Time, a totally different dimension which exists alongside our own. The Aborigines believe (*I'm describing this in the present tense with some uncertainty because I'm aware how difficult it is for indigenous people to cling on to their belief system in changing times*) that when they are born, their soul emerges from DreamTime and returns there when they die. It is the place where their ancestors live. DreamTime is not only a sacred place but also a sacred time, described as an *all-at-once* instead of *one-thing-after-another* time in which past, present and future merge together.[3] It is the home of the great heroes whose stories are recounted in myths. When the great deeds of the heroes are ceremoniously re-enacted, those taking part enter the time when the deeds originally happened – not in the past but in a present which has an eternal existence side-by-side with daily life. The aborigines have cult totems forming a "doorway into this eternal DreamTime". When they perform ceremonial rites, the doorway opens for them to enter this sacred space.

The aboriginal peoples see this as the same space that we enter in our dreams, slipping through the doorway as we sleep into a place in which time as we know it ceases to exist. When, in our dreams, we meet friends or relatives, we are just as likely to see them as they were twenty or thirty years ago, or the way they will look in the future, as the way they are today. This is what is meant by an *all-at-once instead of one-thing-after-another* time. It is time-out-of-time.

One of the main areas I want to highlight in this book, is the similarity between this Aboriginal DreamTime and the 94% of the universe which scientists are spending billions of pounds and dollars searching for.

I don't think it's too outrageous to suggest that these two realms of existence might be rubbing shoulders with each other or are even different names for what is basically the same realm.

And not only did the Aborigines find it first, but could have saved the scientists a bit of cash by pointing out the way:

- Both are talking about a realm which exists alongside our normal day-to-day existence.
- Both are talking about a completely invisible world.
- Both have the possibility of further dimensions wound around inside them.
- Both are talking about a dimension which only weakly interacts with ours i.e. we're not in contact all the time but can access this space only through specific portals or doorways.

- Both are talking about an area in which time as we know ceases to exist.

During the first part of this book we'll look at portals into DreamTime and examine the way they let us peer inside this other realm or dimension. The largest and most dramatic portal would seem to be near-death experience. If this is the realm where our spirits go when we die then those who've already tried this experience out for size have most to tell about what they've discovered.

However, you'll be pleased to know I'm not recommending this as a new-fangled spiritual practice and strongly suggest that you don't try it at home. We'll move on instead to a doorway which is much more accessible and pleasant: the doorway of creativity.

Chapter 6

Creativity

It writes all manner of things that I don't intend...
The King, Alice through the Looking Glass, chapter one.

I believe I've got a book coming. I feel so excited...I walked up Piccadilly and back and went into a Gent's in Brick Street, and suddenly in the Gent's, I saw the three chunks, the beginning, the middle and the end.[1]

This was how the English novelist Graham Greene described his inspiration for writing The Third Man. I'm still intrigued to know whether Greene was referring to a Gent's tailoring shop or a public lavatory and, should you try to follow his example, don't automatically assume, if someone places their hand across your shoulder in a public toilet in Piccadilly, that it has to be a muse offering inspiration.

The Ancient Greeks believed that all artists had a muse, the true composer of the work for which the author, artist or composer was only a vessel or a mouthpiece. The earliest known muses were daughters of the Earth Goddess, Gaia, worshipped at Delphi before the shrine was rededicated to Apollo.

Jung describes this sense of being guided when he began to write his *Memories, Dreams, Reflections*:

A book of mine is always a matter of fate. There is something unpredictable about the process of writing, and I cannot prescribe for myself any predetermined course. Thus this autobiography is now taking a direction quite different from what I had imagined at the beginning. It has become necessary for me to write down my early memories. If I neglect to do so for a single day, unpleasant physical symptoms immediately follow. As soon as I set to work they vanish and my head feels perfectly clear.[2]

So the notion that creativity links us to something over and beyond ourselves goes back to the dawn of time. We sometimes feel that the poem or novel exists already and all we have to do is simply trace over the words.. And yet another notion is that to be truly inspired the subject of our work has to be of personal significance. Martin Amis, writing in the Guardian Book Club describes the process:

> A work of fiction begins with an inkling: a notion that is also a physical sensation. It is hard to improve on Nabakov who described it as a "shiver" and a "throb". The throb can come from anywhere, a newspaper report (very common), the remnants of a dream, a half-remembered quote. The crucial, the enabling fermentation lies in this: the shiver must connect to something already present in the subconscious.[3]

An example of such an inkling occurred in one of my creative writing classes when I was encouraging my students to explore their childhood memories; as always, I picked up a pen and joined in.

The most significant event of my childhood was the death of my brother and sister; both had cystic fibrosis, for which, in those days, there was no cure. As they spent so much time in hospital, and died before I was four, my memories are hazy: taking out a doll and asking my mother whether our new baby would be bigger or smaller in size... sitting on the grass in Sheffield's botanical gardens with my baby sister and threading her a daisy chain... asking about my sister when I hadn't seen her for a while, only to be told that she had died and the news had been kept from me...

What I remember more clearly is the birth of another child. This time the memories are stronger: learning to knit mittens and bootees and threading them with yellow ribbons... neat piles of baby clothes and terry diapers folded in the airing cupboard... my mother going into hospital... the gut-wrenching shock that a child could actually be born dead... the sight of my mother, her features grey as slate, carried into the house on a stretcher...

Yet as I looked back, the most defining aspect was the surrounding silence. The baby clothes vanished from the airing cupboard; none of the children were mentioned, their names erased from our past. I began to write in my notebook, *It was as though they had never been born...*

And then I stopped and thought: how ridiculous.

When we avoid a subject, it doesn't just disappear. There are things that we don't talk about. Then we sidestep round the areas that touch on things we don't talk about; we tiptoe round the issues that relate to the areas that touch on the things we don't talk about. Yet a wound needs air to help it heal. When we cover it over, it festers.

I tried again. This is what I wrote:

None of the children were ever mentioned afterwards as though, if we never spoke of them, it would be as though they'd not been born.

But there was no wiping out the ghosts of three dead children. Whenever we sat down, they came and sat beside us; they stood wherever we stood and whenever we spoke they listened. When we sat down to eat, they seated themselves at our table. They stayed awake all night to haunt our dreams and when we moved house they came with us. Their memory pulsed between us, backwards and forwards, to and fro like an empty cradle. Rocking.

When I came to the line, *their memory pulsed between us, backwards and forwards, to and fro...* the English teacher inside me bristled: a fine example of redundancy. *Think again, Linda. Did it pulse backwards and forwards? Or to and fro? You can't have both.* But then another voice at the back of my mind, the real Linda, was having none of it. *No, no. We haven't finished yet. Wait and see what's coming next.*

And then I completed the sentence: ...*like an empty cradle. Rocking.* Straightaway, I could see why I needed to repeat myself: to depict the rhythm of the rocking cradle. But what amazed me was the realization that part of me knew what I was going to write before the image appeared in my mind, before reaching the end of the sentence.

On other occasions, I'd had the feeling that, in my most creative moments, my words had a life of their own and all I ever did was trace over them, yet this was the first time I'd actually caught myself in the act. How could it happen? Writing is a conscious process; it takes thought. We think of something to say, then write it down; we think of something else to follow. We don't – like the king in Alice through the Looking Glass - write first and think afterwards.

Or do we?

Here's another example from a writing workshop, this time in the basement bar of City Screen cinema in York. Wafting above our heads are chattering voices from the terrace which overlooks the river and as I take my notebook over to the window, I'm amused by my view of the underside of tables, feet and women's skirts.

I'm taken back again into my childhood: this time squashed behind an old leather couch, eavesdropping on the chatter of my mother and her friends. Like most women in those days, their hands were always busy with sewing, darning or knitting. I might be asked to hold out a skein of wool for them to wind and afterwards would sneak into my hiding place, ears peeled for the kind of gossip never meant for children's ears.

I open my notebook and begin to play around with words to

do with sewing, knitting and stories: *to embroider facts... to spin a yarn... pull the wool over people's eyes...*

Later that evening, I take out my notebook and begin to hammer my ideas into shape:

Threads

Keep still.
hands straight before her, thumbs raised,
cats-cradling the skein of wool
as it's wound around, crossed and wound again.
And later, keeping even more still,
tucked against the cracked, leather couch,
pins and needles in her feet,
she picks the threads of women's chatter
dropped between nattering needles,
craftily learning the ropes:
Knit one; Purl one; Knit two together...
combing apart the strands of homespun wisdom
picked up from behind the seams by a forgotten, only
    child -
waiting like a virgin princess, for the pinprick on her
    thumb -
for the day when she will also learn to spin a yarn,
embroider stories, pull the wool over people's eyes,
when she will also take a skein of wool
and stand a child before her, impatiently cats-cradling.

And when many years have passed,
when the needles stop their nattering,
when the ball is wound and the skein undone,
when the shuttle halts its clatter and the spinning wheel
    has stopped,
she presses her back against the gnarled oak bench
of a Quaker Meeting House,

holding her hands before her, thumbs raised,
enclosing a skeinful of silence
and at last discovers stillness like a virgin sheet of snow.
Her eyes begin to focus on the space between the stitches
on the point between the pinhead and the angel's dancing
    toe.
She has finally cottoned on, removed the wool from her
    eyes
and look: there in the silence, in the gap between the traces
she sees the whole embroidered fabric:
the blue, the green and grey and gold,
the filigree of life,
a winding sheet to enclose the gathered meeting,
knitting them together.
Now she sees, not the warp and weft, but the stuff of all
    existence;
in place of all the clattering, she hears the angels sigh.

She gazes at her finger and no longer sees the pinprick
but how the tiny strands of flesh have knitted back
    together.
Knit one; purl one; knit two together...
She pinpoints the place where the crewel needle
drew forth the droplets of blood
and sees in its place...
a pearl.

In the way that I normally write, I think of a word or phrase, then
jot it down. I consider another, write that down and then, as ideas
rush thick and fast, find that I've actually written something
without thinking about it first. When I reach the lines,

Her eyes begin to focus on the space between the stitches
on the point between the pinhead and the angel's dancing toe...

I write them first, then read them and wonder what they mean. What's all this about a dancing angel?

I recall some theological debate about how many angels could dance on the head of a pin - an issue about which I've never lost any sleep. But I like the image and the lines have rhythm so I leave them. I repeat the process as I reach what I sense will be the conclusion: I know the woman will look down and see something on her finger. What will she see? I've no idea. Then I write the words: *a pearl*. What have I written that for? Well, it fits with *knit one, purl one*; a pearl is small and round like a drop of blood and it's precious. So pain and injury can be transformed into a precious jewel. Yes, OK.

When I'm invited into schools to talk about my writing, the children ask over and over: *Where do your ideas come from?*

I waffle away about this and that: an interesting journey; an odd character but, if the truth be known, I haven't the faintest idea; ideas appear out of thin air like white rabbits out of a hat. I certainly can't force them or order them about. There are times when ideas are as rare as dancing angels and other times when I can't walk across the room without tripping over them all.

The only time I've ever really talked about these notions of creativity and coincidence was the day I met a group of people who understood the very problem: a gathering of authors.

I was taking part in a residential course in which writers involved with the Royal Literary Fund's Fellowship Scheme were studying – amongst other texts - *The Savage* by David Almond.[4] This story depicts a young boy, Blue Baker, bullied at school after the death of his father. Blue writes an illustrated story about a savage who, as the book develops, assumes more and more of a life of his own. The notion of creating something which then goes on to develop an autonomous existence is a common theme in literature - think about the Gruffalo, Pinnochio and Frankenstein's monster for starters – but I was surprised when one of the writers, Brian Keaney, said: *Of course, we've all had the experience of writing something which then turns out to happen in real life...* and was astounded by the number of heads nodding around the room.

Over coffee, I asked Brian what had prompted his remark and he went on to describe the inspiration for *Bitter Fruit,* one of his novels for young people, published by Orchard Books in 1999. I asked him if he would be kind enough to write down his account and this is what he sent me:

There was a knock on my door one morning. When I opened the door I saw my good friend Stephen standing there with tears in his eyes. Now Stephen was a big man who worked in the construction industry, so I was surprised and dismayed to see him in this state. 'What's the matter?' I asked.

'It's Linda,' he said.

Linda was his thirteen year old daughter.

I immediately assumed that something terrible had happened to her. In fact the first thing that came into my mind was that she had been in a car crash. I don't know why. Perhaps because I was also a parent and we lived on a busy road.

'She told me she hates me,' Stephen said.

I nearly laughed out loud with relief. 'Come in and have a cup of tea,' I told him. 'You can tell me all about it.'

When Stephen was sitting down with a cup of tea he began to describe the difficulties he had been experiencing with his daughter. She was staying out until the early hours of the morning. She wouldn't say where she had been. When they tried to ask her about it, she just shouted at them and stormed off. And when Stephen had insisted that she come back at a reasonable hour she had told him that she hated him.

After a while Stephen began to feel better about things. Just talking the problem through with another parent had obviously helped. Soon he got up and went on his way. After he had gone, however, I kept thinking about what he had said and I realized that it would make a very good starting point for a story. I phoned Stephen and asked him how he would feel about me using some of his experience. He was always a generous man and he said he would have no problem with that.

To kick-start the process of devising the plot. I did what I often do when I'm trying to develop a story: I decided to put the central character in the worst place I could imagine just to see what would come out of the situation. I remembered my fears when I had first seen Stephen standing on my doorstep and suddenly I had a burst of inspiration: what if it was not the girl who was killed in a car crash but her father?

Immediately I saw the narrative stretching out ahead of me. In chapter one she has an argument with her father which ends with her telling him she hates him; in chapter two her father is killed in a car crash so that this casual phrase uttered in anger becomes the last thing she ever says to him, an outcome that she will have to live with for the rest of her life. After that the novel just wrote itself.

I had just about finished the first draft when Stephen's wife came to my door, also in tears, to tell me that he had been diagnosed with a very aggressive form of cancer. There was absolutely no hope for him. He was dead within a matter of months, long before my book was published.

I have never been able to read my book without feeling as if I made that happen. Of course it's a silly thing to say. He wasn't even killed in a car crash. Yet I still feel somehow responsible, as if I had tempted fate.[5]

These strange episodes of synchronicity don't just happen with writers. My daughter Mikita Brottman, a professor at Maryland Institute of Contemporary Art, has written Hollywood Hex, a book detailing some of the bizarre events occurring on

Hollywood film sets - events which mirror many of the incidents in the movies being made.[6]

When I invented my fictional angel, my life became surrounded by angels, bombarding me left, right and centre. My second novel was a modernized version of King Lear. Someone quoted from Lear in Quaker Meeting; there was showing of Lear at the local cinema; there were other coincidences along the way but the most significant was that I invented a girl whose mother had recently died of cancer and my own mum died of cancer before the book was published.

Surely this was nothing to do with my writing. How could it be? Writers devise plots about murder, war and haunting without any concern that they might be making these things happen. But when my later novels also contained events similar to those that went on to happen in real life, I began to feel uneasy.

Over lunch at the RLF gathering, I asked whether any other writers had accounts they were willing to share. Shah Husain had written a story which presaged the car crash in which Lady Diana was killed; she'd also written about an erupting underground lake in Iceland which was then followed by a similar real event. I was also intrigued by an anecdote of the novelist, Anne Rooney and asked if she would be kind enough to write it down for me. This is what she sent me:

I was working on a novel set in Venice in 1576 in which a nobleman and his brother embezzle a large sum of money from the Republic. The brother is a bad type, and would do it without a guilty conscience, but the more important protagonist, my heroine's father, is not criminally inclined and I needed a good reason for him to be involved in the crime. He had a personal motive - his son was gambling away their fortune - but I could not square the act with his character. The two were members of a large noble family with many branches, some extremely wealthy.

I was working in the Marciana library in Venice on 16th century manuscripts as part of my research. In the afternoon, I took a break from the very glum accounts of plague deaths to sit in the main reading room and distract myself with other books. I was tired of reading Italian so looked for something else and the first thing I came across was the typescript of an old PhD thesis written in French but about 16th century Venice. I opened it at random and started reading - and there was my motive. The Republic had borrowed a very large sum from the noble families during the late 15th century which they had persistently refused to pay back. The money was needed to pay for salt. When the Republic did finally repay the debt, many decades later, it did not pay attention to which branches of the families had lent the money but just gave it to the most dominant figures. So here was my reason: the minor branch of the family had not been repaid their salt money. The bad brother could convince the good brother that the money was rightfully theirs. I already had a character in the book whose family worked on Torcello gathering salt, including a boy who was in prison for smuggling salt, so it tied in well.

I did feel rather spooked. It wasn't the only strange coincidence around this novel, but it was the most useful. I had been looking for a reason for ages, and to have picked up that particular book, of all the books on open shelves, and turned to that particular page.... it was very strange. The novel has a central conceit of being written from a diary, and it seems that history is rearranging itself to make things I've invented true. At times, I almost feel as though I'm discovering it rather than inventing it.[7]

I mulled through these conversations on my journey home. Of course, writers cannot make things happen: Brian did not cause the death of his friend any more than I caused the death of my mother. Otherwise we'd only write about nice and happy stuff.

Books would come with a disclaimer: *No imaginary characters have been harmed in the writing of this story…*

Many years ago I was approached by a group of peace activists wanting me to write a film script based on peace.

I was puzzled.

"We're sick of the number of films about war or glorifying war. Why are there no films about peace?" one of them asked. "We thought a consortium of us could come up with the money to produce a film about peace and we thought you'd be a good person to…"

How would the story go? *Once upon a time there were lots of very nice people who lived happily ever after. The end!*

Drama is based on conflict – between people, countries, families, or even different aspects of someone's personality. Without conflict, you'd be left with a documentary about a group of nuns going for a picnic, spring lambs skipping in the sunshine and happy families holding hands on holiday and an audience switching channel before the title tracks had finished.

We cannot ban conflict from fiction or guarantee that no characters will be harmed. Where would the Bible have got to? And the Greek myths? And the Bhagavad-Gita?

On the way home, I reflect on this longer than I wanted.

An accident on the M60 has ground the traffic to a halt, leaving me mulling the problem over for the next two hours. A picture comes into my head of an old-fashioned mincing machine. I shove the picture away. It comes back, bigger. Like Alice when she grows so tall that her head sticks out of the chimney.

I'm hoping there will be readers young enough not to know what a mincer looks like. In the days before food processors, they were used to make burgers or meatballs. You clamped the mincer to a worktop, fed lumps of meat, onion, potato or whatever into the funnel and then turned the corkscrew-like handle. As a child I found it fascinating to watch the long strands of minced meat snaking through the perforated disc into my mother's mixing bowl.

And now the mincing machine has grown so big, its handle is hanging from the driver's window and the funnel peers out of the roof.

So here I am sitting in standing traffic one cold, late-November evening, reflecting on the metaphor of mincing machines, time anomalies and manifestations of the muse.

Our view of time is linear; it has to be. We're born; we grow old; we fall off the log; we can't grow old first or fall off the log first. Because of the way we're born and then we die, time happens in straight lines. First one thing, then the next... one thing after another...

If there are other dimensions which exist alongside ours, this may not need to happen. If people aren't being born and dying, time needn't happen in straight lines. It could be, like the Aboriginal DreamTime, *all-at-once* instead of *one thing after another*. But even without time as we know it, surely things wouldn't just be a huge, chaotic sludge. DreamTime suggests a higher dimension in which it's possible to see further and understand more; so if things aren't organized by time, wouldn't they be arranged some other way?

Like topics?

I imagine folders labeled:

- *Mothers with Cancer,*
- *King Lear*
- *Angels*

When we focus on creativity, we maybe pick ideas out of these ethereal folders When we feed them into our thoughts, it might be like feeding stuff into a mincer.

- Lumps of potato

- Sage
- Onion
- Beef
- Salt

It gets turned around a few times before coming out as long, thin mixed-up strips.

So if our creativity opens a portal into DreamTime then maybe we encounter stuff there from the present, from the past and stuff that hasn't happened yet. What if, when Brian goes into this DreamTime state, his folder doesn't just contain fathers in the present and the past but fathers in the future? And Brian unwittingly pulls down an idea that hasn't happened yet.

In other words, it's not our writing that determines what happens in the future, but the future – and the past - that determine what we write. Because we think of time as moving only in one direction, it gives the false impression that our stories influence future events.

A different kind of example.

I'm on one of my favorite walks through the Andalusian Valley of the Beehives. It's still winter back in Sheffield so I'm exhilarated by the Spanish sunshine and fresh air, the almond blossom and the heady perfume of wild rosemary and lavender. I stride across the river and head towards the hilltops.

I've been having a bit of a crisis: family problems, relationship problems, next-door-neighbor problems, as though the world and its woes have been stuck to my back like the shell of a grumpy old turtle.

I clamber up the hillside where the view opens out over the snow-covered peaks, then find a rock to sit down while I catch my breath. Why do I always attract so many needy people? Why don't I say No more often? How can I be creative with so much stuff weighing me down?

I pour myself a drink.

My parents taught me How to Be a Good Girl and Good Girls always put themselves last; they do Good Deeds; they sometimes do things they don't enjoy and sometimes stuff they hate. If they write books and poems, they write them in their spare time after they've taken care of everybody else. They don't say, *Go away. I'm busy now.* They don't spend the winter months walking in the Spanish sunshine when everyone they know at home is shivering with cold.

I sigh. *Linda,* I tell myself, *you were not born to be a saint. You were born simply to be good enough. Your parents never wanted you to be a martyr; they wanted you to be just who you are.*

I take out my pen and notebook and write down some of these thoughts before they fly away. As I write, I have a sense of something soft and feathery pressed against my palm; of course there's nothing there but the softness grows, like a small bird cupped inside my hand.

What about all my friends who are doctors and teachers? Or lawyers? They don't put up with their next-door-neighbor knocking on their workplace door, demanding to be driven to the shop to buy six oranges, a jar of marmalade and a tin of rice pudding because they can't cope with the profligacy of buying more than one tiny bagful of groceries at once. When other people are working, they don't expect to be disturbed.

My mother told me: *I want… never gets:* it was all right to want for others. *If you never want anything,* my mum said, *you'll not be disappointed.* But she lived in the days of hardship and rationing and it doesn't apply anymore.

The bird is still there. I don't know what it's doing in my hand.

I sit and look towards the olive trees. My parents were modest people who accepted their station in life, but that didn't make them fulfilled and it didn't mean that they didn't want me to be happy.

The bird is completely ridiculous. There is no bird. It's just that I can feel it, warm and quickening. I place my notebook on the grass and cup my hands around this absolutely ludicrous imaginary bird. I think I can feel its heartbeat. And then I have the crazy notion of launching it into the air.

I'm aware of some kind of picture of someone who did that, but I don't know who it was.

Someone that I know?

No.

Some kind of story, an archetypal image. And then I realize that it's Noah. When the waters recede and they hope to find dry land, Noah stands at the prow of his ark and launches a dove into the air.

Why?

Some kind of symbol of hope.

So why am I thinking of that?

Because when I was a child, I was taught that hope was wrong. Good Girls had to shelve their aspirations to make way for everyone else.

I pick up my notebook again and write it down. I write that every child is conceived in hope, every purpose and idea. I write that hope is creativity – because it raises us into the air and without it we'd be stuck in the mud like chickens that can't fly. I don't know how to launch a dove. I don't know if you throw it like a beach ball or just open your palms and wait for it to fly.

I place my notebook back in my rucksack, then turn around to check there's no one watching. Which is a bit stupid in the foothills of the Sierra Blanca when I've seen nobody all day. Then I clamber to my feet and hold the dove inside my palms. I give her a bit of a stroke; I think I ought to talk to her but I don't know what to say. Then I realize that I do know how to launch a dove: all you have to do when it's time for something to leave is open up your fingers and let go. Then I raise my hands to heaven, open out my palms and release her into the air.

Of course there is no dove and I don't even believe in the story of Noah and his ark any more than I believe in a world inside a rabbit hole; so when I get back to my room and switch on the TV and there's a song by Crosby and Nash about a woman releasing a dove I don't take too much notice. And when I pick up my copy of *Natural Grace* [8] and notice the flying dove on its cover, I tell myself that now I've been thinking about doves, I'm just a lot more likely to notice them. And the next day, walking to a Quaker Meeting in Fuengirola[9] and noting Noah's dove on the stained-glass window in the local church, I tell myself that Noah's dove is an archetypal image and most churches will have one somewhere.

But walking back along the promenade, I'm stopped in my tracks by a statue. It's not far from the harbor so would have formed a likely place for the powers-that-be to have commissioned a depiction of Noah standing at the prow of his boat. But the statue isn't Noah. It's a woman. Remarkably like me. Shoulder-length hair; child-bearing hips; no spring chicken and she's standing on the promenade, next to a plaque that says *A gift from the people of Fuengirola to the tourists...* raising her arms in the air, opening out her palms and there between them is a dove setting out to fly.

Chapter 7

Living Backwards

That's the effect of living backwards,' the Queen said kindly: `it always makes one a little giddy at first'

`Living backwards!' Alice repeated in great astonishment. `I never heard of such a thing!'

`— but there's one great advantage in it, that one's memory works both ways.'

`I'm sure mine only works one way,' Alice remarked. `I can't remember things before they happen.'

Alice through the Looking Glass, chapter V

I'm walking in the countryside north of Sheffield on the path that leads through the grounds of Sugworth Hall. Karl, my partner at the time, has wandered off. Always one for wandering, I would look around and find him disappearing out of sight, on a mission for wild mushrooms, wild garlic or anything to make a free meal out of. I slow my pace and find myself reflecting on my dream of the night before.

In the dream, I was out with Karl in the countryside when we came across a rabbit crouched beside a hedge. The rabbit didn't move as we approached and from its weeping eyes, appeared to be a victim of myxomatosis. Karl picked up a rock hoping to put the rabbit out of its misery but – being a great animal lover – couldn't bring himself to hit hard enough. Every attempt resulted in more and more of a bloody mess and the distraught animal suffering more than it did before we arrived.

I grimace and try to put the dream out of my mind as I look ahead where Karl stands motionless in front of a small glade. He turns around and beckons.

Something inside me simply *knows* he's found a rabbit. I want to warn him before I even see it: *Don't try to*....

But Karl is already scouring the ground for rocks. "There's a rabbit," he turns and whispers. "It let me get really close." The only big stone he can see is embedded in the ground. "I think it must have myxomatosis."

"I don't think you should..."

"I'd better try and kill it." He begins to search further afield. "Can you see any big stones or a rock or...?"

The lack of rocks gives me chance to explain about the dream. Karl nods in resignation, relieved at being exonerated from something he'd rather not attempt. The rabbit looks relieved as well, crouching sorrowfully with its weeping eyes.

I gaze around at the manicured lawns and tennis courts, "Maybe the groundsman will kill it." I resist saying, *And make a better job of it.* "Or a fox. A fox might kill it."

Karl nods as we stroll away and I reflect upon the synchronicity. I've never before seen a rabbit with myxomatosis and certainly never dreamed of one. To have such a dream the night before we see one is just too much of a coincidence. And certainly too much synchronicity for the dream also to involve Karl and the business with the rock.

I'm reminded of the account by Jung when he relates the dream he had one night about a kingfisher only to find, on the following morning, a dead kingfisher lying by his path. As he explained, in his home area, kingfishers were rare; he'd only ever seen two or three in his entire life and had no recollection of ever dreaming about one before; there seemed no way the two events could have occurred together simply by chance.[1]

There was another small, odd feature about this event: in my dream, the rabbit was crouched in front of a hedge whereas we found the real-time rabbit in a hollow, inside a small glade. The two events were identical but for one small difference, just as Jung's dream kingfisher was alive but his real kingfisher was dead. Some might argue that these anomalies suggest there's no such thing as synchronicity, but there are other possible interpretations. We'll examine these in our chapter on multiple universe theory, but first of all, back to Time:

We think of time as a straight line – like a train on measured tracks. We cannot see the future because we haven't got there yet. And yet, the notion that we can see or dream about an event before it occurs appears to refute all this. If we can see into the future, then surely somehow... somewhere... in some strange way... the future must have already taken place.

Another example of such precognition concerns a friend called Kieran who, when I first met him, was writing a school text book. As this was his first such venture, Kieran was keen to discuss it with another writer and took to calling round of an evening with a bottle of wine. Or two. Like many others who work at home, I make it clear to friends that they should never simply turn up, but phone first and check I'm not too busy. This was something Kieran did – religiously. I would receive a phone message with his Irish brogue (he was actually born in Liverpool but made much of his Dublin accent) incanting, *It is myself...*

On this particular morning, I'd been invited to a school in Rotherham, about ten miles east of Sheffield. For some inexplicable reason, I'd not been looking forward to the visit, but the students turned out to be a sheer delight. This was no reason, however, to drive back to Sheffield with the roof open in the middle of winter, singing at the top of my voice, feeling that I led a completely charmed life and also that I'd better put my foot down as Kieran would be arriving any minute.

This was stupid. Kieran – like the rest of my friends – never called round without warning. And yet I saw a clear picture of him standing on my doorstep. *Don't be stupid, Linda,* I told myself and then started wondering whether there'd be enough left of last night's casserole to make us both a spot of lunch and whether it was too early in the day to throw caution to the winds and light the fire. As I rounded the corner into my street, I felt surprised that Kieran wasn't standing there already.

And then I thought, *No. The picture was not of him walking down the street but standing on the doorstep.*

As I climbed out the car and walked up my path, that's just where he was – exactly as I'd pictured him – standing on the step, having just pushed a note through the letterbox.

When the picture had occurred to me, I'd been a couple of miles from home and if I'd seen Kieran as he really was at that moment, he'd have been cycling along the main road. So, what I actually saw was an image of something that hadn't happened yet. And of course later that afternoon, after Kieran had left and I picked up my phone messages, there was the one that I'd missed while I'd been in Rotherham: *It is myself...*

Like the myxomatosis dream, this event was of no great earth-shattering import. Kieran just happened to be cycling past and decided to drop by. I mention this because it's not unusual to hear about people who've received warnings of major life events before they've actually happened. They've experienced precognitive dreams about air crashes, bombs, floods and other natural disasters. In *The Holographic Universe*, Michael Talbot has a whole section dedicated to such dreams, but in spite of their credibility, they present a few misgivings: most of us dream occasionally about one kind of disaster or another: we're in a car when the brakes have failed or have a nightmare that we're tumbling off a cliff or drowning. Such events may presage real events or may be a subconscious symbol of our fear. Some of us might experience such a dream on the night before some terrible disaster and of course it may be precognitive or simply have happened by chance. It seems to me however that these small, almost mundane coincidences – like Jung's kingfisher, Kieran's arrival and my sorrowful rabbit, are the ones that really do turn our concept of Time on its head.

Einstein explained that time is actually curved. If it were

straight, then it would depart like a train into a future that hadn't happened yet. If it's curved, it bends around and comes back to meet us, enabling us to glimpse the future before it actually occurs. As Einstein declared in a statement to a meeting of the Spinoza Society in 1932: *Human beings in their thinking, feeling and acting are not free but are as causally bound as the stars in their motions.*

And yet, for those of us born into western culture, the core of our belief system is that we affect what happens. We make decisions which influence – not just our own lives but the lives of others round us; we believe that we have choice; if everything has already happened, it takes away our sense of who we are as sentient beings with free will.

As related in Lockwood's *The Labyrinth of Time*, James Jeans cites Arthur Eddington's well-known remark (1920:41) that "events do not happen; they are just there and we come across them":[2]

In this case our consciousness is like that of a fly caught in a dusting mop which is being drawn over the surface of a picture; the whole picture is there, but the fly can only experience the one instant of time with which it is in immediate contact, although it may remember a bit of the picture just behind it, and may even delude itself into imagining it is helping to paint those parts of the picture which lie in front of it.[3]

If Time has already taken place, we are just like these flies being drawn across the surface of someone else's picture..

A little story about a train:

When I was very young – maybe four or five years old, I was given a train set; I don't remember who gave it me but I can still see its enticing box with a picture of a powerful, green steaming locomotive on the lid.

Our first home was a pre-war Sheffield council house with barely room for my parents, grandparents, sister and myself let alone a train set. I was told I would have to wait until we moved into a larger house before I could take the track from the box and lay it out. The box was stored inside the sideboard cupboard – a cupboard just the right size for me to squeeze inside, pick up the train set and clutch it to my chest.

One day, I was invited to a party. An awkward, unsociable child who never liked parties anyway and this, God help me – was a boy's party – I tried to wriggle out of it, but no, I was told that would be rude and ordered upstairs to put on my one and only party frock. When I returned, my mother had wrapped up the train set in crèpe paper. I stared at her incredulously.

"You have to take a present to a party," she explained. "Train sets are for boys. He's a boy and... you never play with it..."

I was horrified. I tried to grab the train set back before she placed it high on the mantelpiece. I tried to jump and reach it. I yelled; I cried; I screamed. I refused to go to the party. I lay down on the floor beneath the table banging my fists on the lino.

Nothing that I said or did made the slightest bit of difference. The event had been decided. We were a poor family and could not afford another present.

I refused to go to the party. I squeezed inside the sideboard cupboard and closed the door behind me with my fingertips. They prised me out. I screamed and yelled some more. There was nothing I could do. The only thing that made me falter was a promise: *We'll buy you a new train set, one that's a bit smaller, one that you can play with...*

I set off for the party as grudgingly as a child can go with the train set wrapped in the crepe paper that made do for gift-wrap tucked beneath my arm.

I didn't allow my parents to forget about the promised, smaller train set and it wasn't long before it materialized, small enough, they explained, to set out on the table.

And small it was. About the size of a large saucer - a tin circle painted with grass and trees on which was clipped a track the texture of a hairpin. When you turned it over, next to the ticket that said *Made in Hong Kong*, was a keyhole. You wound it up and a train the size of a small caterpillar trundled round. There was a small moment of excitement when it vanished inside a miniature tin tunnel and rolled out the other side.

I wound up the train then sat and watched. At first I was entranced: my first real, working train set. But after several minutes, began to feel I'd been duped. The important thing about a train set is deciding where the tracks will go, fixing them together, hooking on the rolling stock, lowering the train down on its rails and setting it off on its way. There is no fun and no adventure in a train pre-programmed to go round and round for ever till it stops.

Which is why none of us have ever taken too much notice of a theory of time that goes any way other than forwards. We want to arrange what happens: we want to be the engineers, the Fat Controllers who plan the routes, fix the tracks together and decide where the trains will run. We do not want to live a pre-determined life.

We may choose a life of virtue in which we give to charity, put food out for the birds, collect our empty cans together for recycling, and offer our seats to old ladies on the bus. Or we may shout abuse at charity collectors, poison the pigeons in the park, kick empty beer cans down the street at midnight, and honk our horns to terrify old ladies dithering at the crossing.

But if our sole purpose is to sit around and wait to be wound up, before getting slower and slower and slower till we stop, what is the point?

We pour scorn on Eastern ideas of fate. If we hear about a coach crash being described as the will of God, we want to scream out, *No! Someone should be held responsible. Someone should have checked the brakes. Someone should be called to account.*

I remember running a creative writing class at a Muslim girls' school in Bradford where I read the extract quoted earlier about the death of my three siblings and was moved to find that many of the girls had similar stories to tell. But these deeply religious girls described these tragedies as shameful: a punishment for wrongdoing in some previous existence.

And I can't accept that version of events; my mother had as much right to give birth to a healthy child as anybody else. I expect medical staff to save lives not shrug off premature death as being the Hand of Fate.

If our future is already written and nothing we do can change it, most of us would prefer to crawl inside the sideboard cupboard, squeeze the door shut tight and refuse to ever come out.

Party or no party.

* * * *

One of the most well-known prophetic dreamers was Abraham Lincoln. His friend and biographer, Ward H. Lamon, described the dream in which Lincoln was in the White House, hearing the sound of terrible wailing and weeping. He followed the sound until he came to the East Room where, to his horror, he found a corpse laid out in funeral clothes on a catafalque. Soldiers were standing guard and Lincoln asked them who had died. "The president," he was told. "The president has been killed by an assassin."

Another much more prosaic dream:

A woman is sitting eating breakfast with three other people and during the course of the meal, she tells them about the dream she had that night.

In the dream, just as they were finishing breakfast, a farmer arrived with a large bucket containing thirty three eggs. Later, as she was standing on the stairs, someone handed the woman another three eggs. An unremarkable dream but odd enough for the woman to relate it that morning over breakfast.

A little while later, after the meal, a farmer really did arrive at the house and present the woman with a bucket which he said contained – not thirty three – but three dozen, thirty six eggs. The woman placed the eggs in a basket, paid the farmer and then, as they were packing for a journey, gave the eggs to her husband to take upstairs.

A short while afterwards, her husband called down and told his wife that what she had dreamed really had occurred: he'd counted the eggs and the basket contained, not three dozen, but only thirty three eggs. He asked his wife to go upstairs and count them all herself. The woman did this, but as she was counting, someone called her from downstairs and told her that there had been a mistake; three eggs had been taken from the bucket. The other woman then walked upstairs and handed her three more eggs.

This dream was not foretelling any world-shattering event but again contained the kind of minor detail which excludes the likelihood of it occurring simply by chance. Another important factor here is that the writer actually told three others about the dream straight after it occurred so there were witnesses to the event.[4]

Another dream seemed so odd that the dreamer noted its details in his diary the morning after it occurred. He saw a native American canoe sailing across the town hall square of his home town and described the dream as not just weird, but particularly vivid. It was nine years later when the real bizarre event occurred. The dreamer was standing in the Lord Mayor's parlor in the town hall as his father was lord mayor that year and while he was talking, he glanced out of the window and to his amazement, saw a fully-painted native American war canoe apparently sailing through the square. The man walked across to get a better view before realizing that a number of props, with the war canoe on top, were being delivered to a local theatre.[5]

Both the above accounts were collected by the Yorkshire-born writer, J.B. Priestley, best-known for his stage plays such as *An Inspector Calls* and popular novels like *The Good Companions*. Priestley had a lifelong obsession with time, having himself experienced precognitive dreams. During an interview with the TV presenter, Huw Wheldon, he described – as most writers are prone – his work in progress, "Man and Time". Wheldon suggested – perhaps a little unwisely - that viewers might contact Priestley with any experience they'd had themselves which seemed as he put it, "to challenge the conventional and common-sense idea of Time." [6]

Priestley must have been biting his lip as, over the next few weeks, he went on to open letter after letter containing accounts of precognitive dreams, strange prescient hunches and episodes of déjà vu. He organized these as best he could but having no workforce other than himself and his secretary, found himself overburdened. He says he actually gave up counting when the letters passed the thousand mark. Basically he was searching for accounts that could be corroborated, either by entries in journals or by correspondence or in conversation. Such accounts went on to fill several chapters. Some – like the two quoted above – described events before they happened; others – like my dream about the myxomatosis rabbit – enabled the dreamer to avoid something unpleasant.. For example:

The most vivid and outstanding experience that has ever occurred to me was one night when I woke up in a cold sweat absolutely sure that I had knocked down a small boy with my car. The dream remained with me for two or three days afterwards but, eventually, as all things do, it was put to the back of my mind. It was only a few weeks afterwards when driving into Manchester, that I had to swerve and brake violently in order to avoid an accident. I jumped out of the car and was staggered when I immediately recognized the boy as being the same child as in my dream...I did not hit the boy but was only inches away from hitting him, which thankfully proved one aspect of the dream wrong.[7]

Priestley goes on to suggest that such a writer may of course be deceiving himself when he thinks he recognizes the boy. Alternatively, forewarned by the horror of the dream, the driver may exercise much more care so a tragedy is avoided. In short, as Priestley says, "the man was able to *change the future* by the fact that it had already been revealed.

Reading this brought to mind a slightly similar experience. Having returned from an afternoon walk in the Derbyshire countryside, I'm driving along the stretch of road between Wardlow Mires and Stony Middleton. Quite suddenly, out of nowhere, I see a mental image of a car bearing down towards me over the brow of the hill on the wrong side of the road just as a car is overtaking on my right. It's a ridiculous idea. This stretch is no bad place for pulling out in front of a slow tractor, but my little MR2 is no slow-moving vehicle. And nobody in their right mind would overtake over the brow of the hill. Nonetheless, I find myself thinking, well, if such an event happened... what would I do?

Steer off the road and into the wide verge on my left. My much-loved, old sports car might get its paint scraped on the dry-stone wall or even stuck in mud, but I'd avert a head-on crash. Then I notice the deep ditch. OK, then. No, the best thing would be to brake hard while being careful not to skid. With this foolish dilemma resolved, I concentrate back on the road just in time to see a car careering towards me on the wrong side of the road over the brow of the hill as a quick glance in my wing mirror tells me, as I'd instantly suspected, that someone else is overtaking on a stretch where there's only room for two.

But of course I know what to do. My foot is already there on the brake. The driver overtaking has time to tuck himself in front before the other car hurtles towards us. He slaloms into a bit of a skid, but stays in control and no, I don't shake my fist or shout abuse. I smile smugly, rather proud of my skilful driving and awesome powers of anticipation.

I describe the incident later to a friend who refuses to believe that this could be anything other than coincidence. "Drivers are always anticipating situations," he insists. "You probably do it all the time without noticing. You only remembered it because something actually happened similar to the event you were thinking of. If it hadn't, you'd have forgotten all about it."

And yes, I could see his point. I always anticipate situations when I'm driving. I anticipate what I'm going to have for tea, and if I'm going out, what I ought to wear and whether to take the car or splash out on a cab. I anticipate the possibility of a cake or chocolate shortage and anticipate where I might buy some on the way back. I might anticipate a wine shortage...But think about driving maneuvers..?!?

So, I know coincidences happen and given all the events of a lifetime it would be even more of a coincidence if they didn't. And whereas to me, the myxomatosis dream just has to be a premonition, this event may have happened by mere chance. It just seems very unlikely

Another example from Priestley, written by Stephen King-Hall, a well-known writer in his time who was, for many years, a naval officer. The incident occurred in 1916, almost half a century before Priestley's television interview. It seems incredible that anyone could recall so vividly an event occurring fifty years before and you might be forgiven for wondering whether his memory could be trusted. However, these kind of events leave such a marked impression that most people remember them for ever. It's almost as though these are not just the most important events of our lives but in a sense, the only ones.

One afternoon in 1916 I was officer of the watch in the Southampton as we approached Scapa Flow. A mile ahead I saw a small island, and I knew that as we passed it a man would fall overboard. The sea was flat calm. The Commodore, navigator and other officers senior to me were on the bridge. An officer and a number of men were on the forecastle clearing away the anchor. I thought to myself, it must be one of these men who will fall overboard. But what could I do..? We got nearer and nearer the island and the feeling grew stronger...

Staking everything on this feeling, Sir Stephen gave the order to put out the lifeboats, muster the sea-boat crew and so forth. The orders were sharply challenged.

...The Commodore said, "What the hell do you think you are doing?" We were abreast the island. I had no answer. We were steaming at 20 knots and we passed the little island in a few seconds. Nothing happened!

As I was struggling to say something, the cry went up: "Man overboard" from the Nottingham (the next ship in the line, 100 yards behind us) then level with the island. 30 seconds later "Man overboard" from the Birmingham (the 3rd ship in the line and then abreast the island). We went full speed astern; our sea-boat was in the water almost at once and we picked up both men. I was then able to explain to a startled bridge why I had behaved as I had done. This is a brief outline of a fully authenticated case of precognition...[8]

Although the obvious conclusion to draw from these events is that we need to re-examine our cozy conception of Time and the way it's normally viewed, many people meet so much ridicule and disbelief from their friends and families that they simply carry on as if nothing extraordinary has taken place at all.

Priestley found many of the letters he received referred to this "popular opposition to the idea of precognitive dreams." He goes on to explain:

And what to me was curious and then significant was that in most instances, when a dream had been told to husbands or wives or other members of the family or friends or workmates, and this dream had come true, these other people might marvel for a little while but always left it at that. The prevailing notion of Time was not then challenged. Our contemporary idea of ourselves was not questioned. Something odd had happened, that was it; it could not be fitted into the accepted pattern, so it was ignored. Nobody, man or woman... pointed out that, if one, just one, precognitive dream could be accepted as something more than a coincidence – bang goes our conventional idea of Time! [9]

These people were educated, intelligent and curious enough to watch a late-night arts and culture program and write an intelligible letter, so why do educated, intelligent and curious people simply "leave it at that"?

An explanation may be offered by an occasion when I spent some time with my son, Marcus, living in New York. Marcus had been given tickets for a cabaret-style show featuring a hypnotist in Times Square. Marcus, our friend, Nancy, and myself sat towards the back behind a pillar which we hoped might help us avoid the embarrassment of being hauled up on stage. The hypnotist exuded confidence and good humor (well, he *was* American) and asked us all to clasp our hands and hold them out before us. As forty or fifty of us sat with our hands clasped together, he then told us that our fingers were being forced apart by an unseen force and we would no longer be able to squeeze them together.

With a restricted view as well as being quite small, I couldn't really tell to what extent the unseen force was raging round the room, but it seemed to ignore our table. I sat with my hands comfortably clasped together and waited for the force to arrive but was somewhat disappointed. I had no intentions of spoiling the show and was in fact quite eager to find out whether or not I could be hypnotized; I just failed to experience anything at all. Marcus felt the same.

The hypnotist walked around checking people's hands, offering reassurance if they felt alarmed or distressed, ignoring Marcus and myself but, at the end of this short experiment, gave me, to my surprise, something of a public showdown. He drew everyone's attention to the fact that I was the only one sitting, so he said, with my fingers clasped together. It was probably as well that his Brooklyn accent was not so easy to decipher as what I did catch (*Yanno a female who keeps her fingers tightly closed always has her legs wide open..*) produced ribald laughter from the audience but hardly the same reaction in a polite English lady. I smiled – I'd like to think – good naturedly – as he went on to suggest that I was uptight, showing off and determined to be different. Needless to say, the prospect of further disapproval failed to encourage the unseen force in the next trick which was supposed to make my palms stick to my scalp.

Yet everyone else, presumably – apart from Marcus and myself - had their palms stuck, just as their hands had been driven apart. I was a showman's gift: for if someone can be ridiculed for failing to conform during the first five minutes, the fear of such humiliation will deter others who might consider wavering later on. And the unseen force which was raging round the room, as I'm sure I don't need to tell you, is the unseen force of public opinion and the fear of being seen as different.

This pressure to conform is one of the strongest forces that we know, stronger even than our instinct to survive. Why else would an Indian widow fling herself upon her husband's funeral pyre? Why else would young men enlist in wars without any understanding of what they're fighting for? Why did people fail to speak out in the early days of the Third Reich against the persecution of the Jews? It is this force more than any other that blocks our curiosity. A weird experience that's ridiculed is – sad to say, for many people - a weird experience best forgotten.

Chapter 8

Time and The Dark Arts

`It's a poor sort of memory that only works backwards,' the Queen remarked.*

Alice through the Looking Glass, chapter 5

I'm in Sheffield University library, searching for the books of Dunne and the Russian mystic philosopher, Ouspensky whose writings influenced J. B. Priestley. I have to confess that finding books in libraries has never been one of my talents - something to do with the way that they're all arranged by numbers. And to my frustration, everything to do with time anomalies, human consciousness, dreams and synchronicity, rather than being neatly housed within the departments of physics and psychology, keeps circling back to the same category – not the same number, which would make life easier – but the same compartment in the minds of librarians and academics: *Magic... Alchemy... Astrology... Witchcraft... The Dark Arts...* and dark they are. The lights refuse to work; the books may - or may not be - on the top shelf, but I can't reach and I can't find anything to stand on and it looks as though nothing's been taken out of this section for the last fifty years.

And, distracted as always, there's one volume I just have to take down because it's the only one that's been borrowed, referred to, referenced or thumbed through for many a furlong of pristine book battalions. Its dark green binding is so frayed it peels away from the stitching as I cradle it in my hand, leaving its pages a collection of loose and crumbling leaves. The frontispiece informs me that this volume is not as old as it appears, but is in fact an 1886 facsimile of the 1584 edition: The Discoverie of

Witchcraft by Reginald Scot, Esquire. [1] An encyclopedia of a book, a huge tome worthy of a PhD in Persecution Studies:

> ...a hollowe peece of wood or a chest is placed in the church, into the which any bodie may freelie cast a little scroll of paper, wherein may be conteined the name of the witch, the time, place, and the fact &c. And the same chest being locked with/three severall locks, is opened everie fifteenth daie by three inquisitors or officers appointed for that purpose; which keep three severall kaies. And thus the accuser need not be knowne, nor shamed with the reproach of slander or malice to his poore neighbor.

> Item, there must be great persuasions used to all men, women and children, to accuse old women of witchcraft. Item, the little children of witches, which will not confesse, must be attached; who will confesse against their owne mothers.

Forgetting all about time anomalies, I stand mesmerized, my insides tumbling like a heavy-wash program. Here in my hand are passages from the actual Inquisitor's Handbook: How to discover a witch - with all the examples of terror and torture to be tried upon her until she finally confesses.

> Item, if anie denie hir owne confession made without torture, she is nevertheless by that confession to be condemned, as in anie other crime.

Having been shocked to read Priestley's statement that people in 1968 were reluctant to challenge their notions of Time, I'm suddenly face-to-face with the backlog to all this, streaming through the centuries. Women like myself who see glimpses of the future have been reviled and persecuted, tortured and burnt over hundreds – no, thousands of years..

Item, the judges must seme to put on a pitifull countenance and to mone them; saieng, that It was not they, but the divell that committed the murther, and that he compelled them to doo it; and must make them believe that they thinke them to be innocents.

Item, a witch may not be put in prison alone, least the divell dissuade hir from confession, through promises of her indemnitie. For some that have beene in the gaole have proved to flie awaie, as they were woont to doo when they met with Diana and Minerva, &c: and so brake their owne necks against the stone walles...

The possession of supposed psychic ability – or the merest hint of it - led to somewhere between twenty and a hundred thousand women *(their numbers, like their names, erased by time)* right across Europe being burned at the stake less than five hundred years ago. After the birth of Shakespeare. After Sir Walter Raleigh had first glimpsed the coast of North Carolina. These women suffered the most appalling tortures – both to themselves and members of their families - until confessions were made and they resigned themselves to getting it over and done with by being burned alive instead.

Item, if any man, woman or child doo saie, that wuch a one is a witch; it is a most vehement suspicion and sufficient to bring hir to the racke...

Item, though a conjurer be not to be condemned for curing the diseased by virtue of his art; yet must a witch die for the like case

Item, the behavior, looks, becks, and countenance of a woman, are sufficient signes, whereby to presume she is a witch...

Another reason for keeping quiet about my so-called psychic personality– was the reaction I received from a very dear, Quaker Friend, Jessie Baston.

Jessie was an ardent peace campaigner, organizing meetings, writing outspoken letters to politicians and campaigning to channel to charity the portion of her tax that would be spent on nuclear weapons and, to crack it all, a staunch Christian who talked about Jesus as though he were alive and well and just taking a bit of extended annual leave. To me, she lived the kind of virtuous life that would put most of us to shame. One evening, when she asked what had brought me to the Quaker Meeting, I talked about the death of my mother and my encounter with the angels, assuming that Jessie would have similar stories to relate. I was shocked, gutted, in fact, when she murmured sadly: "I've never had that kind of...awareness... awareness of the presence of God." She paused. "Of course, I pray, pray regularly and many a time I've prayed that... that I might be given a Sign, but..." She shook her head and appeared quite tearful... it's as though... as though He's never answered." What she said next really shook me to the core: "I suppose that means God doesn't think of me as good enough. Perhaps if I'd lived a better life, he might have..."

What a load of twaddle. Was there really a God seated in heaven with a placard saying, *Linda. I am here. But only for You. Don't you go telling that old renegade, Jessie Baston.* The idea that I was somehow more saintly had me shaking my head in horror. I insisted: *No, no, no ...*

But Jessie's words troubled me. So much that for many years I kept quiet about my so-called "signs" afraid anyone might think I was claiming some kind of moral high ground. But the conversation made me wonder: where do such notions come from?

Well, the Catholic church puts forward the names of those who experience miracles for sainthood. Two decent peer-assessed miracles and you can write the letters St in front of your name. *(I did once, for a bit of a laugh, try to pass myself off as a nun when applying for a train ticket on the basis that I might enjoy a seat to myself and get some work done. The online booking system has never allowed me to forget this and sends tickets every time to Sister Hoy. But just imagine if you could simply write "Saint" in the title box instead..?).*

Now, there may well be a link between what some people think of as miracles and precognitive ability and dreams, but surely that's not holiness; it just means all of us are different. It's a concept described by Jung when he says:

> *The difference between most people and myself is that for me the "dividing walls" are transparent. This is my peculiarity. Others find these walls so opaque that they see nothing behind them and therefore think nothing is there.*[2]

In the same way that I've an amazing memory for words but can't remember anyone's phone number and can't draw for toffee but can play music by ear after hearing it only once and you also have your own special talents and your weaknesses, this surely doesn't mean I'm favored by God any more than it means I deserve burning at the stake.

> Item, if the child of a woman that is suspected to be a witch, be lacking or gone from hir; it is to be presumed, that she hath sacrificed it to the devil...

Thank goodness none of my children have left home under mysterious circumstances.

> Item, it is not onlie a vehement suspicion and presumption, but an evident proofe of a witch, if any man or beast die suddenlie where she hath beene seene latelie...

Item, if she have anie privie marke under hir arme pokes, under hir haire, under hir lip, or in hir buttock, or in hir privities: it is a presumption sufficient for the judge to proceed and give sentence of death upon hir.

Had I been living in earlier times I would have been terrified of anyone finding out that I've a mole at the top of my leg, have recently witnessed the inexplicable demise of several of my zebra fish and my lodger's cat died on Christmas Day.

Item, if they will confesse nothing but upon the racke or torture; their apparel must be changed, and everie haire in their bodie must be shaven off with a sharpe razor.

And yet there's a completely irrational anger often directed towards anyone who claims to have experience of the paranormal. As Rupert Sheldrake described in a lecture at the Royal Society: *This is one of those pathological areas of regular science where there's a denial of evidence... a blindness to evidence and, in fact, a willful ignorance.*[3]

Item, if they have charmes for taciturnity, so as they feele not the common tortures, and therefore confesse nothing: then some sharpe instrument must be thrust betwixt everie naile of their fingers and toes...for by meanes of that extreme paine, they will confesse anie thing.

And it's been a huge relief to me to realize I'm not alone. J.B. Priestley and Jung possessed some of the greatest minds of their generation and both had the courage to write candidly about events they knew that others might ridicule.

Item, little children may be had to the torture at the first dash...

Item, at the time of examination, there should be a semblance of great a doo, to the terrifying of the witch: and that a number of instruments, gieves, manacles, ropes, halters, fetters &c be prepared, brought foorth and laid before the examinate: and also that some be procured to make a most horrible and lamentable crie, in the place of torture, as though he or she were upon the racke, or in the tormentors hands: so the examinate may heare it whiles she is examined, before she hir selfe be brought into the prison...

I return to Sheffield University. In spite of any fears that CCTV cameras might be tracking my progress round the shelves on Sorcery, Alchemy and Magic and zooming in on the mole on my leg, I resume my search for the works that inspired J.B. Priestley. I ask the librarian for a torch and stool and discover a vast new section containing most of the books I need, barely one of them borrowed since the Beatles first hit town which is why, presumably, no one's bothered replacing the light bulbs.

Yet I'm delighted to relate that Dunne's theories from almost a hundred years ago not only make a cracking good read – until you get to the charts and diagrams that look like the formula for a new biplane made out of brown paper, sealing wax and empty biscuit tins - but suggest ideas similar to those put forward by physicists and cosmologists during the last few decades.

John Dunne, born in 1875, served as a soldier in the Boer War and then became an aeronautical engineer. In 1904 he invented a hydrofoil, named after him and went on to build and fly both biplanes and monoplanes. (add illustration (4)...

In 1906-7, he designed and built the first British military airplane. In spite of this, his first book was about neither time nor aeronautics but his other main obsession, fly-fishing. J.B. Priestley describes him thus:

He was a man of intellectual integrity, and as courageous as a thinker and writer as he had been as a man of action...

He may be said to have challenged the conventional positivist idea of Time on its own ground. He did not start from any strong religious prejudices. He had no secret love – as many of us have – of the miraculous. He had not been visited by any mystical revelations. He was not a sentimentally poetic character, outraged by the contemporary world. He was a hardheaded military engineering type, whose hobby was not fantastic speculation and juggling with ideas but fly-fishing. He was, as no doubt they said at the United Service Club, 'a sound fellow' even though he did fool around with airplanes in 1906, when sounder fellows knew that these things would never have any real value.

But something happened to him that he could not explain – this 'displacement of time' – and just as he had worried away at his aeronautical problems, so now he worried at this Time business...tackling the problem in a tough realistic spirit, one more genuinely scientific than that of those scientists who had a suspicion that the problem was there but ignored it. Almost all of them ignored Dunne too. Like many another original thinker before him, he was a nuisance.[4]

The "something that happened" to Dunne was a completely inexplicable series of precognitive dreams. The first seemed insignificant: he dreamed that his pocket watch had stopped at half-past four. Waking in the middle of the night, searching around for his watch, he found that it had done just that. A ridiculous coincidence. The second event was more bizarre: whilst invalided home from the Boer War, he dreamed of an expedition arriving in Khartoum with three ragged men, dressed in khaki, their faces almost burnt black by the sun. The men informed him that they had set off from the Cape.

The following morning, Dunne opened his Daily Telegraph to read about an expedition which had done just that – three men, answering this description, had arrived in Khartoum from the southern tip of Africa.

In the next dream, Dunne was standing on high ground from which small jets of vapor were spouting upward. He realized he was on a volcanic island which was just about to blow up and became determined to rescue the inhabitants. Travelling frantically from one official to another, he kept telling them that four thousand people would be killed unless they were carried away by ship straightaway. Once again, it was the Daily Telegraph which informed him a few days later about a volcano disaster in Martinique in which survivors had been carried away by British steamer; strangely enough, the number of dead was reported to be – not four thousand – but forty thousand – an anomaly which Dunne explained by the fact that when he read the paper, he first read the number as four thousand. It was, he said, almost the kind of dream he would expect if he had read the newspaper first.

These precognitive dreams continued and Dunne's great scientific brain flew backwards and forwards in an attempt to explain how they could occur. As he said: "I cared not a whit whether Time were a form of thought or an aspect of reality or (this was later) compoundable with Space. What I wanted to know was: How it got *mixed*?"

One factor which J. B. Priestley noted about the letters he received from TV viewers was that they mentioned over and over again that precognitive dreams had a particular texture: they were so extraordinarily vivid that the writers felt they somehow *knew* these dreams were presaging real events. Assuming you're not Priestleyd-out with precognitive dreams by now, I'll share one more example.

I dreamed that I was wandering around Sheffield city centre, looking for the Quaker Meeting House. My frustration of not being able to find it had me breaking down in tears. This is so unlike me; I rarely burst into tears, especially in public.

Eventually I stopped a young man who – I realized on waking - resembled someone I knew who later became a clergyman. He'd no idea where to find the Meeting House, but said that if I were looking for a religious service, I'd be welcome to join him as he was just about to take one himself. I followed him inside a large building near the Peace Gardens, down some stairs, where a group of people were engaged in... I can't remember what... but I remember feeling strangely at peace there and joining quite happily in the service.

The total clarity of this dream convinced me that the same event was about to happen soon. The only conclusion I could draw was the sudden advent of dementia. Did it really come on so quickly? Wasn't I a bit too young? I kept asking my friends if they know what the first symptoms were: what about when I walked into the kitchen and couldn't remember what I'd gone there for? What about when I couldn't remember my phone number?

The following week, I'd been invited to Preston in the north west for a friend's surprise party. After a few drinks, I remember telling the story of my dream and quizzing other long-suffering friends about the symptoms of dementia: what about when I made myself a nice picnic and then walked out the front door, leaving it in the fridge?

The next morning, anxious to catch my train home so as not to miss an important Quaker meeting, I endured a catalogue of frustration – a delayed taxi and every traffic light at red and then the lack of notice boards on the station resulted in my standing on the platform watching the only train to Sheffield disappear into the distance. However, at 10.15 I'd be in time for the Quaker Meeting in Preston. But how would I find it in a strange town where most of the cab drivers were Muslim?

On the next platform was a large **Information Office** sign.

Just the ticket.

Inside, a woman was seated at a computer. I knocked on the

window.

Her eyes didn't move from the screen. "I haven't logged on yet.".

"I wondered if you'd got a phone book I could have a look at."

She didn't look up.

"Or a map of Preston. A street map. Do you have an A-Z?"

The woman still stared at the screen. "We don't do anything like that. I've got to log on."

"I'm looking for the Quaker Meeting House."

When there was no response, I offered, "You could google Quakers. They've a very good website."

The woman sighed and spoke to me as though I were a two-year old: "You can't google when you've not logged on."

I glanced at the minutes ticking by on the station clock. "Might anyone else know where the Meeting House is?" I suggested. "It'll be starting in five minutes."

The woman sighed again and picked up a microphone the size of a large foghorn. She bellowed across the station with all the subtlety of a sound-check at a stadium rock concert. *Can you hear me? Over...*

Receiving you loud and clear. Over. Something of an under-statement if ever I heard one.

Can anybody tell me where the... what's it called?

"Quaker Meeting House"

Where the Quaker Meeting House is? Over..

*Where the **What** is? Over..*

*Meeting House. Over.*What's it called?

"Quaker Meeting House."

Where the Quaker Meeting House is. Over..

***What** Meeting House?*

***Quaker** Meeting House. Over*

It's all right. I'll walk into town."

Quaker. "Is that what you said?"

What?

"It's all right. I'll walk into town. It's nearly half past..."
Quaker. Over... "That's right, isn't it?"
What? Over...
"It's all right, thank you very much. I think I'll...."

I take a deep breath and manage not to ask why some dipstick who can't tell their dongle from a day out in Blackpool has been given a job beneath a huge sign saying **Information Office** in a place where nobody knows f.... all. But being a polite English lady and seeing how it's now 10.26 I leave the woman logging and hotfoot out the station.

Back on the road, I follow a large sign that says **Town Centre** before realizing it's been erected by the same cerebrally-challenged Prestonian that put up the **Information Office** sign as I find myself on the outer ringroad, below a large motorway sign for **Blackpool.**

And then there's nowhere to cross to get back and I have to dart through speeding traffic to clamber over the central barrier. Then I finally see the town centre back where I've just come from but everyone I ask for directions goes, *What? What Meeting House?* And sends me first to the Jehovah's Witnesses and then to Morrisons supermarket and lastly to the Chinese Eating House and I start feeling slightly demented and in the end stop a young man in the street. He's on his way to church, he says, and if I'm looking for a religious service, I'd be most welcome to join him...

I stand and blink. I thank him and stare tearfully at the ringroad traffic. I've been misdirected – so what? There's no need to burst into tears.

I begin my return towards the town centre when I see a young priest . "I'm very sorry," he explains. "I don't know of a Quaker Meeting, but I'm just about to take a service myself and if you'd like to join us, you would of course be most welcome."

He might be wondering why I gawp at him like a goldfish on a go-slow. "It's a beautiful old building, well worth a visit. We've a Burne-Jones window and a lovely organ..."

So I'm led by Fr Andrew Teacher inside the warm and welcoming church of St George the Martyr[5] on Friargate and am amazed to find myself inspired by the whole caboodle – incense, statues, stained glass, candles and the magnificent organ. The sermon is a corker – inspirational, witty and well-delivered. Quakers are always delighted when the ministry at Meeting somehow hangs together, but this service hangs together because it's been planned like that. And the small congregation isn't just composed of middle class intellectuals. I travel back to Sheffield with a sense of rapture and my view of the Anglican church shaken upside down like a snow globe.

So, it's the texture of the dream that convinces me it really is about to happen. But there are two significant differences: the incident happens in Preston, not in Sheffield, and I'm led inside a traditional church rather than down some stairs. In a similar way, with my myxomatosis rabbit dream, I see the rabbit crouched beside a hedge, rather than in a hollow. When Jung describes his dream about a kingfisher, it's not a live bird he sees the following day, but a dead one. It seems as though, with prescient dreams, no matter how similar they are to real events there has to be some kind of fault line in the scenery.

You might use this to argue of course, that there's no such thing as a dream that foretells the future, that these discrepancies negate any such conceit. But Dunne's theory of serial time is based on the notion that the future we see in our dreams has to be slightly different. And that's because... wait for it... he suggests that all of us have lived our lives before. What we see when we look inside the future is not the future at all.

But the past.

This is Dunne's ground-breaking hypothesis:

Every Time-travelling field of presentation is contained within a field one dimension larger, travelling in another dimension of Time, the larger field covering events which are "past" and "future", as well as "present", to the smaller field... [6]

Now this may seem about as clear as a cauldron of clam chowder. But Dunne was suggesting that we live inside a universe in which different times are encased one inside another like a set of Russian dolls or Chinese boxes. The crux of his argument is that it's possible for us to travel in between these different layers through what he called The Effect: his expression for finding a portal into DreamTime.

In order get a grip on Dunne's ground-breaking concept, I'd like to adapt an analogy of Priestley's by describing one of my favorite journeys – from my home in Sheffield across the Pennine hills, to Manchester Airport.

I drive west, leaving the city behind and entering the Derbyshire Peak District National Park. On my left lies the westerly gritstone of Stanage and on my right, the boulders of Derwent Edge. A modern bridge spans the twin reservoirs of Ladybower and Derwent, both sites of villages flooded to provide Sheffield with some of the best drinking water in England.

The road then twists and turns uphill through conifer plantations. You now understand how the Snake Pass got its name as the road coils more and more steeply. The pines are replaced by moorland, rocks and boulders, the reservoir below dwindles to a river, then a stream. We pass the Snake Inn where stranded travelers have been known to spend many a night in snowy weather. We may catch sight of walkers, traversing the Pennine Way to Kinderscout plateau or through Doctor's Gate towards the boggy mass of Bleaklow (*bleak, yes, but certainly far from low*). After changing gear to negotiate the last few hair-raising bends, the road levels at the watershed where before too long, there's a view of Manchester in the distance. One short flat section before the road starts its descent and we can see the outskirts of

Manchester ahead.

So my journey's a series of landmarks. And, although I like to think of myself as Living in the Now, marveling at the sunrise and such stuff, when I've a plane to catch, I feel a tad edgy and mentally tick places off: *Right, that's the bridge across the reservoirs, next the Snake Inn…and the Watershed* means I'm half way there.

All of us have our own journeys in which landmarks turn into points in time: *I've got to here, now that's behind me. Next, I need to get through…* And if we have people to meet or flights to catch, we might even – as we mentally tick off the landmarks – keep glancing at the clock.

Before I relate this to Dunne's theory, let me just describe a journey back from Manchester in the early hours after a late-night flight. Driving over the Snake Pass, I'd passed the watershed and was negotiating hairpin bends down towards the Snake Inn. This wilderness is devoid of houses and street lights; if you dare take your eyes off the sweeping bends, all you can see is an empty sheet of black. As I rounded a corner, I saw a light ahead and prepared to dip the headlights but the beam stayed still. I rounded the next bend and there, across the road, was a car with its headlights blazing and its driver door wide open. No one stops on a bend in the middle of the night unless there's an emergency. I checked the rearview mirror but there was nothing to break the emptiness, so I pulled over as far as I could, applied the hazard warning lights, left the headlights on and stepped out. What I saw froze me to the spot. There was a body on the road. From what I could see, it was a woman, wearing a long, grey coat. The driver held a wheelbrace high in the air before smashing it down on her head. My heart turned over. The body juddered. I glanced behind me, pleading for another light to appear out of the void. Nothing. The hills were totally empty. I strained my ears: not even the faintest hum of a distant car.

The only sound was the thudding of the wheelbrace.

I hesitated. Striding across the road to confront a homicidal maniac hardly seemed a preservation plan. Could I just drive off? I have to confess, I considered it. Then realized I would never forgive myself if I stood and watched a woman being battered to death before turning and racing off into the night. Maybe if I looked supremely confident... I took a deep breath and projected myself into the role of angry-teacher-on-playground-duty-breaking-up-a-fight as I forced myself to cross. The man ignored me, raising his arm to give one last sickening thud. The huddled mass at his feet jerked. The man dropped the wheelbrace then bent down, lifted up a leg and dragged the body to the side of the road. It was a sheep. I gulped. So much for the sad victim in the grey coat. "Is there anything I can..." I squeaked.

"I ran straight into it," the man explained. "It was just standing there... in the road. I couldn't help it." He dragged the dead sheep further towards the ditch. "I had to shift it. It would have caused an accident."

"Can I do anything?"

"No. No. I know the farmer. I'll give him a ring and tell him." He paused. "It's a bit late now. Maybe leave it till the morning."

So, back to Time. Rather than imagining my drive across the hills, just consider that I'm in a plane, beginning my descent towards the airport. For once, it's a lovely day in Manchester and even the tops of the Pennines are sparkling in sunshine. Let's suppose as well that, rather than the usual seat over the wing, I've a wonderful view.

As I gaze out the window of the tilting plane, I see the whole stretch of the southern Pennines. The main feature is the highest point, invisible from the road – the boggy plateau of Kinderscout. The main other feature is the shape of the reservoirs which – again, unlike the view from the road – I can now see in their entirety – all three - with Howden tucked inside the valley. The Snake Pass is a slender thread uncoiling left to right.

I'd have to search hard to find the various points I tick off on my journey: I might make out the Snake Inn as the sun glistens on the windscreens in its car park; I may notice where the reservoir dwindles to a river, then a stream. But now I'm now free from all constraints of time, I can take in features willy-nilly. I might notice a car overtaking over the brow of a hill unaware of another vehicle heading towards it on the same side of the road. I might even see (though we'd be perilously low if I did) a sheep standing in the road and a car snaking round the bend.

When we think about the passage of our lives, we see a kind of journey. We think of starting out...*the house where I was born, my first school...* we think of crossroads where we've had to stop and make decisions: *Should I go this way or that?* We think of turning points and unfortunate collisions. At some time or another, often completely out of the blue, we have to deal with death. Sometimes it just appears out of nowhere, standing in the road.

However, just suppose there was someone else observing this same landscape, like a passenger gazing out of a low-flying plane. Their view would take in so much more. Part of their perspective would be what we think of as our past and part of it would be what we think of as our present and some of it would be stuff that hadn't happened yet, just like the airline passenger who sees a sheep standing in the road. The tick-off points on our life-journey would just appear as features on their wide, broad canvass.

Dunne suggests that if we really can glimpse inside the future, then there has to be another kind of time running beside our own – a time we can slither inside when we're asleep and dreaming. He describes it as a set of Chinese boxes but the picture that came into my head much more mundanely was the foam lagging that we wrap around a central heating pipe. An odd picture, but as it appeared just after reading Dunne's book and in the time that's most crucial for me - just before falling asleep - I gave it some serious thought.

My foam lagging suggests a future that, rather than existing "out there" in the distance is wrapped all around us. Its foamy texture suggests it may have other dimensions secreted inside. Amazingly, I discovered later that "space-time-foam" is one of the expressions now used by theoretical physicists to describe the possibility of superstrings and multiple universes – but more of that later. The other important analogy is that, no matter how tightly we squeeze the foam together, it always has a crack running down the middle. We need the crack for us to seep inside another time. In the words again of my great guru, Leonard Cohen: *There is a crack, a crack in everything. That's how the light gets in...* [7]

This relates to Dunne's description of yet another precognitive dream connected with, as he describes it, "the veriest triviality"...

...reading a book, I came upon a reference to one of those combination locks which are released by the twisting of rings embossed with letters of the alphabet. As I read this, something seemed, for one fleeting instant, to be stirring, so to say, in my memory...in a little while it came back. I had dreamed, during the previous night, of precisely such a combination lock.

The chances of coincidence, where two such vague, commonplace events were concerned, needed no pointing out. But I could not remember having seen, heard, or thought of such a lock for a year or more. [8]

Well, if Dunne had been a cyclist, a hundred or so years later, he wouldn't have had such a problem. Having already had several bikes stolen, I use these locks frequently and they're the bane of my life – fiddly and awkward to line up, and of course I've no memory for digits... but because of my familiarity with them, knowing the sense of relief when they finally spring apart... I think Dunne has missed a trick. I would see this not just as a precognitive dream but, more importantly - like my dressing table mirror and vision of the pipe lagging - as something of a revelation. Because Dunne's Theory of Time which he goes on to elaborate throughout his book and spends the rest of his life researching - works just like the combination lock we use to secure a bike.

If we were to imagine another kind of time running alongside ours – and if we were to imagine, rather like the water pipe and lagging, that they run in two concentric circles, one inside the other – and we imagine the narrow crack that runs all the way along the lagging and just suppose – for the sake of argument that there's a narrow crack in the water pipe as well – if they were able to rotate, there would be the occasional moment when both of the gaps came together. This would of course be the point where we'd get water all over the carpet and have to phone out for a plumber. And if we continue this analogy with the combi-nation lock – assuming there were only two rings and three numbers to remember (which would make life a good deal easier for some of us), when the time came that the crack on both rings coincided – when we'd turned it to the right number - that would be the time when the gap appeared and you could see right through – and Time, or your bicycle, would be unlocked.

Well, we can't go back and point this out to Dunne. But we can read about his great Experiment with Time in which he suggested that if people wrote down their dreams immediately on waking, there would be many more dreams remembered and more synchronicity observed. That of course is obvious. But Dunne's reasoning was this: why do some people have precog-nitive dreams and not others? Maybe these dreams are universal, but most of us forget them within the first few moments when we wake. If we kept a notebook and pencil on the bedside table and noted down our dreams before getting out of bed, then many more people would experience precognition.

And this is exactly what happened. His book sold widely and many readers tried his experiment. They recorded their dreams and any later similarities with real life events so that, when Priestley asked for examples of precognitive dreams thirty or forty years later, many of his respondents had kept their original dream notebooks and were able to offer accurate reports. As we've heard before, the episodes ranged from long narratives to small, almost insignificant detail. Priestley, now up to his armpits in letters about weird dreams, was particularly impressed with the following because he knew the writer to be a sound, sensible chap who worked alongside him in the BBC's engineering department:

Dream experience: I dreamed that (specifically) a sparrowhawk was perched on my right shoulder; I felt its claws. There was no associated dream: this was one of a number of isolated and quite disconnected dream situations on that night.

Waking experience: While I was studying in the lounge of my "digs" (being almost totally absorbed in my reading material), my landlord, who had been clearing out the attic, entered the room with a number of items of wooden refuse which he offered my colleagues as fuel for the lounge fire. One of the items was a stuffed sparrowhawk mounted on the baseboard of (presumably) an original glass case. I paid little attention, until one of my colleagues, having detached the bird, came quietly up behind me and dug its claws into the shoulder of my jacket with sufficient force to enable it to remain standing on my shoulder. I felt its claws. It was only then that I remembered my dream.

Comments: The probability is, obviously, extremely low; I did not previously know of the existence of this stuffed bird. The interval was short – only two hours elapsed between waking (when I recorded the relevant dream, with other material, in a notebook), and the moment when the waking event took place. [9]

The number of such reported episodes convinced Dunne that he was far from alone in his experience of precognition. However, another reservation I might add – although I wouldn't want to doubt the integrity of Dunne's experiment– is that he did take dream analysis literally. He produced his main writing in the nineteen twenties and although he refers at one point to psychoanalysis, he takes no account of Freud and Jung's symbolic interpretation of dreams. For Dunne, an umbrella is an umbrella; a candlestick is a candlestick and a train entering a tunnel is just that. He regarded dreams this way partly, I suspect, because of the era in which he lived but also because his expertise lay in the fields of engineering and mathematics. As Priestley himself says, this was a great strength: Dunne recognized a scientific problem and thus sought out a purely scientific explanation. Had he been living nowadays, many of his interpretations may have been quite different.

So, back to his theory which it may be helpful to repeat:

Every Time-travelling field of presentation is contained within a field one dimension larger, travelling in another dimension of Time, the larger field covering events which are "past" and "future", as well as "present", to the smaller field...[6]

Dunne's notion of a "smaller field" would be my journey by road to Manchester with the various pointers I pass along the way. His "larger field" would be my flight path to the airport where my view would encompass the past, present and future of my previous journey.

Dunne then takes this a step further by assuming that the larger field might also be contained within another, even larger.

Suppose for example, that I were flying – not from Manchester – but from London to New York. I'd still be gaining height as I flew over Manchester and, in the unlikely event of no cloud cover – if I could just make out the airport – planes taking off and landing on the runways would look like tiny flies around the strips of bacon rind we put out for the birds.

Dunne then goes on to suggest that all these different "fields within fields" could be extended into infinity, so that Time, rather than a single point, is like a ripple of water with larger and larger waves following behind. He calls this Serial Time. Although so many years have passed since he first produced his theory, it's only recently that theoretical physicists have finally caught up with him. The model they've produced looks remarkably similar to the kind of foam lagging that we wrap around our hot water pipes.

It's known as multiple universe theory and we'll examine it in Chapter Twelve.

And before we leave strange visions, here's another account from Reginald Scott:

> You shall read in the legend, how in the night time Incubus came to a ladies bed side, and made hot loove unto hir: whereat she being offended, cried out so lowd, that companie came and found him under hir bed in the likenesse of the holie bishop Sylvanus, which holie man was much defamed therebie, untill at the length this infamie was purged by the confession of a divell made at S. Jeroms toombe. Oh excellent peece of witchcraft or cousening wrought by Sylvanus!

Scott himself was not so easily duped, as he goes on to explain:

> Thus are lecheries covered with the cloke of Incubus and witchcraft, contrarie to nature and veritie: and with these fables is maintained an opinion, that men have beene

begotten without carnall copulation (as Hyperius and others write that Merlin was) speciallie to excuse and maintaine the knaveries and lecheries of idle priests and bawdie monkes; and to cover the shame of their lovers and concubines.[10]

Chapter 9

Finding the Key

...alas for poor Alice! When she got to the door, she found she had forgotten the little golden key, and when she went back to the table for it, she found she could not possibly reach it: She could see it quite plainly through the glass and she tried her best to climb up one of the legs of the table, but it was too slippery; and when she had tired herself out with trying, the poor little thing sat down and cried.

Alice in Wonderland, Chapter One

I've never kept a dream diary because I have so many dreams – most of them seemingly of no consequence whatsoever - that if I were to write them all down before getting out of bed, it would be lunchtime before I even started breakfast.

However, I do use the time after waking and before getting out of bed to run through my dreams, reflect on them and sometimes, if I want to find out more, go back inside them. The scientific name for this is *lucid dreaming*. Most people call it bone idleness. However, it does throw up occasional examples of Dunne's distortion of time.

The other morning, for instance, I was lying awake and conscious but still in my idle, dream-like state, when I saw a picture in my mind of a gushing tap. The picture was followed one or two seconds later, by the real-life sound of water gushing from a pipe in the adjoining bathroom. As though I somehow knew the pipes were about to make a noise and had already conjured an image to explain it.

Although I've suspected such time-distortions before, this was the first when I was definitely not asleep.

A similar event had occurred a couple of weeks previously at the annual Scientific and Medical Network Conference at Winchester University. Our rooms were in the students hall of residence where sleep was often interrupted by the banging of those so-difficult-to-close-quietly fire-doors.

I dreamed that a cleaner, walking into the adjacent kitchen, armed with a mop, sweeping brush and bucket, was unable to close the door behind her. I was awakened within the next second by the sound of the kitchen door banging, convinced that this event had been anticipated by my dream.

When we talk about such incidents, there's a conventional explanation that our dreaming state has the ability to compress time: we hear a door slam and then invent an explanatory dream so quickly that it seems to have happened already. However, my half-awake experience with the gushing pipe convinces me there must be some other factor at work.

Another more famous example, recorded in the 1870's by A. Maury, the French science writer:

I am dreaming of The Terror. I am present at scenes of massacre; I appear before the Revolutionary Tribunal; I see Robespierre, Marat, Forquier-Tinville, all the most villainous figures of this terrible epoch; I argue with them; at last, after many events which I remember only vaguely, I am judged, condemned to death, taken in a cart, amidst an enormous crowd, to the Square of Revolution; I ascend the scaffold; the executioner binds me to the fatal board, he pushes it, the knife falls; I feel my head being severed from my body; I awake seized by the most violent terror, and I feel on my neck the rod of my bed which has become detached and had fallen on my neck as would the knife of the guillotine. This happened in one instant, as my mother confirmed to me, and yet it was the external sensation that was taken by me for the starting point of the dream with a whole series of successive incidents. At the moment that I was struck, the memory of this terrible machine, the effect of which was so well produced by the rod of the bed's canopy, had awakened in me all the images of that epoch of which the guillotine was the symbol. [1]

As he explains in this last sentence, Maury assumes that after being hit on the head, he has then constructed the dream which appeared to him very lengthy but must in fact have lasted for only a fraction of a second.

Basically, we don't understand how time can possibly flow backwards and therefore refuse to engage with the notion that such a thing can happen. As a defense against such a wake-up call to our dormant sense of how-the-world-ought-to-work, we arm ourselves with any explanation on offer; if we read somewhere that it's possible for time to be so compressed in dreams that we mistake the order of events, then we repeat this explanation whenever such a happening occurs. In the same way, when people hear about near-death experience, they tend to say: *Oh, yes, I've heard of that. It's caused by drugs...* And that's the end of their reflection on the subject.

Here's another time-distorted dream: I was sitting, Alice-like, on a grassy bank with friends while behind us in the distance, children were singing a playground rhyme: *Oranges and Lemons, say the bells of Saint Clements...*

For those unfamiliar, this is a long and complicated game based on the traditional melodies of London church bells. Two children form an archway through which the others process, being captured as the archway falls:

Here comes a candle to light you to bed;
here comes a chopper to chop off your head...

This sounds uncomfortably akin to Maury's dream above and is in fact a reference to the infamous Tower of London and its grisly executions. The game concludes with the captured children standing behind either one of the arches and taking up position in... what?

I began to wake. Why ever was I dreaming about a game of Oranges and Lemons? What a ridiculous subject for a grown woman!

But then, as I went back inside the dream and the children acted out the last part of their game, I suddenly understood. Over the last few weeks I'd been worrying about a family crisis; my son and his partner were separating and I was concerned about their children, worried that they'd finish up being pulled this way and that in a family tug of war.

And that's how the game finishes: with the two opposing teams attempting to drag each other across the grass. And I was amazed to realize that I must have already been aware of how the dream would end before the song even started. I'd dreamed this whole long, convoluted game just because, when it reached its conclusion, it would bring me face to face with my real-life fear of a family tug-of-war.

Both these dreams are examples of the way that DreamTime, as the aborigines claim, can be *all-at-once* instead *of one-thing-after-another*. But aborigines are not the only people to share this notion. In Man and Time, J.B.Priestley talks about the Great Time of primitive people:

It was not passing time but the Great Time that had meaning and reality...

The Great Time belonged to the myths, the gods, the mighty spirits, the magical creators; and when primitive man worshipped, performed ceremonial rites, or engaged himself in any meaningful act – for when he went hunting or fishing he might be deliberately imitating some mythological hero – then he entered the Great Time. His world was sustained not by the meaningless passage from dawn to noon and noon to sunset, but by this Great Time, in which all creation, power and magic existed. [2]

The assumption has been made of course by intellectuals and academics, that DreamTime and the Great Time are the imaginings of naive and innocent people whose very existence is a relic from prehistory.

I remember an exhibition depicting Pete Marsh, the Late Iron Age man exhumed from a peat bog at Lindow Moss in Cheshire. As I read how his fingernails had been elaborately manicured and that these people enjoyed a varied diet, wore elaborate jewelry and imported wine from France, I realized that, unconsciously, I'd taken it for granted that people from the distant past had next-to-no culture, limited language and wouldn't know a Merlot from a flagon of moonshine.

Because we're supposedly descended from apes and – although some apes can be taught to count and recognize pictures on a card – most would have a job assembling a flatpack wardrobe, changing a car tire or even remembering how many bananas make five. With nothing to challenge my prejudice, I'd assumed some kind of progression: the further back you went, the less intelligent people were; those of us living now, with all the advantages of technology and education, must surely be the cleverest.

But if we're all that bright, why have more people died in war and genocide during the last hundred years than ever before in our history?

And what about Plato?

And Aristotle?

My school history books had been illustrated with orangutan- like cave people huddled in the dirt, scrabbling for roots, and Iron Age men daubed with mud, not reaching out with manicured hands to savor the bouquet of the latest Beaujolais nouveau. Geography lessons had portrayed indigenous people wearing the heads of dead animals and stamping round the campfire in some kind of primitive hoe-down and had somehow conveyed the impression that these people had all the intelligence of Tweedledum and Tweedledee.

Hopefully, you'll have enjoyed the benefit of a much more enlightened education. And this is important because what I'm suggesting – particularly in relation to DreamTime – is that people whose lives are more simple than ours may have access to wisdom, knowledge and understanding which those of us in more technologically-advanced societies have left a long way behind.

Research[3] carried out by Professor Dieter Kruska, the German biologist, shows how the brains of mammals kept in captivity shrink drastically in size. Without the need to be on the look-out for potential predators, without the challenge of hunting, without the need to travel far to find a mate, without the need to do anything very much apart from pressing a few buttons and waiting for the next meal to be delivered, every part of the brain of caged, laboratory animals is reduced in size within the space of only a few generations.

No one as far as I'm aware has dissected the brains of humans housed in blocks of flats, pressing their smartphone keys and sending out for takeaways and compared them with the brains of those who have to hunt for food, construct their own shelters and watch out for predators; but I'll warn you that these experiments were not just conducted with rats but with dogs and cats and monkeys...

So it's not impossible that native, indigenous people for whom life presents more of a challenge may be more intelligent and in matters of other-dimensional-travel understand a great deal more than we do.

In answer to a question at the conclusion of a lecture at the Royal Society in 2004, the scientist, Rupert Sheldrake goes on to ask:

Why have we lost so much of the sensitivity that our ancestors had? There are many stories from travelers in Africa who say that it's taken for granted... that members of a tribe will know when somebody's coming, when somebody's needed somewhere else, and they'll just go and they'll find someone who needs them 50 miles away. They respond to this all the time. Before the invention of telephones, this was what people did, and there are reports from the American Indians, Australian Aborigines, travelers' reports. Typically, anthropologists didn't study it because they were convinced it was impossible. [4]

This point is illustrated by a section of An Experiment with Time[5] when John Dunne questions why it seems to be only in his dreams that he is able to see the future. Why don't such events occur during his waking life? He reflects that maybe we have such experience while we sleep because then our minds are empty.

In order to test his theory, he tries other ways of blanking out his thoughts. What if he were to take down a novel, concentrate on the title and then try to imagine what the book might be about? His first experiment he described as "a gorgeous success". He feels quite elated. He'd taken a novel, sat in silent contemplation, waited for ideas to emerge, opened the book and found his projections were spot on. Fortunately, before he had time to inform the scientific community, he suddenly realized the reason for his great success: he'd pulled down a book he'd already read before.[6] He next tries the experiment in the library of his gentleman's club where he lists odd words that have come to him at random: *kangaroo, narwhal, woodknife*

I then drifted into a little inner library, which is an excellent place for a nap. I chose a comfortable armchair, and, for appearances sake, equipped myself with another volume...opening this in the middle.

Immediately my eyes fell upon a little picture of an ancient dagger, underneath which was inscribed Knife (wood). I sat up at that, And began to dip into the book, turning back after a moment to page 11. There I came across a reference to the horn of a narwhal. Reading on, I found on the succeeding page the words, *"The old man, kangaroo..."* [7]

Although Dunne himself doesn't pick up on this, I suspect the main catalyst is the situation he describes in his first paragraph – his main intention isn't really the pursuit of his experiment but finding somewhere comfy to sit down for a nap. And the time when the connections suddenly come to light is the moment I find most crucial – the seconds just before sleep.

Another later attempt at his experiment produces what he describes as a *"very curious image"* (It may be helpful to remember that this book was first published in 1927)

It was that of an umbrella with a perfectly plain, straight handle, a mere thin extension of the main stick, and of much the same appearance and dimensions as the portion which projected at the ferrule end. This umbrella, folded, was standing unsupported, upside down, handle on the pavement, just outside the Piccadilly Hotel.

I happened to pass that way in a bus next day. Shortly before we got to the hotel, I caught sight of a most eccentric-looking figure walking along the pavement in the same direction, and on the hotel side of the street. It was an old lady, dressed in a freakish, very early-Victorian, black costume, poke bonnet and all. She carried an umbrella in which the handle was merely a plain, thin, unpolished extension of the main stick, of much the same appearance and dimensions as the portion which projected at the ferrule end. She was using this umbrella – closed, of course – as a walking stick, grasping it pilgrim's staff fashion. But she had it upside down. She was holding it by the ferrule end and was pounding along towards the hotel with the handle on the pavement.

I need hardly say that I had never before in all my life seen anyone use an umbrella that way.

Dunne goes on to explain his conclusions:

These experiments showed me that, provided one were able to steady one's attention to the task, once could observe the 'Effect' just as readily when awake as when sleeping. But that steadying of attention is no easy matter. It is true that it makes no call upon any special faculty, but it does demand a great deal of practice in controlling the imagination. Hence, to anyone who is desirous merely of satisfying himself as to the existence of the 'Effect', I should recommend the dream-recording experiment in preference to the waking attempt.

But for studying the problem, the waking experiment is of distinct value, because one can follow a great deal of what one's mind is doing. [8]

An example of Dunne's "Effect" for me came on a walk around Ladybower Reservoir in the Peak District National Park.. It was a beautiful summer day. My normal route would have been to stride for a short distance by the reservoir then turn up through the woods, thus avoiding all the traffic din from the Snake Pass. However to my joy, the road was closed for repair and the whole area bathed in silence. For the first time, I could walk undisturbed along the entire length of the reservoir before clambering through the plantation to the Roman road along the ridge.

I set off with much elation but soon foresaw a problem: my walk would be doubled in length. Unless I found somewhere to refill my already half-empty flask, I'd be too thirsty. Almost straightaway, I heard the trickle of water; there was a fresh spring, tumbling crystal clear into a mossy pool. Thankfully, I drank my fill, replenished my supplies and then began my climb.

Fifteen minutes later, a bit puffed out, I was ready for a rest. The floor of the forest was muddy. What I needed, I thought, was a stout, flat rock to sit down and have a drink. No sooner was the thought in my mind than I looked ahead and saw, between the conifers, a large, flat rock. I slipped the rucksack from my shoulders and staggered through the pine needles to enjoy a welcome rest.

At the top of the hill, it was picnic time and I needed more than a rock. Somewhere to spread out my food with a view. It was time to savor the vista back to the reservoir and gaze ahead to the Roman road that led towards Win Hill. And there before me was the perfect spot; I could not have designed it better.

My trek went on in exactly the same way. When I lost the path and decided to take a shortcut, I needed a stile to cross the wall. And there one was. When I looked for another rock to sit, it was there. And when I needed what all women on a hike require – a large tall bush – one sprang up in my path.

I did not take this seriously. Just saw it as a bit of luck: six items on my walk exactly when I needed them. But when the same happened on my next walk, I considered it more carefully: maybe I'd heard a trickle of water in the distance and that had increased my thirst and only then had I looked around and seen the spring. Maybe I'd unconsciously seen the rock as I clambered around the corner and that had prompted me to think of taking a hard-earned rest.

But then such events began occurring regularly, yet only when I was hiking. I didn't, for example, wander round the supermarket thinking how nice a bottle of Merlot might be and then see a whole stack of them on special offer. There were times when I thought about catching a bus, but that didn't make one suddenly materialize: I'd stand at the stop just like everyone else, waiting for a 22 like a frustrated bingo player with one last square to cover.

And yet the coincidences continued. When I was nearing the end of my Beehive Walk[9] in Spain, I noticed on a large rock by the river, something strangely circular and small. It looked like an animal dropping. There were no animals about, but it was something I recognized - whatever was it? It took me a while to remember.

A few years before, on the Scottish island of Isla I'd set off with a burst of energy on my mountain bike to a bird hide and wildlife centre. I was soon to learn that Scottish miles are longer than English miles and their hills are much steeper as well. Their rain's a lot wetter and the Scottish wind excels at blowing the English back where they came from. I parked the bike and staggered into the centre with legs like jellied eels. A DVD was playing about otters; I watched it. I watched it again. I watched it because I felt so weak that each time I tried to stand, my legs congealed like cow bits in lumps of Scottish haggis. I opened my flask and drank my tea and ate my picnic and learned all there was to learn about otter excrement – how otters mark their territory by leaving their almost circular turds neatly on top of rocks. The otter poo was a little coil called...what..? Sprain? No. Stain? No. Whatever was it?

I waited so long in the information centre for life to return to my legs that I could recognize otter excrement in a Scottish mist after a tour around several distilleries, but I never bothered looking because my next stop was on the Isle of Jura where I saw otters every day. I camped by the loch and there they were, dipping and diving. But this half-remembered word kept whittling away and it wasn't until I'd stopped thinking about it and was almost back at the car, that the word leaped out like an otter's head from the loch: a spraint.

Back at my hotel with a couple of hours to spare before the evening meal, I sifted through the discarded book collection in the foyer and selected a couple of novels. The first one opened with a long description about – not just otters – but otter spraint – about the derivation of the word – something to do with a combination of spraying and straining. A word I had encountered only once before ever in my life.

So, Dunne's "Effect" went with me on my travels. When I visited my daughter, Mikita, and her partner, David, in California, it was there on a stroll around Lake Casitas. When I was thirsty, a water fountain appeared. Having been warned about rattlesnakes, I was reluctant to nip behind a bush: there are more dignified ways for an English author to meet her end than being bitten on the backside with her pants down and as I was cogitating on this, a portaloo appeared. Further on, I needed to unpack my rucksack and there was a seat large enough to spread my stuff. As none of these items were expected, I was becoming more and more convinced that I hadn't unconsciously glimpsed them already.

The next day, I ventured to Ventura with its magnificent views of the ocean and wide, furling waves so beloved of surfboarders. I clambered eagerly on to the sand, slipped off my shoes and filled my lungs with fresh, Pacific air. A mile or so away, I could see the marina which seemed like a good first stop.

I strode along, relishing the warm sand beneath my feet, when the thought occurred to me, completely out of nowhere that this might be a place for dolphins. All my life I've searched for dolphins but have never seen them in the wild. I'd left my binoculars in the car and had a nagging notion that I ought to go back.

But I was so much enjoying my walk and was already halfway to the marina. I'd never seen dolphins before so why should today be any different?

I hesitated and stood still, looking out to sea. There was a black fin. I stared. Then a dolphin reared out of the sea in all its glory, less than thirty yards away. I didn't need binoculars; I could see perfectly well without. The dolphin arched again out of the warm shallows. Then I saw another fin behind. There were two of them. And another behind that. And another. Four dolphins swimming away from the marina and if I'd walked on any further – if I hadn't stopped and turned to look at the ocean – I'd have missed them.

I think of these events as Dunne's "Effect" because, similar to precognitive dreams, it's another way of seeing stuff that hasn't happened yet.

But if that's the case, why doesn't it happen all the time? And am I the only person that it happens to? I've never known anyone else talk about such stuff when they go out for a walk.

After a bit of reflection, I realized that I don't know other people who hike the way I do. Of course, I meet other people on my travels. Normally, they're in couples or a group, chattering away, regarding their ramble as a social event. When I do meet lone walkers, they're normally listening to their iPod, walking their dog, jogging, chatting on the phone, horse riding, doing all sorts of complicated stuff with satellite navigation or riding a mountain bike. Or several of these at once.

I just enjoy the solitude.

During the long, cold English winter, I tend to stay indoors, only venturing out on the moors at the start of spring or when I'm in sunnier climes.

I find then that, for the first few walks, my brain buzzes with a backload of stuff: a bit like vigorous exercise when you're totally unfit – my mind finds it hard to relax; it simply feels overstretched. But by the third or fourth walk, the busyness has shifted and I'm left with empty space in my head like a field of virgin snow. When this happens, it's much easier to achieve Dunne's "Steadying the attention" or "controlling the imagination". My mind skates on silence. It's similar to a Quaker meeting but with added birdsong, gurgling streams and much better scenery.

And doubtless this is why Aborigines and other indigenous people have found Dunne's Effect so much easier than us: as their lives contain fewer distractions and less noise, they're more able to empty their minds and pay attention to the silence. In order to achieve The Effect, we need to note the words of Thoreau: *Our life is frittered away by detail... Simplify, simplify, simplify! ...* [10].

For most of us, the opportunities for making space are rare. In our *I'm-late, I'm-late, eat-me-drink me* culture, we have too much going on. Silence is so unusual, it suggests that something's broken. The radio needs new batteries, the iPod needs recharging or the Wi-Fi's Donald Ducked. And this would seem to be the reason for not finding the doorway into DreamTime: we live in a world without any mental space. *It's always tea-time and we've no time to wash the things between whiles.* We're surrounded by stuff. Barracked by bills and demands. Assaulted by e-mails: oblivious to the cacophony.

She knelt down and looked along the passage into the loveliest garden you ever saw. How she longed to get out of that dark hall, and wander about among those beds of bright flowers and those cool fountains, but she could not even get her head though the doorway; `and even if my head would go through,' thought poor Alice, `it would be of very little use without my shoulders.

Maybe all these demands make us seem more important – I don't know. But the doorway into DreamTime becomes more and more like the elusive door that leads into Alice's garden. It's always locked and the key is always out of reach. And the answer for Alice was to take enough pills because this might make her taller and this one make her smaller – but she was so busy taking the pills and drinking from the medicine bottle and seeing what effect they had – that she soon forgot that her original quest had been to take the key from its place on the glass-topped table and use it to open the door.

Chapter 10

Tweedledum and Tweedledee: Entanglement

They were standing under a tree, each with an arm round the other's neck, and Alice knew which was which in a moment, because one of them had "DUM" embroidered on his collar, and the other "DEE". `I suppose they've each got "TWEEDLE" round at the back of the collar,' she said to herself.

Alice through the Looking Glass, Chapter Four

So, to recap on our doorways into DreamTime. We now have:

- Near-death experience
- Creativity
- Dreams
- Emptying the mind

And before we add to the list, a bit more about the texture of this state: how do we know we've found a portal into DreamTime rather than simply a snooze? Or doing a bit of painting? What if Time doesn't actually move for us? Can it still count as DreamTime?

At the afore-mentioned Scientific and Medical Network conference in Winchester, we heard a fascinating talk by the American doctor, Larry Dossey about remote viewing. A group of us were discussing this over lunch when someone remarked: *Some of those accounts were amazing. I could feel the hair standing up on the back of my neck...*

One of the ways we recognize DreamTime is that the opening of these portals has a different kind of timbre to our normal everyday life: there is this sense of being in the presence of something over and beyond ourselves. When people talk about events, their voice will often change; you may see a moistening at the corner of their eye. Simply reading or hearing about such incidents might produce a quickening of our hearts or a feeling that we're coming out in goose pimples

And sometimes, we *just know.*

Which isn't the kind of knowing like realizing we know the answers in a pub quiz. It's a gut reaction rather than a connection in the brain. Just as precognitive dreams have a definite texture, so does this kind of knowing. When I *just knew* that my friend, Kieran, was standing on the doorstep and *just knew* that Karl had found a sick rabbit on our walk, it's almost as though the ideas had been planted from outside.

A Quaker woman I once met told me that she was walking on the cliffs and saw a figure walking below her on the beach. He was too far away for her to make out his features, but she told me: *As soon as I saw him I just said to myself: that's the man I'm going to marry. I **just knew.***

And marry him, she did. They shared many happy years together. Which brings me to our next portal into DreamTime: Entanglement.

It has long been known that newborn chicks will become attached to and follow the first large moving object they see after hatching, so for this experiment a group of chicks were "imprinted" with the image of a robot called a Tychoscope, relating to it – rather poignantly - as though it were their mother. The Tychoscope was programmed to wander randomly around a room. But when the cage of chicks was brought in, its movements changed; it began spending much more time in the part of the room closest to the chicks. There seemed no possibility of the robot deciding that it wanted to get to know the chicks better, so the only conclusion to draw was that the chicks were somehow able to influence the movement of the robot, "willing" it towards them. The experiment was repeated with 80 different groups, each of 15 chicks; overall, the robot moved 2.5 times more in their direction than towards chicks who hadn't been maternally imprinted.

This research was carried out by René Peoc'h and the Swiss Fondation Marcel et Monique Odier de Psycho-Physique who then went on to experiment with a second group of chicks, placed in a cage in a darkened room but with a candle on the Tychoscope. Again, the chicks appeared to manipulate the movements of the robot, willing it over to their side of the room so they could have more light. What makes these results particularly amazing is that the Tychoscope was being driven by a random generator located 23 kilometers away. Not only were the chicks able to influence the movement of the Tychoscope but do so at a considerable distance. As described in Scientific Exploration:

> It was found that the Tychoscope spent two and a half times longer on the half of the surface closer to the chicks, compared to its motion when the cage was empty ($x' > 1 1. 11 < 0.00 1$). Using chicks that had not been conditioned to adopt the robot as their mother, the robot moved in its normal random motion (Peoc'h, 1986). [1]

But if baby chickens can affect the movement of a robot, what about human beings? Can we affect the workings of machinery? Might it be possible for us to focus on the fruit machine and cause it to stop on the jackpot? Or cast our vibes over the roulette wheel so it skids to a halt opposite our pile of chips?

Well... surprisingly, although the results have been quite limited, studies have suggested that yes, there is a link between people and machines. One well-documented case described by Michael Talbot in The Holographic Universe[2], concerned the physicist, Wolfgang Pauli:

Pauli's talents in this area (psychokinesis) are so legendary that physicists have jokingly dubbed it the "Pauli effect". It is said that Pauli's mere presence in a laboratory would cause a glass apparatus to explode, or a sensitive measuring device to crack in half. In one particularly famous incident, a physicist wrote to Pauli to say that at least he couldn't blame Pauli for the recent and mysterious disintegration of a complicated piece of equipment since Pauli had not been present, only to find that Pauli had been passing by the laboratory in a train at the precise moment of the mishap.[2]

Pauli was no fool; as far as scientific rigor was concerned, he was Mr (or should that be Herr) Perfectionist. No one could be further from New Age, tree-hugging, crystal gazing, fluffiness. Scathing of any theories that lacked scientific rigor, his famous phrase about a weak argument was: *Das ist nicht nur nicht richtig, es ist nicht einmal falsch!* Not only is it not right, it's not even wrong. And yet Pauli's personal presence came to have such an effect on laboratory equipment, that he began to consult the great psychiatrist, Jung. It needed a mental breakdown before Pauli was able to reconcile himself with the factors causing this extraordinary effect, events discussed later in a series of letters between himself and Jung.[3]

In The Holographic Universe, Talbot writes that he has "experienced first hand many of the paranormal phenomena ...discussed" He describes his experience as something similar to that of witnessing a poltergeist:

> ...its activity very definitely seemed connected to my moods – its antics became more malicious when I was angry or my spirits were low, and more impish and whimsical when my mood was brighter – I have always accepted the idea that poltergeists are manifestations of the unconscious psychokinetic ability of the person around whom they are most active."[4]

I was relieved to read about this. All my life I've had strange relationships with machinery and have always found it acutely embarrassing to have to explain that, when I'm upset, the machinery round me malfunctions. When I'm fine and dandy, everything works a treat. There have been occasions when my car has broken down with its only possible malfunction due to the fact that I was heading somewhere I seriously didn't want to go. I remember an ex-boyfriend calling round to collect some of his last remaining stuff and by the time he'd departed, the electric kettle had whistled its last threnody, the central heating boiler hung up its jacket, the landline phones taken themselves off on a Quaker retreat and several lights had died.

After ending another relationship, I fused my way through several different sound systems. Trying to explain to the nice, young, helpful salesman about the difficulty with my personal karma, I sensed he thought he was dealing with some freaked-out, old hippy who didn't know her graphic equalizer from a half-ounce of waccy backy. Deep in the depths of my soul, I *just knew* the stress of my boyfriend still being in the house was tangible. No bottles of wine were deep enough: the pressure had overflowed. I thought it only fair to return the sound system and leave it in the shop but the helpful young salesman was having none of it. "It can't be broken," he insisted. "It's a different batch from all the rest."

I tried to discourage him from plugging it in whilst I was standing there. "I'll go and stand out in the street," I offered.

But the salesman's finger was already on the button and the grin on his face suggested he assumed that I was joking. Less than one minute later, all of us were standing in the street because the shop had filled with smoke as my fourth sound system burst into flames.

A little bit of reassurance on the subject of people and machinery, it might be worth mentioning that everything I've read so far suggests our influence is relatively minor. Just for fear you're worried about taking a transatlantic flight in case the pilot's wife has just walked out on him or concerned that your local nuclear reactor might go into meltdown because one of technicians is worried about losing her job... I've read nothing so far to suggest that our effects on machinery could be completely catastrophic.

Yet.

The university department which carried out the experiments with chicks also used human volunteers – not with mummy robots this time but random coin-flip generating machinery. They found that yes, people did appear to influence a coin to land on heads or tails, but their influence was relatively small. Several million coin flips had to be produced by a random-flip-generator before patterns demonstrated the effect of human interference. In the next chapter we'll examine ways in which these effects came to be enhanced.

But what about the contentious issue of thought transfer - not just between people and machines - but between two people?

I first became aware of such connections when my children were very small and I realized they stopped crying as soon as I stopped what I was doing and headed toward the crib. As a teenage mum, I was determined to overturn everyone's worst expectations by becoming The World's Greatest Mother. I read every possible book on childcare and became familiar with the phrase: *How a newborn child will soon learn to recognize the sound of its mother's footsteps...* but what a load of twaddle. My newborn children didn't recognize any other sounds; how could they? And it made no difference whether I was wearing slippers, boots or heading towards them in bare feet; the time when they began to coo and gurgle was when I put down what I was doing, washed and dried my hands and headed off to see what on earth was wrong with them this time.

I would never, of course, wish to compare my offspring with French Bulldogs or Dalmations, but this is exactly the same process Rupert Sheldrake describes in his book: Dogs who Know when their Owners are Returning Home.[5] Tyson the bulldog might appear to be scratching at the front door in response to his owner's footsteps on the drive or the familiar sound of the Toyota being backed into the garage, but, on investigation, the dog's excitement can be traced back to the time when his owner stops work several miles away and takes the car keys from her bag. These dogs also trot towards the window and stand waiting even when their owners' return home at completely random times or in a cab.

And it's not only dogs who demonstrate this empathy with their owners. A psychic parrot in Manhattan has a vocabulary of 950 words – apparently the most accomplished language-using animal in the world. The owner claims her pet is able to speak in meaningful sentences and wakes her from dreams by commenting on what she's dreaming about.

Rupert Sheldrake described this pretty polyphonic parrot in the Telepathy Debate in which he participated at the Royal Society of Arts in London in 2004. [6]He set up a filmed experiment in which the parrot owner was asked to open a collection of sealed envelopes containing random images. Another camera in a separate room filmed the parrot who was asked to describe what his owner was looking at. In 71 trials, it was right 32% of the time and as there were 19 different images, this result was a great deal higher than would have been expected by chance.

I remember an incident when my son, Marcus was just big enough to toddle. As we couldn't afford a car, my father-in-law used to collect us on a Sunday afternoon to drive us round to their house for tea. Marcus – who saw the trip as the highlight of his week - would stand at the window watching out for Granddad's green Mini car appearing over the brow of the hill.

But this wasn't Sunday; it was a Thursday. Nonetheless, Marcus quite suddenly stopped what he was doing and clambered over to the window seat. "Granddad..." he pointed through the window excitedly. "Mini car..."

I explained to Marcus that he'd got it wrong, that it wasn't Sunday, that Granddad never came for us on Thursdays. In fact, as he worked all week, he never came on any other day. But Marcus refused to climb down and kept insisting. "Mini car..." and pointing down the street.

There was no car when I went to look. And it was a couple of minutes later that the green Mini appeared. From my comprehensive reading, I should have put this incident down to: *How soon a tiny toddler will learn to discriminate between the engine sound of different vehicles several miles away...*

But I didn't. I did, however, think back to a theory I'd read in my many books on child development suggesting that a young child passes through all the different stages of human evolution. A young fetus, for instance, has gills, with no function at all since our ancestors left the swamps; a newborn child has a grip similar to that of an ape – a tiny baby can dangle from your index finger (*just believe me – don't try this at home*). And of course, babies learn to creep and then crawl in exactly the same way – if we're to believe evolutionary theory – as our ancestors did. Might it be possible, I pondered, that certain psychic abilities were a similar sloughed-off stage in our evolution? Might it simply be that, as we've developed more and more complex forms of language, we've allowed what was a once a vital skill to disappear?

It was a few years before I was able to discuss my theory with an expert. I was fortunate enough to gain a place at Totley Hall teacher training college in Sheffield. My sociology tutor was an anthropologist we knew only as Miss Ward. During one of her fascinating seminars, I expounded my ideas and to my relief, she nodded sagely. "That's right," she said, "a lot of indigenous people are telepathic. That's how the old bush telegraph used to work."

I remembered these examples when I later read Sheldrake's' claim that one of the commonest areas of telepathic experience is between mothers and their new-born children. He demonstrates this with studies showing the physiological links with nursing mothers whose breast milk rises to the surface – often, as I remember to my great embarrassment - whilst walking round the supermarket - at the same time as their babies are waking up and crying a couple of miles away.

Sheldrake also describes an experiment carried out by one of his colleagues, Sir Rudolph Peters, Professor of Biochemistry at Oxford who investigated the case of a mother whose son suffered severe learning disabilities.[7] The boy had very poor vision but obtained brilliant results on his eye tests. His bewildered ophthalmologist sent the boy's mother out of the room and then found that the boy's scores rapidly deteriorated. He could apparently see very little without his mother present. Was his mother somehow relaying to her son the images that only she could see?

Sir Peters set up a series of controlled experiments at his laboratory in Cambridge. He placed the mother in a different laboratory about five miles away and showed her a series of cards with numbers or letters randomly placed and asked her son, at the other end of a phone, to guess what she was viewing. Just as with the psychic parrot, the son achieved a 32% success rate over 163 trials – considerably over and above what would have been achieved by chance.

Michael Talbot mentions the fact that "primitive cultures nearly always score better on tests of extra-sensory perception than so-called civilized cultures."[8] All of which leads back to the notion of indigenous societies, with their firm sense of a spirit world and DreamTime, retaining concepts and abilities lost to those of us with more technical sophistication.

This is reinforced in David Bohm's *On Creativity*. In his introduction, Leroy Little Bear of the University of Lethbridge describes discussions at the university among a group of Native American colleagues about the similarities between quantum theory and Native American thought. Leroy Little Bear had been struck by the similarities between his Blackfoot ways of thinking and David Bohm's seminal work *Wholeness and the Implicate Order*[9]

As Leroy explains:

> Blackfoot philosophy includes ideas of constant motion/constant flux, of all creation consisting of energy waves and imbued with spirit, of everything being animate, of all of creation being interrelated... the constant flux notion results in a spider web network of relationships. In other words, everything is interrelated... all creation is a spirit. Everything in creation consists of a unique combination of energy waves... what appears as a material object in space is simply the manifestation of a unique combination of energy waves. [10]

David Bohm had been studying the way in which quantum particles behave. When they've been formed from the same atoms and are similar in make-up – like twins – they appear able to connect with each other, no matter how far apart they travel.

So, if we take two twin particles – let's call them Tweedledum and Tweedledee – travelling in opposite directions, they will always travel at exactly the same angle to each other. If one of them gives out a positive charge, so will the other. It is just as though there's some kind of invisible network linking them together and this ability to communicate is constant - no matter how far apart they go. At first this seems impossible. How can such minute particles know what their partners are doing? And over such huge distances? They can't shout; they can't see each other; they don't have smartphones. And yet, as communication between them appears to be instantaneous, they seem to transmit messages faster than the speed of light.

Virtually all scientists accept Einstein's statement that nothing can travel faster than the speed of light. As Frank Close, professor of theoretical physics at Oxford University noted in the Guardian after claims from CERN about faster-than-light neutrinos: "the only thing that travels faster than light is a rumor."[11]

And so as this instantaneous communication has been observed over and over again, particle physicists have hardly been able to believe the evidence of their own eyes.

The main explanation, put forward by David Bohm, suggests that, alongside the universe as we know it, lies another deeper order of existence which he calls the implicate, or enfolded, order. Our own level he refers to as the explicate, or unfolded, order. Everything is connected by this vast, invisible interlocking fabric that knits the whole universe together. Bohm suggests that communication can take place between tiny quantum particles because of the way they're connected through this vast, invisible, interlocking fabric.

Look at the way we might view the separate waves in the ocean, he argued. As one wave rises, another falls back; one wave wraps itself around a sandcastle, another drowns an ice cream cone. One picks up a baby turtle and carries it out to sea; another lifts a crab from a rock and sets it down elsewhere. They have different sizes and perform different tasks, appear completely separate when looked at from above and yet, below the surface, all the waves are part of one great whole. All of them make up the sea.

In order to make his theory more accessible, Bohm devised the analogy of a goldfish in a tank with two closed-circuit TV cameras, one at the side and one facing the front. He asks us to imagine the TV footage viewed by aliens who've never seen fish before.

These aliens notice that when one fish turns away, the other one faces the front; when one fish waves its left fin, the other waves its right; yet both rise to the surface together and sink at just the same time. Surely, they must have some invisible means of communication. How else would each fish know what its partner was doing? Can they read each others minds?

Of course, the two fish don't send secret messages across the buried treasure and tiny shipwrecks of the fish tank. The aliens are looking at two completely different viewpoints of one and the same fish.

And here's another illustration:

Dim's Sun

Dim lived in Australia and wasn't very bright.
She'd lie on the beach and sunbathe from morning until night;
She'd phone her best friend, Maddy, back home in the UK
To tell her about the goings-on with the sun in the sky each day.

Maddy seldom saw the sun for Manchester was dull;
The sun was a miserly twitch now and then
Between Liverpool and Hull.
Dim's sun was a whole lot brighter; it beamed and scorched and shone;
It singed the fur on kangaroos and made surfing a lot more fun.

When Dim phoned her best friend, Maddy, having switched off the television;
Maddy was just eating corn flakes and toast and the sun had barely risen.
"What an amazing fact," Dim said, "that when my sun goes to bed
Your sun wakes up and shimmers and brings light to you instead.
And when your sun starts yawning and decides to call it a day
My sun wakes up and stretches and decides it's time to play.

And when my sun feels lazy and stays in bed much of the

time,

Those are the coolest months of the year, our Australian wintertime.

That's when your sun's at its brightest, shining all day long.

How do they talk to each other and know which side of the world to shine on?

And if mine wakes up as yours goes to bed, how do they synchronize?

How do they shout across all that sky?

Do suns telepathise?

Since Bohm's hypothesis, a host of other theories have speculated on the possible shape and location of this deeper substance which appears to link the universe together. Is it formed from a layer of strands like an intergalactic web? Or is it made out of the dark matter we believe collects inside black holes? Or might other dimensions all be coiled together like a wound-up hosepipe so that – when looked at from above, they simply appear to be flat? Or might it be something like a ball of string? Or is everything we see simply an illusion? Is our existence a virtual aspect of an intergalactic hologram, a representation of reality which we only think we see?

These theories may sound like the drunken ramblings of a group of friends who insist they're just beginning to unravel the secrets of the universe as it's time to leave the pub; or the pitchings of a third-rate sci-fi scriptwriter after a bad night on the cheap vodka; however, they are all perfectly respectable theories put forward by theoretical physicists to explain the invisible links between Tweedledum and Tweedledee.

Chapter 11

Love; the double doorway

"I've cut several slices already, but they always join on again!"
"You don't know how to manage looking-glass cakes," the Unicorn remarked. "Hand it round first, and cut it afterwards."
Alice through the Looking-glass, chapter v11

Christiaan Huygens, born in 1620, was a Dutch mathematician and astronomer, honored as a Fellow of the Royal Society. Considered the world's first theoretical physicist, he discovered amongst many other extra-terrestrial phenomena, the Saturnian moon, Titan. Mons Huygens, a mountain on the moon, has been named after him, as has a crater on Mars, an asteroid and the Huygens software package for microscope imaging. In 1695, his book *Cosmotheoros* advocated the existence of extra-terrestrial lifeforms and he was also known for his invention of the pendulum clock. This device dramatically increased the accuracy with which time could be measured and became the bane of everyone who had to work hard for a living. Having patented his first clock, Huygens designed others which may explain the fact that, at one time, he had two clocks both on the same wall hanging in the same room.

Huygens noticed that although the clocks were originally out of synch, before long, they began to tick in unison. He stopped the clocks and reset them a fraction of a second apart only to find that, after a short while, they began ticking together again. Huygens kept restarting them: one ticked; the other tocked, but before long, they were ticking and tocking together, yet always in opposite directions. Like two friends walking side by side one with his right foot forward, the other with his left, one slowed down and the other sped up, so they could keep in step,

But how could the clocks communicate? They might have been Huygens' invention and his pride and joy but they were still clocks. Other scientists repeated the experiment with different clocks in different places and noted the same effect. They gave it the name of entrainment and throughout the years, examples of entrainment have been discovered in almost every aspect of science: in the worlds of chemistry, pharmacology, biology, medicine, psychology, sociology and astronomy an amazing variety of unconnected stuff has been found ticking and tocking together. In the insect world, bees have been known to co-ordinate their wingbeats to act as one large cooling fan; fireflies have been found to synchronize their flickering to form one large flashing LED display and, as has long been known, women who share the same household often find their menstrual cycles begin to harmonise. One moves forward a few days and another drops back until they reach the terrifying state of all being premenstrual on exactly the same day. What evolutionary benefits could possibly be gained from this, no-one has so far discovered.

Scientists have also found entrainment in the electric signaling patterns in the human brain: when the higher nervous system of one person is stimulated, it can affect the same part of the brain in their partner who's receiving no such stimulation and is, in fact, in a different room at the time.

One such experiment in Mexico used flashes of light. These flashes were found, through E.C.G monitors, to have a marked effect on the brain patterns of the viewer. However, their partners sitting in an electrically-shielded room over fourteen meters away from the flashes also showed similar signs of stimulation to the same part of the brain. A further study by Bastyr University and the University of Washington showed the same results with flickering light. As Lynne McTaggart writes in The Intention Experiment: "It demonstrated that "the brain-wave response of the sender to the stimulus is mirrored in the receiver, and that the stimulus in the receiver occurs in an identical place in the brain as that of the sender. *The receiver's brain reacts as though he or she is seeing the same image at the same time.*[1]

In spite of the statements by David Bohm and others that all of us are connected on some deep, harmonious level – no matter how much we to aspire to unite with the creative flow of the universe - we can't help feeling more connected to some people than to others: there are those with whom we'd willingly share our Leonard Cohen albums and our last piece of chocolate cake and those who – let's face it - to use a colorful phrase of my younger son, Bevan's: "you'd think twice before pissing on if they were on fire."

And just as Huygens' clock didn't swing in synch with any old passing pendulum and bees don't flap in time with those from a colony from out of the neighborhood, so it's no surprise to find that our level of entrainment varies according to who we're with.

The experiments described in the previous chapter at Princeton University showed people affecting the generation of random numbers by simply focusing their thoughts. The results were of minor significance but were completely transformed when partners were used instead of individuals. When the experiment switched to what they called "bonded couples", the effects were almost six times greater, as though some resonance between the couples had been harnessed and turned outwards.

Another series of experiments, initiated by the US psychiatrist, Elizabeth Targ, came to be known as The Love Study. Carried out – somewhat appropriately - in the San Francisco Bay area, this study recruited couples, one of whom suffered from cancer. Subjects were placed in sealed rooms with no possibility of communication or of outside interference. The "healing group" were then shown pictures of their partner and asked to send "compassionate intent" towards them. The receivers had no idea when this compassionate intent would happen, what form it would take or for how long it would last. Wired up to every conceivable item of monitoring equipment, it was found that - each time they were asked to focus - the senders displayed all the symptoms of intense concentration: a sharp intake of breath, a change in blood pressure, in brain waves, heartbeat and in skin conductance. However, these changes were immediately mirrored in their partners; they too changed their breathing patterns and their heartbeat, their brain waves and their skin conductance even though they were in isolated rooms with no knowledge of when the healing thoughts occurred. [1]

Previous studies into remote viewing – or telepathy - have tended to pair participants with strangers to ensure they can't have secretly established some kind of number sequence or series of images to transmit. It's no surprise that these studies are often disappointing; they ignore the fact that what's become known as non-local transference tends to develop with people closest to us: our partners or our children or our closest friend or twin. The closer we are, the more we can anticipate what they're about to do or say. We may find ourselves thinking about a close friend or relative just before they phone, but is this simply because we know roughly how often they phone and what time of day? Is it thought transference or just that people can be quite predictable? Is it thought transference that warns you your husband is just about to shrink his woolen socks on the hottest wash? Or the simple fact that after seventeen years he still hasn't learned to use the washer? Is it telepathy that tells you your friend will order a double short with his last pint at the bar and then suggest stopping off for kebabs as he totters along the precinct singing *Oh, Danny Boy...*? Or just that you know him so well?

One night, nodding off to sleep, I had a completely ludicrous picture in my mind of digging with a spade and discovering a hoard of treasure. It didn't make any sense – it was in the days when I never had time for gardening - probably didn't even own a spade - and was even less of a bounty hunter. It was then that my husband, fast asleep beside me started muttering in his sleep: *Just like digging for treasure,* he intoned. *Just like digging for treasure.*

So, I would say the answer to these questions is: both. The closer our relationship, the more likely we are to predict what someone is about to do or say, but also the more likely that we'll have a strong intuitive sense of knowing when we're in their thoughts (such as when they're about to phone) or whenever they're going through some traumatic event or crisis.

Here's such an account from Jung:

I recall one time during the Second World War when I was returning home from Bollingen. I had a book with me but could not read, for the moment the train started to move I was overpowered by the image of someone drowning. This was a memory of an accident that had happened while I was on military service. During the entire journey I could not rid myself of it. It struck me as uncanny, and I thought, "What has happened? Can there have been an accident?"

I got out at Erienback and walked home, still troubled by this memory. My second daughter's children were in the garden. The family was living with us, having returned to Switzerland from Paris because of the war. The children stood looking rather upset, and when I asked, "Why, what is the matter?" they told me that Adrian, then the youngest of the boys, had fallen into the water in the boathouse. It is quite deep there, and since he could not really swim he had almost drowned. His older brother had fished him out. This had taken place at exactly the time I had been assailed by that memory in the train..."[2]

Here's an example from the Quaker, Rufus Jones on a visit to England in 1903:

The night before landing in Liverpool I awoke in my berth with a strange sense of trouble and sadness. As I lay wondering what it meant, I felt myself invaded by a Presence and held by Everlasting Arms. It was the most extraordinary experience I had ever had. But I had no intimation that anything was happening to Lowell [his son]. When we landed in Liverpool a cable informed me that he was desperately ill, and a second cable, in answer to one from me, brought the dreadful news that he was gone... [3]

Throughout this book we've listed ways in which we seem able to access what Aborigines describe as DreamTime. We've looked at meditation, dreaming and emptying our minds; we've examined creativity and near-death experience and before we leave this list, I'd like to add a quote from my daughter, Mikita, about thought transference during psychoanalysis:

I am convinced that the psychoanalytic situation, under certain circumstances, can produce unique connections between two minds. At special moments in this highly charged situation, thoughts do appear to cross the boundary that separates one individual from another. Most psychoanalysts have experienced such moments. They are very difficult to describe, and almost impossible to pin down. They often involve phenomena that seem embarrassingly trivial or unattainably fleeting... [4]

I've recently discovered that, as I've been writing The Effect, Mikita – who's been working in California and is known for her books on film and popular culture - has been working on a book called Phantoms of the Clinic. Completely unbeknown to me, Mikita has also been studying examples of thought transference and has quoted from Sheldrake, Pauli, Jung and David Bohm. And not only has she mentioned string theory and the relevance of thought transference in primitive culture but has referred to Sheldrake's psychic parrot and included exactly the same quotation from him as the one I've included myself.

Mikita, a practising analyst as well as an academic, describes the unique relationship of the analyst and patient:

> In this strange and unique fifty minutes, the external world is bracketed and set aside, and something else is allowed to emerge. The time and place are turned over to the unconscious with its magical beliefs, odd rituals and deep shadows. The order and connections of "reality" are temporarily replaced by the order and connections of thoughts, fantasies, wishes and dreams...such experiences occur all the time... but they grow especially involved in relationships that are emotionally intense – in love, in family relationships, and between analyst and analysand. the more heavily involved the relationship, the more intricate the psychological dynamics.[5]

Which brings us around to relationships. As Mikita describes, this needn't be a sexual relationship; it can be the bond that exists between psychiatrist and patient or a parent and a child or between siblings and especially twins or the love between two friends.

When I take my place in Quaker meeting, I sit for a few moments gazing round, ticking a kind of mental inventory of who's there. To say that I bless them all might sound a bit pious, but I certainly feel as though I give them all a great big mental hug. These Friends can be obstreperous, pedantic, petty and take a pitifully long time to reach the point and yet I love them dearly.

The Quaker meeting, like so many other spiritual places, is a circle of love; not just for me but for all who gather there. It's also a place where people empty their minds and sit in silence and this is why, I suspect, it's not just a doorway into DreamTime, but a double door: it scores twice - a doubling of what Dunne calls

The Effect. Doubtless this is why we so often find ourselves focusing on the same subject or even thinking the same thoughts.

An even more powerful example of this relates to near-death experience. When we talk about entering DreamTime, it's like a tiny chink or tear in the fabric separating one dimension from another. We see through for a split-second before the gap is closed and we're back firm and square in our own dimension. When someone's dying however, it's as though the fabric has to part – like a pair of opening curtains – to make space for them to pass. They don't just see a momentary glimpse, but long-dead relatives, a dark tunnel and an all-encompassing light. Those we read about earlier paused on the threshold , had a look around, realized they'd arrived on the wrong day, turned around and went back. People who haven't arrived on the wrong day, so to speak, carry on inside. The curtains stay open and if someone you know is in this state and especially if you're close beside them at the time, you may experience the greatest double doorway of them all when you feel for a moment, as though it's happening to you. When my mother died, I had a sense of her elation, so strong it felt as though the two of us were lacing up our hiking boots, striding through the gates of heaven and sharing our joy together.

This doesn't happen to everyone. I know those who've cared for much-loved parents or partners, day-in, day-out without experiencing any of this shared bliss. That may be through the effects of mega-high doses of palliative drugs or because the person was simply too weak to share anything at all; it would seem however to be no reflection of the depth of feeling or the amount of love between them.

But for those who do have this experience, it can be so vivid they remember it for ever. This account was told to me by Philip Hunt, a Quaker Friend. Philip's lucid memory extends as far back as the latter end of the First World War when he was a child of two. He met his wife-to-be at a social gathering in Oxford in

1939. Eleanor was a newcomer and as she knew no one there, Philip was asked to "be kind to her." He says, with a twinkle in his eye, that he would like to think he "was kind to her" for the next fifty years and a day as they stayed together from then on until Eleanor died in February, 1989 at the age of seventy five,

Eleanor had grown up on a dairy farm where one of the cows was kept for the family's own use. This cow, unfortunately, was infected with tuberculosis and as a result of drinking infected milk, Eleanor had to have a kidney removed. So, when in later years, a cancerous growth was found on her other kidney, its removal was not an option. Her body rejected all attempts at chemotherapy and within six months, Eleanor was admitted to the Home Towers hospice – an establishment for which Philip has nothing but praise – for the dedication of its staff and, what he describes as a "spirit of joy" in spite of the terminal illness of its patients.

Philip has a vivid recollection of the phone call which summoned him to Eleanor's bedside and the subsequent three hours he spent beside her. He relates:

It was as though she was a long, long way away. She was mentally very busy... occupied... and said quite suddenly, "Yes, I would like to cross over to the light, but I can't quite find the line." She didn't say this to anyone – not to me – but as a statement of her position at the time. Eventually, she seemed to come back. She opened her eyes, raised herself, looked me straight in the eyes and said: "Oh, my love," and then... her eyes glazed over. Her eyes had always sparkled so much, and then they just glazed over and went dim. I felt certain that she had left whatever it was she was doing in order to come back and say goodbye. I felt convinced that, wherever she was, she was happy. Prior to this I had had some vague sense of an afterlife, but the whole experience left me with a strong belief that death is not the end.

Another account of a loved one returning to say a last farewell comes from Jung who describes an event which happened some time after his wife had died:

> ...after the death of my wife, I saw her in a dream which was like a vision. She stood at some distance from me, looking at me squarely. She was in her prime, perhaps about thirty, and wearing the dress which had been made for her many years before by my cousin, the medium. Her expression was neither joyful nor sad, but rather, objectively wise and understanding, without the slightest emotional reaction, as though she were beyond the mist of affects. I knew that it was not she, but a portrait she had made or commissioned for me. It contained the beginning of our relationship, the events of fifty-three years of marriage, and the end of her life also. Face to face with such wholeness one remains speechless, for it can scarcely be comprehended.[6]

If I had to invent an expression for those who've returned from near-death experience, I'd call them Afterbirders. "After-bird" was an expression for after-hours drinking before the British licensing laws were relaxed (rhyming slang: *birdlime/time*). Pub customers would leave at 11.15 and shout a hearty goodnight before strolling round the block and nipping in through the back door and picking up their drinks from where they'd left them on the bar. So, if people find that Closing Time (*another Leonard Cohen song here*) is not in fact The End, but simply signals the introduction to the real Afterbird session –what happens after that?

Does the session last for ever?

Is this what the Irish would call, *the real craic* with an endless supply of Guinness and all of it for free?

Are there complementary trays of bagels and samosas, falafels, dim sun and barbecued spare ribs?

Does the stomping good band play all night long?

Do we finally put the world to rights, win the darts match, watch Sheffield United win the cup and the premier league and find the love of our life as we fall into each others arms as we're both dancing on the same table?

The accounts of those who've experienced the celestial Afterbird sound ecstatic and sublime with enfolding light and heavenly music and yet... to be absolutely honest... and not wishing to sound ungrateful... I could imagine myself getting bored. I could see myself wandering round for a few days, taking in the ambience, catching up with all my deceased friends and relatives, marveling at how young and sprightly everybody looked... but what about after that?

Time is the way we measure change and without time there would be no change. As Priestley expresses it:

If we try to imagine ourselves in a world without sound or movement, with nothing stirring, without even our breathing or heartbeats, we must agree that we cannot have Time there. Time may not be merely something happening, but unless something is happening, there cannot be Time.[7]

In a dimension where Time came to an end, everything would stay the same. But my idea of Heavenly bliss involves a bit of variety. No matter how blissful, I wouldn't want time to stand still for too long; I'd still want something to happen. Like stopping off at some idyllic spot after a long journey, it would be wonderful to have a swim. Ecstatic to find a table set out on the beach with mouth-watering food and a bottle of Merlot as I take off my shoes and wriggle my toes in the warm sand before raising my glass as the sun sinks over the bay.

But then what?

I'd want to wash my hair and change my clothes After only a short time, I'd be restless, itching to move on. There's a word I've learned from my colleague, Tim Birkhead, the renowned ornithologist at Sheffield University who, in his excellent book, The Wisdom of Birds,[8] writes about *zugunruhe* – the restlessness of caged birds when it's time for them to migrate. Tim quotes the unknown author of *Trate du Rossignol (A Treatise on the Nightingale)* writing in 1707:

> In the month of February or March or mid-September, those nightingales who are in the room or in the cage, become impatient and resist much then during three or four days of full moon, and fly against the glass or the frame of the cage, the evening, the night and the morning, as if they feel in themselves then something I do not know what which obliges them to leave the place where they are; what they do not do another time. And it is this instinct and inner guide that makes them fly by a favorable wind directly to the place where they want to go[9]

And maybe it's not only nightingales who feel their wings flutter against the glass when they have to sit through some tedious meeting or listen to some boring person droning on and on. And it's not only the feet of zugunruhe birds which pace up and down when they're stuck indoors in spring: we all know that feeling when it's time to pack our bags and move on.

So, no matter how exquisite and sublime our afterlife might be, there would still come a time when many of us would feel like checking out and heading for the door.

And many of the world's great faiths suggest that this is what we do: call in somewhere that is our celestial home; rest and spruce up; meet old friends; account for our conduct in some kind of life-review, and then set out again as someone or something else. It's known as reincarnation.

There's a poem by Rumi, the thirteenth century poet known as Jelaluddin Balkhi in his homeland of Afghanistan, who portrays this beautifully:

...Where did I come from? What's the purpose of this life?
I really don't know.
My soul has arrived here from somewhere else; I'm certain,
And that's where I'll surely return.

This drunkenness began in some other tavern or lodging house.
When I return to that place again,
I'll be sober. Meanwhile,
I'm like a bird from another continent, sitting in a cage.
I know the day will come when it's time for me to fly away...,
...I know I didn't come here of my own accord, and I know I can't
    leave that way.
Whoever brought me here will have to take me home. [10]

One of the reasons why reincarnation seems possible is because of déjà vu – those moments when we appear to have a fleeting realization that we've done something before, but in a previous life. Maybe with a tiny detail askew. Déjà vu is too unpredictable to be scientifically measured, but straw polls suggest[11] that it's reported by about 70% of us. Some encounter it rarely; with me it happens frequently but in clusters: possibly as often as several times in one day (notably, around major changes in my life) but then not for several weeks. An important factor seems to be location.

Such a location was in York at the Galtres Hotel on Petergate. I was working as writer-in-residence at the nearby university and this medieval building was just a few minutes away. I remember the stairway where the walls and floor seemed at such an odd angle, I wondered whether I might have consumed one too many glasses of the hotel's excellent mulled wine as I staggered up to bed. On the corner was a large cupboard used as a priest-hole for concealing Catholics during the times of persecution.

And I remember checking out one morning, waiting for the till to whirr through my various extras – and as they served excellent food as well as the mulled wine, this was taking a little while - when I suddenly had the sensation that I'd stood on that very spot before, but on this other occasion, a clock was striking. At that moment the minster clock, very loud and very near, began to chime the hour; my mind stayed inside this experience and I then thought: *Yes it's just the same except that the door then opened and a man walked in.* This happened. The door opened and a man walked into the restaurant. And then I thought, *Yes, but the man on this other occasion walked right across the room and he was carrying a heavy bag...* I blinked and stared as he walked across in front of me - a workman carrying a heavy bag of tools.

On my next visit, I arrived back late after an evening out and was surprised to find it was the workman who let me in. He explained that, as he had to repair the floor in the restaurant, he was only able to do it after the customers had left. York is a medieval town built on a Roman town, built on an earlier settlement and the floors in the buildings round the minster are often known to shift. He was repairing a large crack that had appeared in the step down to the restaurant.

There's an expression the Irish use: they talk about *thin places*. By this they mean the walls that normally exist between different worlds are less robust. There are places where we can see through – from one time to another or from one world to another as though there's a crack or a distortion in the fabric.

Throughout the years, many such places have become well-known as places of pilgrimage, frequented by those searching for what I've come to call The Effect. Many have become shrines or churches. Whether they're sometimes turned into restaurants as well, I'll leave you to imagine.

So, does the frequency of this kind of experience really mean that all of us have lived a previous existence? Does it mean I've lived a life before in which I've stayed in the same hotel in York in which there was another workman mending a different crack in the floor?

Dunne and his predecessor, Ouspensky write about serial time - where we live our entire lives again but with the chance to make improvements every time; more traditional notions of reincarnation suggest we live again but next time our existence is completely different. We're born at a different time in a different location; we have different parents and a different name; we'll have a different birthday and different children. This concept therefore excludes any real explanation of déjà vu which only makes sense if we've actually lived not just any life but *the same life* before.

I considered this when I was travelling through India and visiting Hindu temples. As I wound the circular route towards the shrine of one temple, I became fascinated with the intricate carvings on the frieze, depicting first a fish and then a tortoise, then a pig or a boar and afterwards a kind of half-man/half-lion. It then went on to portray a very small man or dwarf before the depiction of figures that seemed much more familiar. The temple was several centuries old, so why should its frieze illustrate evolutionary theory, not widely understood until the ideas put forward by Darwin and Wallace in 1858?

On enquiry, I was told the frieze represented various incarnations of the god, Vishnu who had begun as a fish, been reincarnated as a reptile, then returned as a mammal and later as half-man-and-half-lion before, over many lives, developing into the highest level of existence, that of man.

I realize this theory might explain why human babies exhibit so many of the signs of evolution mentioned earlier – gills and an ability to creep and then to crawl, but for some reason, I don't warm to the notion of a previous existence as a fish. I was in my mid-twenties before I even learned to swim. And I've never had a déjà vu moment thinking, *Oh yes, I think I've swum through this little bridge before… maybe in a dream or in a different life…*

Another quandary arose when I experienced a vivid sense of déjà vu whilst standing at the supermarket checkout. Thinking, *Oh yes, I think I've done this before* may not seem so unusual in a local supermarket where we shop all the time. But I did have that vivid sense of another time: a split-second recall of a similar supermarket I know I've never shopped whilst chatting with a familiar friend I'm certain that I've never met. And what made this so odd is that I was born in the days before supermarkets became universal. For this to have happened in a previous existence, I'd have to have been a good twenty years younger.

Another problem with traditional views of reincarnation is the notion that we can be weighed down by bad karma or original sin and our misfortunes are not simply due to chance but some kind of retribution for our wrongdoing in some previous existence.

However, Dunne and Ouspensky's concept of reincarnation addresses these misgivings. It also means we only have one birthday to remember and get to keep not only the same parents but, conveniently, the same name. We're born again without bad karma because we've enjoyed a previous existence in an almost identical time. The theory was developed by J.B.Priestley and described vividly in his stage play: *I have been here before*. [11] Set at Whitsuntide high on the North Yorkshire moors in the Black Bull Inn, Priestley introduces us to the eccentric German scientist, Dr Görtler, who has an uncanny way of knowing what is about to happen to the Black Bull's other visitors. As with most good stage plays, it's an eventful weekend during which the wife of Mr Ormund, one of the guests, decides to leave him and Mr Ormund is intent on suicide. Dr Görtler, however, suggests that, rather than being the peaceful way out, Ormund intends, this is the mistake he has made in every life he's lived so far:

Dr GORTLER: We do not go round a circle, That is an illusion, just as the circling of the planets and stars is an illusion. We move along a spiral track. It is not quite the same journey from the cradle to the grave each time. Sometimes the differences are small, sometimes they are very important. We must set out each time on the same road but along that road we have a choice of adventures.

ORMUND: I wish I could believe that, Görtler.

DR GORTLER: What has happened before – many times, perhaps – will probably happen again. That is why some people can prophesy what is to happen. They do not see the future, as they think, but the past, what has happened before. But something new may happen. You may have brought your wife here for the holiday over and over again. She may have met Farrant here over and over again. But you and I have not talked here before. This is new. This may be one of those great moments of our lives.

ORMUND: And which are they?

DR GORTLER: When a soul can make a fateful decision. I see this as such a moment for you, Ormund. You can return to the old, dark circle of existence, dying endless deaths or you can break the spell and swing out into new life.[11]

The ways in which we *swing out into a new life* are also the subject of another great concept we now need to explore: Hugh Everett's Multiple Universe Theory...

Chapter 12

Multiple Universe theory

"Why, sometimes I've believed as many as six impossible things before breakfast."
(Through the Looking Glass, Chapter 5)

Sunday morning.

In the way that's now become routine, I plan to attend my local Quaker Meeting but... as I open my front door, the neighborhood is covered by a huge white duvet - except that it's not so warm. Every year it snows in Britain; every year we're unprepared. *What? Snow? In winter?* The local radio informs us that snow ploughs and gritting trucks have been "caught unawares" – no news there then - and recommend that no-one takes out their car unless their journey is absolutely vital.

I start scraping ice off the windscreen. I could heed the warning and walk into town. It would only take half an hour and I'm relatively fit, but there's quite a few frail and elderly Quakers who will at this very moment be plodding into town from a good way out and if I take the car, I could offer them a lift back home when the gritting trucks might have made a start.

It takes a while to sweep off the worst of the snow and the windscreen freezes almost as fast as I clear it, but after ten minutes scraping and scrunching, I decide it's safe. I take out my car key and then curse in a most unquakerly manner – I've forgotten about the lock. I should have done that first and warmed the key for now, of course, the lock is frozen solid. I'll have to go back indoors, fill up a jug of hot water or find a lighter to warm the key – it'll take another five minutes and that means I'll be late. And this is the week when I've promised to take the children's group; maybe they won't be able to tear themselves away from sledging, snowballing and-snowman building - but a promise is a promise.

I gaze at the iced-up lock. It seems ridiculous and a bit of a long shot but if there really is some force out there that wants us to be some use, then maybe it could melt the lock for me. I don't give it a serious meditative oooohhhm, but a flick-of-the-wrist, ok then, *how-about-it*? mental text and the key slides into the lock. And turns. And then I'm cocooned inside my car with the heater blasting out, skidding and sliding along my side street into the main road.

I check the time. I'm late. And what always works against me are the thirteen sets of traffic lights between my home and the meeting house. If I have to keep stopping, I'll be seriously late and any parents with young children might be giving up.

I have a backwash from the business with the lock – a small sense of elation. It's a beautiful sunny day, even though it's freezing. There's something very special about being the first person out in virgin snow, like walking on a pristine beach just after the tide's gone out. So, knowing how I still have this bit of a mission to perform, a thought flashes into my head: what if the traffic lights were all green..? What if I could sail straight through? Again, it's no great meditative ooohhhhm, but then the first lights are at green and then the next and then the next...and I giggle a bit at the absurdity that I might somehow lead such a charmed life that this kind of thing could seriously happen. (*I might just mention here for anyone in the US or elsewhere accustomed to staggered lights that in the UK, they're not normally linked together; in other words, with each set of lights there's a 50/50 chance of them being red or green*)

So, I pass thirteen sets of traffic lights and all of them are green. Then I park up by the meeting house and see a woman and child just leaving. People I don't know. But I call out and check. The woman seems quite upset. "They said there would be a children's group," she explains. "It's the first time that we've been. I know you can't expect people to turn out in this weather, but I've no one to leave her with at home so we walked in anyway."

I explain to her that I am the children's group.

"Thank God," she says as I take over and lead the shy little girl downstairs and have a chat and find stuff for her to do and all is well. And after the Meeting is over, I pick up elderly Friends who've tottered into town on foot and are grateful for a lift on the freshly-gritted roads.

And over the next few weeks, I ponder and ponder on this and each time tell myself that, of course such things are impossible: we cannot control the way things turn out with just a brief, click-of-the-fingers kind of thought.

But I can't let go of this problem. I whittle at it. Because if such things are possible, it turns our whole notion of how the world behaves on its head. Of course, coincidences happen. If you toss a coin thirteen times and it lands on tails every time, that would be quite amazing and finding all the traffic lights at green would be a similar probability. But for such an event to happen on the only day when I think, *What if...?* And within the same couple of minutes that I'm thinking, *And what if the ice melted on the lock...?*

If it *were* actually possible for me to change the traffic lights, then they would not only change for me but for everyone else as well. If anyone were unfortunate enough to be driving across my path then the lights would all be at red. Not only that, but they may have changed quite suddenly. Somebody might have been heading towards one of my junctions on red, slowed down, saw them change to green, put his foot down and accelerated and then... woops, they suddenly change back to red and as he tries to brake, he skids on the ice... and all so I can get to Quaker Meeting on time. How ridiculous!

My mind goes back to the episode when my mum was terminally ill and I sent out the mental SOS I'm convinced brought

Father William to my mother's bedside. He'd been standing in Broomhill at the time, waiting for the 52 bus. What if the bus had been coming round the corner before his summons arrived? Would it have dematerialized? Would other people at the bus stop have all been stepping forward, counting out their change and then find that the 52 had suddenly disappeared into thin air?

I don't think so.

And yet, in spite of all these misgivings, I feel convinced that this sort of thing really does keep happening. The possibility seems a bit scary. If it really is a special talent, I ought to treat it with respect. I shouldn't really use it to try and win the lottery or get my ex-boyfriend back or even keep practising, the way we do when we've discovered a new technique like whistling or blowing smoke rings.

The issue comes back to baffle me during the next few weeks. I am an open-minded person. The fact that I don't have any real faith in one explanation or another gives me the chance to brainstorm: *how could all this be possible?*

Well, one explanation would be that the world as we know it does not exist objectively but is a figment of our imagination or of our conscious thought. Maybe we can make anything happen if we think about it in a certain way. So, maybe everything around me: my home, my pet rabbit, my family and my fish tank... my friends, my favorite music and the English countryside... all are just dreams... a figment of my wishful thinking.

But then, if everything were down to me, there are certain things I would never have conjured into existence at all. These include:

- Concentration camps
- Cluster bombs
- Instruments of torture
- Famine and disease
- People sitting next to you on trains with tinny sounds

> emanating from their headphones
- Babies that cry on planes
- Premium-rate automatic call-systems with labyrinthine choices that take you back to the option you tried twenty minutes earlier...

I don't have to reflect for long to convince myself that actually, no, I haven't invented the world and all that's in it. If I had, everyone would be nice and lovey-dovey and there would be special soundproof capsules on planes for babies that keep crying.

There is another explanation. An even-more-ridiculous longshot and it goes like this:

What if...?

What if ours is not the only universe? What if other dimensions exist alongside ours but we can't see them? What if there's another universe just the same as ours with exactly the same characters and scenery and history except that on one particular morning when it's been snowing through the night, all the traffic lights into Sheffield city centre are on green? What if such a world exists and what if it's possible to step inside it... not by travelling there on Starship Enterprise but just by an act of consciousness... a mental click of the fingers?

Or what if such a world does not in fact exist but comes into being when we will it into existence?

And for this to happen, there wouldn't be only one such world waiting for us to step inside, but other worlds, created to accommodate other choices we might make. Or that anyone else in the world might make. Or anyone who's ever existed. Or might exist at sometime in the future. This means that there would not have to be just one other dimension, but millions of them. Billions. Trillions. As many alternative universes as there are grains of sand on a beach. And that is what our world would be like – a small grain of sand among trillions.

But if this were a serious possibility, why had nobody else come up with such an idea before?

In the sci-fi spoof The Hitchhikers Guide to the Galaxy[1], Douglas Adams created the Total Perspective Vortex, "the most horrible torture device to which a sentient being can be subjected," showing its victim "the entire, unimaginable infinity of the universe with a very tiny marker that says *You are Here* which points to a microscopic dot on a microscopic dot." This encounter is more than its victims can bear as their brains explode with the realization of their infinitesimal significance. The vortex is said to demonstrate that, "in an infinite universe, the one thing a sentient intelligence cannot afford to have is a sense of proportion."

Might it be possible that this theory makes perfect sense but whenever anyone comes up with the s idea, they reject it outright because the implications are so scary? Knowing that our planet is one of billions orbiting various stars and knowing that our star is one of a hundred billion in the Milky Way and that the Milky Way is one of a hundred billion other such galaxies is mind-boggling enough. But if it turns out that just about everything we do has a billion alternatives as well...?

I discussed the notion with a friend of mine, a scientist, who considered himself a free-thinking, open-minded person, amenable to new ideas. He scoffed. "Humph. Don't be ridiculous," he said. "That's stupid."

Feeling somewhat foolish, I kept quiet about my new theory for some time – until I came across Mysticism and the New Physics[2], in which the American author, Michael Talbot, to my intense relief, describes experience similar to mine. He's also seen or dreamed about events before they've happened and witnessed psychokinetic phenomena, and yet he's a scientist. I was even more relieved to find that after long periods of study and analysis, the explanations he came up with sounded amazingly familiar:

> ...in order to preserve the concept of free will and yet still acknowledge that at least some aspects of the future have already coalesced and can be accessed from the present, I concluded that more than one reality must exist. It occurred to me that, in a sense, many parallel universes must exist and the human mind itself must play some role in determining which of these probabilistic futures manifests as real...[2]

Having reached these conclusions, Talbot then discovered an article in Physics Today by the physicist, Bryce S. DeWitt explaining that:

> quantum physicists had discovered not only evidence that the existence of reality is dependent on the human mind, but also evidence suggesting that subatomic events split the universe into an incomprehensible number of parallel universes. [2]

Multiple Universe Theory, first put forward by the US scientists, Hugh Everett and John A. Wheeler in 1957, suggested that the universe (or multiverse in this case) is actually composed of many - possibly even infinitely many - worlds all existing in parallel. This multiverse is constantly splitting in two. When I will all the traffic lights to be green – that shifts me into a universe of green traffic lights but, no, they don't turn green for everyone. Those poor souls left behind are still tapping their fingers on the steering wheel wondering when the lights will change as normal.

Mark Oliver Everett, vocalist and creative force behind the cult rock band, Eels, is the son of Hugh Everett. A BBC documentary[3] filmed and directed by Louise Lockwood traces the relationship between Mark and his father whilst explaining something of Hugh's multiple-universe theory.

Born in 1930, the only child of a strict military family at an age when other teenagers idolized baseball heroes, recording artists or film stars, Hugh was sending fan mail to his great hero, Albert Einstein. From the start, he seemed an eccentric figure. Mark remembers him wearing a suit and tie at the family dinner table and finding little time to converse with his two children. In fact, researching the television documentary is the way in which Mark becomes acquainted with his father who – although the two inhabited the same house for 20 years - he feels he never really got to know.

A student at Princeton University, Hugh switched from studying maths to quantum mechanics and soon became acquainted with the work of the Nobel prizewinning physicist, Niels Bohr who visited Princeton in 1954. Bohr was one of the Copenhagen scientists whose theories addressed the apparent anomalies of the quantum world. If quantum particles have the ability to exist in two places at once, and if everything in the world is made of quantum particles, why can't everything be in two places at once? Why can't you, for instance, be lounging on the sofa, reading this book and running round the jogging track both at the same time? If quantum particles can be both solid matter and waves, and if we are made of quantum particles, why can't we also dissolve into waves when we feel like it?

Bohr's answer to this was relatively straightforward. Matter, he argued, was divided into:

1   subatomic particles
2   all the bigger stuff.

Subatomic particles do not obey the laws of classical physics. Electrons, for example, rather than orbiting like tiny planets, form an irregular smear. When we observe a quantum particle, it changes. Rather than continuing in some kind of now-you-see-me-now-you-don't, quantum state, once observed, it becomes a tiny bit of stuff. On the other hand, Bohr claimed, everything larger than the subatomic level is subject to a different set of rules – the rules of classical physics.

Bohr felt he had solved the dilemma, was awarded the Nobel Prize and assumed there was little more to be said about the matter. But young Hugh Everett refused to believe that particles changed the way they behaved simply because they were observed. His skepticism was reinforced by Schrödinger who postulated the famous theoretical experiment with the theoretical cat in order to show that no creature can keep its reality state on hold until it knows whether anyone's watching or not. Hugh Everett argued that everything in the universe – both large and small – obeys the same laws of quantum mechanics. However, some kind of split occurs whenever there's a choice or a decision to be made. Both outcomes happen but, because they happen in different dimensions, we are only aware of the outcome that happens in our own world. We may grieve for the dead cat, but we cannot see the world in which the cat lives on, goes for a night out on the tiles, keeps the neighbors awake with its caterwauling and delivers a couple of mice on the doorstep for breakfast.

Everett, assisted by his PHD supervisor, Wheeler, worked night and day on the mathematics associated with numbers that reach to infinity before publishing his results, standing back and waiting for the impact. It was a theory that not only challenged the findings of the world's leading scientists, but challenged the basis of reality. The twenty-four-year-old genius waited for the storm.

There was a deafening silence.

No one, basically, took the slightest bit of notice.

Wheeler took Everett with him on a journey to Copenhagen to explain his theory to the great Niels Bohr.

Bohr was not impressed.

Everett twiddled his thumbs and practised his whistling while he waited for the walls of academia to crumble and when nothing happened at all, he left the university, took to heavy drinking and even heavier smoking. The nearest he came to a moment of glory was in 1977, twenty years after he had written his great, icono-clastic thesis, when he was invited to give a lecture in Austin, Texas. Even though the scientific world had greeted his ideas with one great Paddington stare, the concept of multiple-universe theory had, by now, spread throughout the zeitgeist. The notion of parallel worlds had become the stock-in-trade of science fiction writers and Hollywood producers; every Joe and Larry knew about wormholes and sliders, portals, teleportation devices and Heisenberg filters. Ordinary people were taking to their hearts what the world of science had failed to grasp. It was a great shame that, before he could take his share of fame and glory, Everett died of a heart attack aged only 51. It may have been a blessing that he died before his daughter's suicide. She described herself as *going off to meet my father in a parallel universe.*

So, if the notion of a multiple universe inspired so many sci-fi writers, why did it produce one of the biggest yawns the world of science has ever known?

When we watch a movie about a parallel universe, we simply accept the possibility of another world - exactly like ours except for some tiny detail - existing in some other dimension. We don't think about the maths involved because the numbers are greater than any of us would ever think were possible.

When I first came up with my own multiple-universe theory, I wondered whether there might be as many other worlds as there are grains of sand on a beach. I wouldn't want to count them but had I the time and inclination, I'd find these grains all had different colors, shapes, size and weight – except that, every now and then, maybe one in a thousand – I'd find two that looked pretty much the same. If I placed the identical ones in a box and went on checking for grains that matched them on every beach around the country, I may find quite a few truckloads. Possibly even a mountain. And again, if I had the resources and nothing better to do than check every grain of sand on every beach on every coastline of every continent and island, the mountain would start to grow. It might become a country in its own right.

As telescopes become more and more powerful, our universe – or what we know of it – appears larger. The more we explore, the more we find. Latest estimates suggest that our spiral galaxy of the Milky Way contains about a hundred billion stars and that there are a hundred billion such galaxies in our known universe – a number greater than most of us can imagine. And just as the calculation of our grains of sand would be a practical impossibility as we'd die long before we'd completed the first beach and couldn't possibly take account of grains being formed and washed away – so the task of counting the number of stars and possible planets in the universe can never be any more than an approximate calculation.

If the number of stars is large enough, then somewhere – the laws of chance dictate – there will be planets like our own. And if there are enough planets like our own, there will be people just like us. And if there are people just like us, there will be so many that you and I will exist somewhere inside another time and space. Not only that, but somewhere inside that time and space will be multiple versions of us both. We'll exist in the realm we can view through telescopes and also in the realms we can't see – inside the 94% of the universe that so far appears to be missing. If the numbers are large enough, then anything that is possible will already have occurred. And anything which is possible will occur some time in the future. The concept is expressed by the Argentinian writer, Jorge Luis Borges in his *Library of Babel*. This library *"composed of an indefinite perhaps infinite number of hexagonal galleries"* is Borges' depiction of the universe. It's a *"sphere whose exact centre is any hexagon and whose circumference is unattainable."* Its infinite rooms contain every book which already has been or can be written. These include:

> ...the detailed history of the future, the autobiographies of the archangels, the faithful catalog of the Library, thousands and thousands of false catalogs, the proof of the falsity of those false catalogs, a proof of the falsity of the true catalog, the Gnostic gospel of Basilides, the commentary upon that gospel, the commentary on the commentary on that gospel, the true story of your death, the translation of every book into every language, the interpolations of every book into all books, the treatise Bede could have written (but did not) on the mythology of the Saxon people, the lost books of Tacitus.[4]

Although there are those who tried to organize and simplify the Library by destroying worthless, nonsensical books, Borges points out that their destruction has made no measurable significance. In what would seem to be a perfect representation of Multiple Universe Theory, he writes:

> although each book is unique and irreplaceable, since the Library is total, there are always several hundred thousand imperfect facsimiles – books that differ by no more than a single letter or a coma.

The books to which Borges refer all contain permutations of the same twenty three characters, together with spaces and full stops. There is nothing else. And yet the library extends to infinity. He explains in his concluding paragraph:

> I hereby state that it is not illogical to think that the world is infinite. Those who believe it to have limits hypothesize that in some remote place or places the corridors and staircases and hexagons may, inconceivably, end – which is absurd. And

yet those who picture the world as unlimited forget that the number of possible books is **not**. I will be bold enough to suggest this solution to the ancient problem: **The Library is unlimited but periodic.** If an eternal traveler should journey in any direction, he would find after untold centuries that the same volumes are repeated in the same disorder – which, repeated, becomes order: the Order. My solitude is cheered by that elegant hope.[4]

The Library of Babel provides us with a matrix in which the variations of twenty six characters extend towards infinity. It would be impossible to calculate the variations occurring in our own lives – even in a single day – even in a few minutes - the variations, for instance, of whatever you might do whilst reading this page: reading only one paragraph;, reading two; being distracted after only a few words; deciding the whole idea of The Effect is a complete load of twaddle and throwing it in the bin; deciding this book contains some of the most original ideas you've encountered and writing an appraisal on the internet; intending to write an appraisal but deciding you can't be bothered; eating a sandwich, drinking a glass of beer... the permutations are endless. And each of those permutations results in tiny blips of difference... some of which may not affect your life – or mine - in any significant way and some of which may change the course of events for either or both of us for ever: your sandwich may contain a fishbone on which you choke; your appraisal might result in this book selling more than I ever hoped and being encouraged to write the other books brewing in my brain; I might write to thank you and we might arrange to meet and then to marry; your glass of beer could be the start of a long decline into alcoholism; your contemplation of the immensity of the Library of Babel may be akin to tumbling inside Douglas Adams' Total Perspective Vortex in which the concept of your infinitesimal significance causes your brain to explode...

I began this book with a turning point: a place where my own path forked. My life was running on nice straight tracks – well, a bit wobbly, but straight ones make for a better metaphor - until I encountered twenty seven angels, as welcome as a platoon of parachutists on a runway. My immediate reaction was to taxi onward, sweeping them out of the way in a fanciful flurry of feathers. But instead I crept downstairs and spoke to Something Out There that I had no belief in and asked whatever-it-was for help. That small action became for me a portal into the unknown. Like Alice finding the key into the secret garden, I had no idea what other weird, nonsensical stuff I would discover. The next day I found myself at the Quaker Meeting House which has been my spiritual home ever since. During one of my early Quaker meetings were sown the seeds for writing a modernized version of King Lear. This novel opened the door to an international publisher and a place with a literary agent. I thus became a professional writer. If none of this had happened, I would be somewhere else instead of sitting here writing and the page in front of you would be an empty sheet of paper.

Everyone else who's ever lived can name similar turning points.

So, Everett and the Library of Babel provide us with models of a universe which can split off into infinity. What this projection fails to engage with however, is how or why we might choose one path rather than another...

Chapter 13

Groundhog Days

"How curiously it twists! It's more like a corkscrew than a path"
Alice through the Looking Glass, ch. 11

At the start of the 1985 movie, Groundhog Day,[1] Phil Conners (played by Bill Murray) is a miserable, arrogant, self-absorbed character, pouring scorn on the inhabitants of Punxsutawney, the small rural town to which he's sent as TV anchorman to cover this quaint annual tradition.

And then he finds himself stuck there, reliving the same day over and over, standing in front of the unfeasibly-named Gobblers Knob *(which I hope might have a drastically different meaning in the US)* using his gifts of prior knowledge to indulge his lust and greed. Knowing when the security guards will turn to help a pedestrian, he takes the chance to rob their holdall. He seduces women and gets as drunk as he wants with no prospect of a hangover but none of this brings him one step closer to happiness.

Phil Conners becomes suicidal: he jumps from the church tower, crashes his car into a quarry and tries to electrocute himself but still wakes in the same bed in the same room with the same music playing every morning. Until he discovers love *(well, it is a romantic comedy)* and this transforms him. He gives a wad of bills to the old man spare-changing on the street. He buys coffee and pastries for the TV crew. He carves an ice sculpture of an angel. He uses his TV spot to give an inspirational talk about the good people of Punxsutawney. He becomes overwhelmingly loved and admired.

And Rita, the TV producer, falls in love with him. They spend their first night together and the next morning, Phil wakes to find that Punxsutawney is covered with snow. It's no longer Groundhog Day. Tomorrow has arrived. He has reached Nirvana.

For many eastern religions, this state of Nirvana represents our escape from the wheel of life: - we are born over and over again until our mindfulness, our karma and our meditation lead us to a state of bliss.

This Groundhog Day existence is a depiction of Dunne's concept of serial time, Ouspensky's Roundabout and the insight of Priestley's Dr Görtler. It goes against the grain of our traditional western concept of time as being a straight line extending into an unknown future, calling into play instead Einstein's insistence that time is curved, coming round and back again to meet us. However, it dispenses with the destiny dilemma. We can still decide where the tracks will run; we can still plan our route; we can still be the Fat Controllers with our hands on the points and the signals. We can still be in charge because at every point in our life we make decisions and each time we make a decision, a new path opens up before us.

Dunne, Ouspensky and Priestley's concept of serial time has several limitations, the obvious one being that our choices cannot move sideways; all of us are stuck inside our sets of Russian dolls or Chinese boxes with decisions only affecting what happens when we live our lives again. With multiple universe theory our possibilities are endless. We have scope and power; we have potential. In another story by Borges, *Garden of Forking Paths*,[2] the main character, Ts'ui Pen, sequesters himself inside the Pavilion of Limpid Solitude (*this wonderful appellation should really form the title of the next Eels album or at least a new name for my garden shed*) to write a novel which takes the form of a labyrinth, dedicating it thus: *I leave to several futures (not all) my garden of the forking paths.* His novel is described by Albert, the curator of the manuscript:

> In all fictions, each time a man meets diverse alternatives, he chooses one and eliminates the others; in the work of the

virtually impossible-to-disentangle Ts'ui Pen, the character chooses – simultaneously – all of them. He creates, thereby, "several futures", several times, which themselves proliferate and fork...Fang, let us say, has a secret; a stranger knocks at his door; Fang decides to kill him. Naturally, there are various possible outcomes – Fang can kill the intruder, the intruder can kill Fang, they can both live, they can both be killed, and so on. In Ts'ui Pen's novel, **all** the outcomes in fact occur; each is the starting point for further bifurcations. Once in a while the paths of the labyrinth converge: for example, you come to this house, but in one of the possible pasts, you are my enemy, in another my friend...[3]

The notion that our world is actually a labyrinth has become the stock-in-trade of science fiction writers. One such is Philip K. Dick who describes it thus in VALIS:

"This is an irreal world. You realize that, I'm sure. VALIS made you realize that. We are in a living maze and not in a world at all."

There was silence as we considered this.

"And what happens when we get outside the maze?" Kevin asked.

"We're freed from space and time," Mini said. "Space and time are the binding, controlling conditions of the maze – its power."[4]

So, if we wrap the concept of Groundhog Days and multiple universe theory together and call it Groundmut Theory, what we need to do next is look for any other evidence to suggest that Groundmuts, as they say, have legs. Are these Groundmuts fluffy, airy-fairy, tree-hugging creatures? Or do they have their feet placed firmly on the ground?

Our first piece of evidence would seem to be that, from the

very dawn of time, people assumed that death was not the end. In fact, if we had to name one factor which separated early man from other mammals, we might suggest the burial of the dead. The earliest archaeological sites discovered right across the world are cemeteries and within them have been found a miscellany of objects doubtless intended to accompany the spirit to some other realm of existence: jewelry, tools, weapons, goat horns and musical instruments have all been discovered inside the graves of our earliest ancestors.[5] People from these early times seemed to take it for granted that, after death, they would be moving on elsewhere. We don't know why. When they saw a saber-toothed tiger devouring its prey, they had no reason to assume that this creature was going anywhere but inside the tiger's inside. When they hunted and roasted animals themselves, there was no reason to assume that their dinner would have another life in the hereafter. Why should human beings be any different

One possibility is that our ancestors were more in touch with DreamTime than we are today. Living in a world of less distraction and sharing sacred rites, they may have spent more of their lives inside this realm – rather than seeing, as we do, only an occasional glimpse,

The Ancient Greeks took it for granted they had lived their lives before and would do so again. Priestley describes their concept as: a *vast roundabout, with the eternal gods and their unchanging stars where the engine and the music are, in the center, unmoving.*[6]– a theory expounded by the philosopher and mathematician, Pythagoras in the 6th century, BCE.

And the writer of the book of Ecclesiastes in the Old Testament tells us:

The thing that hath been, it is that which shall be;
and that which is done is that which shall be done;
and there is no new thing under the sun...[7]

In pre-Christian times, the main structure for people's belief system was the cyclical pattern of life; sacred sites and rituals were based upon the equinox, the solstice and phases of the moon. The recurrence of the tides and planets, of night and day, of the moon and of the seasons were the foundations of pre-Christian life. It would make sense, therefore, for such people to imagine their lives also were cyclical: like the sun, the moon, the tides and the seasons, they would also disappear for a while and then return. And just as each springtide is a little bit higher or lower than the last, and just as every night is a tiny bit longer or shorter and just as every summer is never quite the same, so it would make sense to assume their lives would contain small discrepancies each time they returned.

Evidence from the past also suggests that many people expected death to be followed by some kind of life-review at which their conduct would be judged. Some of the earliest accounts of life-reviews are from Ancient Egypt when – from around 2,500BC onwards - papyrus scrolls containing spells or instructions for the afterlife were buried with the dead. People paid up to half a year's wages for an elaborate scroll which would remind them of the correct words to be recited when their heart was weighed:

> Hail to you Great God, Lord of Justice... I have not done falsehood...I have not deprived the orphan of his property, I have not done what the gods detest... I have not caused pain, I have not caused hunger, I have made no one weep, I have not killed, I have not made anyone suffer...I am pure, pure, pure![8]

Those who passed the life-review were rewarded with an afterlife; those who failed were offered to a ravenous creature - part-lion, part-crocodile and part hippopotamus. You may be relieved to hear that no one having a modern near-death experience mentioned glimpsing such a creature lurking behind the defibrillator.

This Groundmut concept offers the only explanation I've encountered for the near-death experience of a life-review. Here's an account reported by Thomas de Quincy in his *Confessions of an English Opium Eater*[9] when he tells of a relative (his own mother, he explained many years later) who, as a child, fell into a river and almost drowned. He says:

> She saw in a moment her whole life, in its minutest incidents, arrayed before her simultaneously as in a mirror giving her the ability to simultaneously comprehend the whole as every part.[9]

We take it for granted that all our actions in a time of stress and danger are geared towards survival: our heart races to pump more blood around the body; our adrenalin levels rise, our senses are on full alert... and then what? *Oh, let's think about our first day at school and that nice teacher... remember when we had tonsillitis and we had to stay in bed... and oooh, my first kiss...*

Survival technique?

Hardly.

Why not spend our last few seconds calling out for help? Or screaming? Or desperately trying to remember how to swim?

This is the personal account of Eugen Guido Lammer a professional mountain guide who suffered a fall after an avalanche in 1887:

> During this deadly fall my senses remained alert. And I can assure you, my friends, that it is a fine way to die! One does not suffer! A pinprick hurts more than a fall like this. And there is no thought of dying either – or only to start with. From the moment I realized that anything I could do to save myself would be useless, it was for me a great liberation. This

person who was being swept across the path of the avalanche, thrown over the body of his companion, hurled into space by the tug of a rope – this was a stranger, more like a block of wood; my real self floated over the scene with the relaxed curiosity of a spectator at the circus. A wave of images and thoughts invaded my brain; memories of childhood, my birthplace, my mother. I could fill hundreds of pages with them! Yet during all this time I was coldly calculating the remaining distance before I would be thrown dead at the bottom... all this without agitation, without sorrow, I was totally freed from the chains of Self. Years, centuries passed during that fall.[10]

In descriptions of near-death experience, one patient after another has seen their life played back as though watching a full-length film; over and over again, it becomes clear that this is not just a way of passing time before the funeral director calls round, but an assessment of their life's work here on earth. As quoted in a letter to the Swiss Lutherian minister and psychoanalyst, Oscar Pfister,

It was like I got to see some good things I had done and some mistakes I had made, you know, and try to understand them. It was like: "Okay, here's why you had the accident. Here's why this happened. Because so and so and so"... it all had meaning.[11]

A factor which goes against orthodox religious belief is that in many of these reported cases, the dying person conducts their own review. They're shown the playback, as it were, but make their own assessment. This is another account from the US writer and researcher, Phyllis Atwater:

I had no idea a past-life review could be like this. I never before realized that we were responsible and accountable for every single thing we did. That was overwhelming!

It was me judging me, not some heavenly St Peter. And my judgement was critical and stern. I was not satisfied with many, many things Phyllis had done, said or thought. There was a feeling of sadness and failure, yet a growing feeling of joy when the realization came that Phyllis had always done Something. She did many things unworthy and negative, but she did something. She tried. Much of what she did was constructive and positive. She learned and grew in her learning. This was satisfying. Phyllis was okay.[12]

In orthodox religion, the life-review is seen as divine judgement. We're judged on our many shortcomings and then ascend to heaven or are cast into hell or out to the hungry hippopotamus/lion/crocodile. In Groundmut theory, we come back again for another bite of the cherry but with the chance to make a better job of it the next time round. J.B. Priestley describes his enormous sense of relief at the possibility that he might one day be able to undo his mistakes in what he calls time-One, his present life.

I am by profession and temperament a dramatist, and I hate ill-contrived and under-rehearsed scenes. But my time-One life can show me – and indeed **will** show me when it turns into my time-Two world – far too many of such scenes. So I welcome the chance not of simply re-living them, though that may have to be done, but of **beginning to put them right...** we may have the choice between building a self-glorifying palace out of our time-One material, until we wall ourselves into a hell of loneliness and desolation. And trying to create in trust and love... a new and more rewarding life. We can begin to do this here and now.[13]

This thought is one that most of us find heartening. We can *Take it again...* as though this life is simply a rehearsal; we can do a *Take Two*...and even a *Take three*...we can try over and over again until we get it right.

We look at our life-review, think through our worst mistakes and bookmark all the stuff we'd like to change. The rest of our past life is then filed away inside the archives. The Ancient Greeks believed that, after death, we cross the Lethe (*from which we get our word, lethargy*) the River of Forgetting, a journey that erases all memory of our past.

Which is just as well because whilst I think I'm writing this book for the very first time it's quite an exciting project but if I could actually remember writing it five or six thousand times already, I'd be sorely tempted to throw the laptop into the fish tank and run screaming down the street...

The other evidence for Groundmut theory lies in our precognitive dreams. As Priestley's Dr Görtler explains:

What has happened before – many times, perhaps – will probably happen again. That is why some people can prophesy what is to happen. They do not see the future, as they think, but the past, what has happened before...[14]

So when we think we're looking into the future, we're actually viewing events which have already taken place; and when we have visions or dreams that warn us of potential danger, we see what happened the last time round; this then gives us chance to take evasive action. In the dream described in Chapter Five from one of Priestley's correspondents, a man was forewarned of an accident with a boy who ran in front of his car. Because of the dream, as Priestley says, "the man was able to *change the future* by the fact that it had already been revealed."

Here is another account of someone's ability to change a future revealed in a dream. This was reported by Dr Louisa E. Rhine – another collector of precognitive dreams - in the

American Journal of Parapsychology:

Many years ago when my son, who is now a man with a baby a year old, was a boy I had a dream early one morning. I thought the children and I had gone camping with some friends. We were camped in such a pretty little glade on the shores of the sound between two hills. It was wooded, and our tents were under the trees. I looked around and thought what a lovely spot it was.

I thought I had some washing to do for the baby, so I went to the creek where it broadened out a little. There was a nice clean gravel spot, so I put the baby and the clothes down. I noticed I had forgotten the soap so I started back to the tent. The baby stood near the creek throwing handfuls of pebbles into the water. I got my soap and came back, and my baby was lying face down in the water. I pulled him out but he was dead. I awakened then, sobbing and crying. What a wave of joy went over me when I realized that I was safe in bed and that he was alive. I thought about it and worried for a few days, but nothing happened and I forgot about it.

During that summer some friends asked the children and me to go camping with them. We cruised along the sound until we found a good place for a camp near fresh water. The lovely little glade between the hills had a small creek and big trees to pitch our tents under. While sitting on the beach with one of the other women, watching the children play, I happened to think I had some washing to do, so I took the baby and went to the tent for the clothes. When I got back to the creek I put down the baby and the clothes, and then I noticed that I had forgotten the soap. I started back for it, and as I did so, the baby picked up a handful of pebbles and threw them in the water. Instantly my dream flashed into my mind. It was like a moving picture. He stood just as he had in my dream—white dress, yellow curls, shining sun. For a moment

I almost collapsed. Then I caught him up and went back to the beach and my friends. When I composed myself, I told them about it. They just laughed and I said I imagined it. That is such a simple answer when one cannot give a good explanation.[15]

So, when I'm driving along and see an image of a car heading towards me on the wrong side of the road, I may be seeing something that happened in some previous existence and this vision of a car about to crash offers me the chance to avoid it happening again. In the same way, the dream of the myxomatosis rabbit didn't depict the future, but may have brought into my consciousness a happening from the past. By dreaming about an event in some previous existence, I could prevent its reoccurrence. And this of course, explains why, when we have déjà vu or precognitive dreams, the details are just that little bit askew: the two events don't completely tally because we're not seeing into the future; we're seeing what happened before.

Another example of a prescient warning was that of Julia, the wife of Ulysses S. Grant. She and her husband were looking forward to an extremely special occasion: General Grant had just accepted the surrender of the Confederate General Robert E. Lee and a reception was being held in his honor. But Mrs Grant felt a great sense of foreboding about the whole event and begged her husband to leave the capital. She kept contacting him throughout the day, relaying her anxiety and suggesting they return to their home in New Jersey. It seemed ridiculous: not only was there to be a reception in the General's honor but they were due to attend the theatre with the president and his wife and, not only that, but be seated beside them in the same box.

After a day of pleading, General Ulysses S Grant finally conceded to his wife's request. The family left Washington and by the time they reached Philadelphia, received news about the president's assassination. Not only were they supposed to have been sitting next to Abraham Lincoln at the theatre, but their names were later found on the assassin - John Wilkes Booth's - list of intended victims.[16]

For anyone who's never had such an experience, Mrs Grant's sense of foreboding must sound extremely odd. How could anyone consider turning down such an important invitation - the event of a lifetime? And yet over and over again, people report that they *just know* when a dream or nagging notion is presaging a real event; the dreams have a totally different texture; they're written in **BOLD**; the incidents are highlighted. Like my dream about the lost Quaker Meeting, I spent the next couple of weeks, simply waiting for it to come true.

So, if people feel so convinced that their dreams of accidents and tragedies are warning them to avoid a real event, how many act on these dreams? Do they normally carry on regardless or wake up in a cold sweat, pick up the phone and straightaway cancel their flight? Or take a different train? And if this is the case, we'd find a disproportionate number of cancellations on planes and trains that crash.

And actually, yes, this does appear to be the case. On a relatively small study of 28 train crashes it was found that vacancy rates were significantly higher on the days of a crash compared with 7, 14 and 28 days before.[17]

The 9/11 planes that crashed into the World Trade Centre's North and South Towers were 74 and 81 per cent empty. And in the Boeing 757 that crashed into the Pentagon, only 64 of 289 seats were taken. In fact, the occupancy rate of all four doomed planes was only 31%, considerably less than was normal.

Another argument in favor of Groundmut theory is that Nature doesn't use straight lines. To think of our lifespan and of time as the only natural straight lines in the whole universe seems odd. Nature draws in circles; it curves but, most importantly, it spirals; even the human genome forms a beautiful spiral pattern: the double helix. Our galaxy, the Milky Way, like so many galaxies, takes the form of a spiral. And interestingly enough, mysterious spiral patterns have been discovered on the world's oldest burial sites. One of the world's oldest buildings so far unearthed, the underground temple of Hypogeum in Malta[18] has a whole ceiling painted with spirals and one huge stone slab after another carved with intriguing spiral designs. If you can't book a trip to the Hypogeum (where visitor numbers are limited), you can view those brought to the archaeological museum in Valetta.[19] Or you could visit the Newgrange site in County Meath in Ireland. Here again are stones dating from around 3,200 BCE carved with a remarkably similar design.

So, were these just doodles? Or fancy bits to decorate the temples? Or could it be that ancient people had wisdom that we nowadays have lost? Might they have understood that life goes round and round and comes back a little bit differently every time? Could these spirals be the logo for Groundmut theory, for the cycle of birth and rebirth?

My last, but probably most important reason for warming to my Groundmut theory is because it makes sense of our normal everyday dreams. I've spoken to countless people about this (*not a scientific experiment, I know, but the best that I can offer*) and everyone is in agreement: all of us dream about places where we've never been.

In real life, when someone starts to tell a joke: *A man walks into the doctors...* I see a typical TV sketch of a doctor's surgery – no doubt because I know both of these to be the introduction to a funny story. When someone says the word *forest*, I think of the pine plantation on the edge of the moors where I go walking. At the word *table*, I see the table in the kitchen of the house I lived in as a child. Every word and concept in the English language has a picture and/or an experience of some kind filed away beside it. Even my latest word, *zugunruhe*, carries a picture of a caged nightingale – the image taken from Tim Birkhead's

Wisdom of Birds.

So, why is it that, when I have a bus to catch in my dreams, it's always a fictional bus, never one that I've actually taken? And why does it never go anywhere that I've actually been in real life? There's a particular house I often dream of with a high, semi-circular veranda, to the right of which is a large grassy garden and yet I've never encountered such a house. There are walks I only take in dreams, but each time, the landscape is familiar – *here I go again*, I think. *I'll be coming up to the lane soon and then across it there's the gate and after that I just need to walk up the path...*

But if every concept and idea has a mental picture filed in our brains to go with it, why would our unconscious minds bother making up a completely new image for every concept and idea encountered in a dream? If we have to miss a bus, why not miss our local bus on the street around the corner? Why make up a fictional bus on a fictional street? Most of us have been on hundreds of walks in hundreds of different locations. What is the point in making up a completely imaginary landscape each time we walk in our dreams? In my role as a writer of books for young people, I've been invited into at least a hundred schools. I've taught in numerous schools. I've been to school as a child. I've seen films and TV programs about schools. So why should every dream about a school involve building a whole new one from scratch? Every corridor, desk, each and every staff room and school office – all of them architect-designed just so I can walk into yet another class and realize that I've got to hoof it again because I haven't planned the work. In a recent dream, I walked along a narrow, cobbled street with small, squat, round adobe cottages where everyone had a seat outside their door. When I walked inside someone's house, it was cool and shady with tiny windows and a clay floor. I have never known such a house or street; I can't recollect seeing one in a film or in a picture. My friend, Pedro, said it sounded like a Mexican house, but I've never been to Mexico. Why should our dream state not simply use our own homes or any of the many people's homes that we already know?

Just as it makes no sense that, when we're in mortal danger, we should start to reminisce about our early childhood, so it makes no sense that when we're at rest and sleeping, our brains should beaver away at the construction of one new building and landscape after another.

The only response I can suggest is that it doesn't. The only explanation I can offer is that our back catalogue of images is far greater than we realize. We do in fact know all these places, but from another life. If we've lived other lives before, then their memory's not obliterated but nor is it readily available; the River Lethe might cause us to forget, but the details still exist in an archive file like a hidden, compressed file on a computer. We may be unable to access these files through the normal route on our desktop but evidence of their existence occasionally comes to light, for example when their names flash by as we operate a search.

When Ouspensky, Dunne and Priestley talked about serial time, they constructed an abstract theory. Dunne filled numerous notebooks with mathematical equations all of which seemed to add up (*I see "seemed to" because I personally can't make head or tail of them although his readers appeared to be impressed*) but to me, this theory contained one monumental flaw: in order to live our lives again in any practical sense, we would have to be reincarnated. And if we're reincarnated then we have to live again at sometime in the future. There's no point in having a life review to highlight our mistakes because next time round we'll be making a different set of mistakes in a different kind of existence: we'll be living a different life at a different time in history.

Ouspensky, Dunne and Priestley knew nothing about Everett's multiple universe theory. Nowadays we do. When we include that in the equation, serial time makes sense. By going into DreamTime - through any of the doorways we've described

- we can slide through the portal into one of the other dimensions which exist alongside our own.

This process is similar to a simple flick-page cartoon, where you draw a character over and over again but with a tiny detail altered every time. Your character's heel might be raised from the ground; in the next picture, her toe; and in the next, her foot is in the air. If you've plenty of patience and your arm's not too tired, you can draw so many pictures that, when you flick through them at speed, your character seems to be jogging.

With Groundmut theory, we can switch into a whole new world in which only one detail is changed. Let's say that you had one major regret in your life. Let's say, for the sake of argument, that you gave up a child - fathered a child then fell out with the mother or felt pressurized into a termination but then found afterwards it was your only chance of parenthood; let's say that this one event had a huge impact and became something you regretted. You could no doubt narrow the fork in the path to one small incident: a conversation, possibly a *No* instead of *Yes*. And now you'd like to go back and change that No to Yes.

We think of this concept as The Butterfly Effect, a term popularized by the American mathematician and meteorologist, Edward Lorenz[20] who suggested that a butterfly flapping its wings in a rainforest in Brazil might lead to the creation of a hurricane in Texas.

So, imagine you were trying to demonstrate to a class of students the effect of a butterfly's wings on the flow of air across the world: were you to film and show the students each small and gentle flap, your film would be a tribute to realism but your students would be bored to death or old and grey before you'd even half-started on your theory. You'd explain the theory instead with a version in which time was speeded up.

We're accustomed to this manipulation of time in film. The simple cartoon described earlier only works if you flick the pages fast enough, just as a movie shown through an old-fashioned projector only worked because the celluloid squares were rattling past the light beam so fast you couldn't see the joins. We're accustomed to TV cameras slowing down the action – to show a foul in a game or to confirm who actually won a race. And we need to apply a similar kind of time manipulation to Groundmut theory. We live out our whole life and then come back and change just one thing. Or two. We live again and change another. The process sounds unbearably dull and tedious, but if we see the process speeding up, like our cartoon, although we may only change a tiny part each time, bit by bit, we finally see ourselves jogging. Or leaping up and down with joy. Or finding our way to Nirvana.

We'll return to this concept in our final chapter, but first of all a few examples of real time manipulation. A near-death experience often involves a replay of someone's entire life, yet this can be contained within the few seconds between being hit by an avalanche and landing in the snow. Such stretching of time has also been witnessed by those involved in car crashes. Recent research has also found another mammal, the bat, makes frequent use of an ability to slow down time. The bat brain processes echo-location data, enabling it to avoid obstacles and home in on its prey. Research carried out by Saillant and Simmons in 1998 found what they refer to as "time-expansion". As Michael Lockwood explains in *The Labyrinth of Time:*

> In effect, bats have been found to possess the temporal analogue of a zoom lens, where greater magnification can be bought at the expense of a smaller visible expanse. As regards the echo-location data, it clearly benefits the bat, from time to time, to exchange a sensory window… with a wider time span but less detail and definition, for one with a narrower time span but more detail and definition. Since this is known to happen in bats, it would seem a plausible speculation that, under the right sort of pressure, something similar might

occur within the regions of our own brains that process the data provided by our senses.[21]

Another example provided by Lockwood, concerns the basketball player, Michael Jordon:

> When asked to explain his inspired maneuvering through a host of menacing defenders, he explained that "time slows down for him." Hameroff, Kaszniak and Scott (1998: 647) speculate that: "Perhaps consciousness comprises a sequence of distinct events, of which Jordon has more per move than his opponents." [22]

So, we'll return later to the concept of time-manipulation. What we need to look at now, to put Groundmut theory into action, is how to access the controls...

Chapter 14

The Control Centre: *to be a queen*

And now for the last brook, and to be a Queen!
How grand it sounds!"
Alice through the Looking Glass, ch. 8

In his multiple universe theory, Hugh Everett doesn't explain how we switch from one universe to another; he only suggests that such a process involves the power of human consciousness.

However, that doesn't rubbish his theory. Most good science starts with somebody saying, *What if... ? What if there were a...?* And most good science starts by trying to *disprove* something. No one so far has disproved multiple universe theory just as no one has disproved string theory or the notion of the universe as a hologram. When we come up with a theory like Groundmut that appears to explain all kinds of seemingly unrelated phenomena, then it's worth exploring until someone proves that it's impossible.

Everett's theory is a mathematical formulation without any interest in spiritual values or the wherewithal of human progress. Everett was a scientist, not a guru. Priestley however, together with writers in most of the world's great spiritual traditions, has a preoccupation with transcendence. With the notion that we are born to raise ourselves higher, to look up and see further. Such writers don't worry necessarily about how, mathematically, other dimensions exist, but concern themselves with reaching them and pointing out the way for the rest of us to follow.

Priestley attempts to describe the path through the voice of Dr

Görtler:

> DR GORTLER: Peace is not somewhere just waiting for you.
>
> ORMUND: Where is it then?
>
> DR GORTLER: You have to create it... ...there is more truth to the fundamental nature of things in the most foolish fairy tales than there is in any of your complaints about life.
>
> ORMUND: Rubbish! Why?
>
> DR GORTLER Because all events are shaped in the end by magic.
>
> ORMUND (scornfully): Yes, I thought we'd come to that. Magic!
>
> DR GORTLER: Yes. The creative magic of our feeling, imagination and will. These are the realities – our feeling, imagination, and will – and all our histories are their dreams.
>
> ORMUND: All very easy!
>
> DR GORTLER (with passion) It is not easy. Life is not easy. It provides no short cuts, no effortless escapes. Peace and ecstasy are not laid on like hot water.
>
> ORMUND (with savage irony): You needn't tell me that. I know it.
>
> DR GORTLER: Yes, but you do not know – you will not understand – that life is penetrated through and through by our feeling, imagination and will. In the end the whole universe must respond to every real effort we make. We each live a fairy tale created by ourselves.[1]

Living a fairy tale created by ourselves hardly sounds the stuff to convince hard-nosed scientists, but I do believe Priestley was right. Everett's theory provides us with the layout, the matrix, the scientific possibilities, but in order to make things happen, we have to imagine them first. We have to create the story of our future.

Dr Görtler says that feeling, imagination and will are *the realities*. When we use them, we write our own history. This is the way we stop our tiny wind-up trains trundling round their circuits because this is how we become autonomous and turn into Fat Controllers. Instead of flies brushed backwards and forwards across someone else's picture, we are the arm that holds the dustmop. What we do makes a difference.

And yet, we've been raised by western science to think of life's ultimate realities as the stuff we can see and touch and measure, like a table or chair or even a slice of cheesecake; we're led to believe that imagination, feelings and will represent the fuzzy stuff that only exists in our own minds.

But David Bohm, the renowned physicist, compares the role of human thought to that of DNA – the blueprint that makes things happen. He insists that *thought is real*. It can be measured by instruments such as the electroencephalograph. He goes on to explain:

> There is no thought without electrical and chemical changes, muscular tensions and so forth…Houses, tables, chairs, cars, roads, farms, factories, and, indeed, all that we see in everyday life are thus extensions of thought. Nature may be regarded as that which takes shape by itself, while human activity leads to the creation of artifacts, shaped by human participation in natural processes, ordered and guided by thought.[2]

Another example of the power of thought is offered by Victor Frankl who endured the Second World War in the most brutal concentration camps. His father, mother, brother and wife either died in such camps or were sent straight to the gas chambers. Frankl came to realize that the ability to survive the barbarism of such camps was not simply dependent on one's physical health and condition. Some perfectly healthy men rapidly gave up the will to live whereas others, less physically fit, developed an inner resistance. More than anything else, this ability seemed to be based on a man's projection of himself in the future – on his beliefs about whether or not he had anything left to live for. As Frankl explains:

> The prisoner who had lost faith in the future – his future – was doomed. With his loss of belief in the future, he also lost his spiritual hold; he let himself decline and became subject to mental and physical decay. Usually this happened quite suddenly, in the form of a crisis, the symptoms of which were familiar to the experienced camp inmate. We all feared this moment – not for ourselves, which would have been pointless, but for our friends. Usually it began with the prisoner refusing one morning to get dressed and wash or to go out on the parade grounds. No entreaties, no blows, no threats had any effect. He just lay there, hardly moving. If this crisis was brought about by an illness, he refused to be taken to the sick-bay or to do anything to help himself. He simply gave up. There he remained, lying in his own excreta, and nothing bothered him any more.[3]

When we talk about people "losing the will to live" this is exactly what we mean. Our will is not a matter of heartbeat and of breathing, but of determination to survive. And what Victor Frankl discovered was that this determination is dependent on a creative act of the imagination – the ability to look ahead to a time beyond the immediate suffering:

> Almost in tears from pain (I had terrible sores on my feet from wearing torn shoes), I limped a few kilometers with our long column of men from the camp to our work site. Very cold, bitter winds struck us. I kept thinking of the endless little problems of our miserable life. What would there be to eat tonight? If a piece of sausage came as extra ration, should I exchange it for a piece of bread? Should I trade my last

cigarette, which was left from a bonus I received a fortnight ago, for a bowl of soup? How could I get a piece of wire to replace the fragment which served as one of my shoelaces? Would I get to our work site in time to join my usual working party or would I have to join another, which might have a brutal foreman?

...I became disgusted with the state of affairs which compelled me, daily and hourly, to think of only such trivial things. I forced my thoughts to turn to another subject. Suddenly I saw myself standing on the platform of a well-lit, warm and pleasant lecture room. In front of me sat an audience on comfortable upholstered seats. I was giving a lecture on the psychology of the concentration camp! All that oppressed me at that moment became objective, seen and described from the remote viewpoint of science. By this method I succeeded somehow in rising above the situation, above the sufferings of the moment, and I observed them as if they were already of the past. Both I and my troubles became the object of an interesting psychoscientific study undertaken by myself.[4]

Those who live the spiritual life do so by raising their eyes. It doesn't matter what they raise them to, so long as they look up. When a congregation stands in church or inside a cathedral, they look up to the vaulted ceiling, to the icons, to the risen Christ, to the sun streaming through the stained glass windows. The whirling dervish raises his arm and tilts his head toward heaven; those who hear the call to prayer raise their eyes to the top of the minaret from where the muezzin is calling. We look to a higher level to seek out inspiration and ennoblement. To the mystic, it is this constant, faithful contemplation of that which is over and beyond ourselves which leads to a higher plane.

This act of contemplation need not be grounded only in the religious or overtly spiritual. With Victor Frankl, the ability to rise above his suffering came from a glimpse of the future, of life beyond the confines of the camp. I had another similar experience through my encounter with what I'd come to call The Bad Effect.

My queasy relationship with machinery had been diagnosed as post-traumatic stress disorder. My helpful cognitive psychologist had been unable to mend my sound system but had tried hard to mend my other damaged bits. The most important technique she'd suggested – which worked a treat - was simply to ensure that bad things never happened. Watch out for stuff that might make me feel uneasy or disturbed and avoid it like the plague. But sitting at home enclosed in bubble-wrap and blankets, watching my fish swim round and round wasn't my idea of life. More like a life-sentence. So every now and then, I peered outside...

All right, OK... I just went back to life as normal: travelled the world, gave lots of parties, went out dancing, got drunk, became ensnared with younger men...

...and sooner or later found myself with the familiar rocks in the stomach, the deep sense of foreboding, the cloying suffocation and the sense of rising panic.

I knew that it would pass. I knew all would be well. I just had to keep my head above the water. I looked forward to Quaker Meeting, an oasis of calm and serenity, but as I walked into town on Sunday, the panic reappeared. What if it got worse? What if I kept fidgeting and disturbing other Friends? What if my bad vibes were so strong, they fused the lights? What if I'd only got by all week being occupied with distractions? What if, without them, I'd just turn into jelly?

I entered the meeting and sat by the door so I could make a hasty exit if required. But then the clock ticked. I'd never noticed it before, but now it ticked and tocked and tocked and ticked. I stood and tiptoed across to the far corner and hunched behind the piano, but as I lowered myself to my seat, I couldn't remember how I normally sat. I clung to the sides of the seat. Like some poor, doomed damsel on a ducking stool, I felt as though I were being drowned. I emitted a silent cry for help. I tried to focus on my breathing – a long, deep, desperate intake inhaling love and peace and calm. But as soon as I exhaled, all the love and peace and calm were replaced by water in my ears and throat and nostrils. I could no longer breathe. My arms were dripping with sweat. I felt sick. I began to hyperventilate. *Try again, Linda. Give it five more minutes.* But I knew I couldn't stay. The only thing left for me to do was to leave.

I was rising out of my ducking stool, when a Friend, John Bouttell, stood up to speak, the last thing that I needed. I'd have to sit down now till he finished. My thoughts refused to focus. John was jabbering on about Jung – the last person on my agenda – as I made a final attempt at inhaling peace and calm like a drowning angel through her last drinking straw. Mentally, I ran screaming from the building, tore along the street and leaped in the town hall fountains.

Jung had said apparently that some people become overwhelmed by adversity and when bad things happen they feel overtaken by them. I blinked. Some of them never recover. Others somehow find a way through. Why was that? Jung wondered.

I blinked again.

Jung said that some people find a way *over* their problems. They do this by focusing on some point in the future when the overwhelming events would all be in the past. Jung compared it with walking up a mountain. There are obstacles to negotiate: there may be a dense forest where we lose our way; we may become bogged down in mud; we may find our path blocked by boulders we need to clamber over and when we've almost reached the summit, we have to find the strength for a last steep pull when our energy is almost spent. In spite of all these obstacles, Jung suggested that it's possible to lift our eyes and focus on the hilltop, to imagine the time when we'll stand on the peak and look back. Some people, he suggested, have the ability to mentally project themselves to this point where they can gaze back at everything they went through but see things much more clearly. This is not to minimize, said Jung, our struggle or the extent of our adversity, but when we look down, we'll be able to see things in perspective – there's the forest where we lost our way; those are the rocks we climbed; back there is the bog where we were almost dragged down and how hard we had to puff and pant to achieve that last steep sprint.

As John spoke, I saw the mountain, Margery Hill, one of my favorite walks. My eyes gazed along the ridge of Derwent and Howden Edge and the windswept moor across to Bleaklow. I projected myself on to the ridge, gazing beyond the outcrops. It was silent. Just the wind. The air was fresh and clear. I saw a stoat stretch over a rock on its hind legs. I saw a mountain hare. I heard a tune-up trill and saw the tiny speck of a skylark as it soared into the air. It burst into mellifluous song. Its liquid notes echoed round and round the circle of the meeting. I inhaled deeply on fresh mountain air and shuffled to make myself comfy, seated on tussocks of heather, surrounded by fresh mountain thyme.

And realized with a sense of amazement that my panic attack had gone. Just like that. I gazed around at the assembled Quaker meeting but everything was just as normal. Before the panic could return, I lifted my eyes back to the hills. I saw the view. I breathed the fresh air. Heard the skylark. It was easy. I did it a few times: hilltop... Quaker Meeting; hilltop... Quaker Meeting... I expected the effect to disappear, but it stayed with me the rest of the day and when I felt a tad uneasy later on that evening, I projected myself back on the hilltop again and straightaway all was well. The problem didn't go away; I'd simply found a way, as Jung described of *getting over it.*

So, in spite of the curvature of space-time – in spite of the likelihood that the future has already taken place, there are ways in which we can exercise control by as Priestley describes, *exercising our imagination, our feelings and will.*

We can raise our spirits and project ourselves into a better future by looking back on ourselves from a higher plane, just like gazing down from a passing aircraft at the tiny cars crawling over the Snake Pass.

Another way of raising our spirits is to immerse ourselves in the sublime. We may view the sublime as mystics do, as the embodiment of perfection or we may find the sublime in art, music or literature or a sense of compassion. We may find it when we fall in love. We can find the sublime in natural beauty or even in tending our gardens or in taking part with others in spiritual observation. All of these occasions, as we've read about before, can be doorways into DreamTime, where we find ourselves enfolded by what Bohm calls the *implicate order.* This, he describes as more than just a place where time melts and we see inside each other's thoughts, but as the control centre, the place where we make things happen.

I can of course make all kind of things happen without going into DreamTime. Things happen in the file I've opened on my computer. I can change the line spacing or the font, insert pictures, check the spelling and count the number of words... but in order to make important changes to my computer, I first have to leave the file I'm working on and access the control panel.

When I'm seated on a train, I can fold down my table, spread out my newspaper, attempt the crossword and plug in my laptop. I can stand up and walk to the bar and buy a drink. But in order to change my destination, I need to leave the train at a junction and find one that's heading in a completely different direction. Or have a quiet word with the man in charge and ask him to change the points.

What Bohm suggests is that this implicate order – rather than some fuzzy, airy-fairy, maybe-it's-there-and-maybe-it's-not whimsical phantasmagoria – is our actual control centre. And if we stick with the notion of multiple universe theory, it's the portal where we switch from one universe into another, the rail terminal where we switch to Eurostar to take us through the Channel Tunnel to go off to find our Eiffel Tower. Learning how to produce what Dunne calls The Effect and finding the portal to DreamTime is more than just the novelty of gaining a glimpse inside the future, but the way we control our destiny.

The idea that we can affect the future by *our feeling, will and imagination,* might sound a bit of a tall order and, at worst, disrespectful for those who have died in spite of the exhortations of prayer. However, the more difficult concept to get our heads around is the notion that this control centre is also where we can influence events *at a distance.*

We've been brought up to see ourselves and our world as separate items in space: this is me, here, and that's a traffic light over there – and the two are not connected. How could we possibly change a traffic light with the power of our minds?

Bohm has offered us the concept of the implicate and explicate order suggesting that there's an invisible web that links us all together, but the writer who's done most to bring Bohm's concept of an energy field into the public domain is the journalist Lynne McTaggart. After many years scrutinizing such concepts as remote viewing, distant healing and psychoneuroimmunology, McTaggart comes to the conclusion that:

> Human beings and all living things are a coalescence of energy in a field of energy connected to every other thing in the world. This pulsating energy field is the central engine of our being and our consciousness... "The field", as Einstein once succinctly put it, "is the only reality."[5]

The traditional scientific view of human beings is that we're like well-oiled bits of machinery. When there's a malfunction, we seek the worn-out or broken part, take it out and replace it. Or use drugs to cure a chemical imbalance. If we see ourselves instead as fields of energy, connected to all other fields of energy, then this opens up the possibility that we can have an affect on inanimate objects, on animals or on other people around us.

The experiments reported earlier with chickens showed that baby chicks can affect the movement of a robot they take to be their mother. A dog-owner, driving home from work, can cause her French bulldog to go rushing to the window; a menstruating woman can affect the menstrual cycle of other women in the same house; couples in sound-proof rooms can somehow send each other signals about the kind of images they're receiving – and all using forms of communication that are invisible, inaudible and often quite unconscious.

Much of The Field is concerned with experiments on the power of remote healing. In an experiment conducted by Elizabeth Targ , the people chosen for their abilities in distant healing didn't come from any particular religious background. What seemed important, as Lynne Mactaggart explains is their "ability to get out of the way":

In Elisabeth's study, it didn't seem to matter what method you used, so long as you held an intention for a patient to heal. Calling on Spider Woman - a healing grandmother-star-figure common in the Native American culture - was every bit as successful as calling on Jesus...

...But what they all seemed to have in common was an ability to get out of the way. It seemed to Elisabeth that most of them claimed to have put out their intention and then stepped back and surrendered to some other kind of healing force, as though they were opening a door and allowing something greater in...it was not an egoistic healing on their part, more like a request: "please may this person be healed". Much of their imagery had to do with relaxing, releasing or allowing the spirit, light or love in. The actual being, whether

it was Jesus or Spider Woman, appeared irrelevant.[6]
Not all of us are blessed with this ability to surrender to some "healing force". Many would prefer to be crawled on in a crisis by a tirade of tarantulas than call on Spider Woman. Many would prefer to surrender to an army of soldier ants than surrender to Jesus. And nowhere is this feeling stronger than with those who've already called for help during a time of desperate need and then felt cast aside. I remember a student once recounting with tears of rage how he'd prayed for his mother to be brought back to life after she'd succumbed to a sudden heart attack. His mother stayed dead and my student vowed never again to ask for help.

It hardly seemed the most suitable moment for a discussion on theology. Nor to explain that when someone's been dead for over half an hour, they can no more be resuscitated than a sloughed-off crab shell. The Fattest Controller in the world cannot raise a corpse any more than it can halt the power of a tsunami, allow you to pass an exam you've never studied for or plaster over a yawning crack in your relationship. All I could offer was a large box of tissues and sympathy.

And yet I have to say that of all the reasons put forward in this book to suggest that something exists over and beyond our physical selves – which, let's face it, is what most of this book has been about - this accessing the control centre is, for me, the most crucial. I am still unable to name what or who it is that's out there but am convinced, as Lynne Mctaggart reports, that the only important thing is to get me and my immediate needs out of the way and simply ask for help. I have glibly referred to my example with the traffic lights because I need have no fear they will never forgive me for writing about them in public. I've never had an intimate relationship with a traffic light; I've never had sex with one; I don't believe any have even seen me without my clothes; and I'm also happy to report that I don't have any traffic lights as members of my family.

However, I have had experiences too numerous to count with people who do fulfill some of the above criteria on whose behalf I have "accessed the control centre" and our lives have been turned round. I have written and will write about none of these as I'm talking about those who are much too close to me for me to regale them on public display. You can of course take my words on trust or scoff and simply ignore them.

And I'm well-aware that there are those whose deep-felt abhorrence of Anything Out There will never shift no matter how much evidence is trowelled on the page. David Bohm tackles this with much insight when he questions the concept of belief and how we come by it. We think of ourselves as intelligent beings who investigate facts and weigh evidence whereas actually, Bohm argues, most of our beliefs are a matter of conformity. We want people to like us; as my experience showed at the hypnotism show, we don't want to be seen as different. As young children, we emulate those we love or admire – our parents, friends, teachers or other role models and tend to parrot what they say. Once we've assembled beliefs, we justify them and carry on repeating them, even in the face of contradictory evidence. To contradict the deeply-held beliefs of our parents and our friends and families might suggest that we don't love them; or that they might stop loving us. And so, when we do encounter evidence suggesting we might be mistaken, we tend to ignore it, ridicule it or feel our undergarments knot together. As Bohm says:

> ...every time the mind tries to focus on its contradictions, it "jumps" to something else. It simply won't stay with the point. Either it continues to dart from one thing to another, or it reacts with violent excitement that limits all attention to some triviality, or it becomes dead, dull or anaesthetized, or it projects fantasies that cover up all the contradictions, or it does something else that makes one momentarily unaware of

the painful state of conflict in which the mind is.[7]

Nowhere are these attitudes stronger than in the realm of religion. For many, the love – or fear - they once felt for their parents is enshrined in their adherence to religious codes and ritual – or lack of them. You can argue and debate until the bottle runs dry in the early hours but these people will never give an inch, no matter how sound your reasoning, because their parents – who may in fact have been dead for many years – are still peering over their shoulder, pointing fingers, tut-tutting, and threatening to withhold their pocket money, or most importantly, their approval and their love.

For many, there's a real struggle to shake off this kind of emotional blackmail. We have to turn around and tell our parents – dead or alive – that, although we love and respect them, that doesn't mean we have to still dress up in that old white cape with the eye slits any more. We don't need to fly the same flag or sing the same hymns in order to keep their approval. Yet once we've survived that struggle and forged our own sense of identity, as Bohm goes on to describe, there are other worse pitfalls in store:

> ...most of those who are not satisfied with such conformity fall into the trap of **rebelling against it**, by projecting an opposing or contrary set of ideals, and trying to conform to these.

> But evidently such conformity is also not creative. For reasons that are hard to specify, a few people escape both these kinds of conditioning to mechanicalness in the operation of the mind. And of these few, a very small number indeed manage to escape the gigantic conflicts, internal and external, which may be initiated by the fear of upsetting the existing state of affairs, on which our security, our happiness, and even our lives often seem to depend. [8]

For those who rebel there's such a hard-won struggle that we're even more terrified of letting go of our new identity than abandoning the belief system of our parents. We feel naked without it. As a close friend remarked about giving up her drug and alcohol addiction, "I kept thinking to myself, *Without my addiction who would I be? I felt scared that, without it, I wouldn't be anyone at all.*

But beliefs don't just apply to us as individuals but to all of us as a society. It was in 1843 that Karl Marx first described religion as "the opium of the masses" and it's now over a hundred and fifty years since Darwin published his *Evolution of the Species* which did so much to challenge the religious ethic of his day. It's over a hundred and twenty five years since Nietzsche announced to the world (interestingly enough, in his book, *The Gay Science*) that "God is Dead." So, in the twenty first century we're on our way to two hundred years of rebelling against our grandparents' fears of hellfire and damnation; on our way to two hundred years of scientists informing us that there is no such thing as an afterlife and there is no point in prayer because there is no one there to answer. And I would like to suggest that the time has now come when we no longer need to rebel against our grandparents' fears of hell any more than we need to rebel against the British tax on tea or the procurement of small children as chimney sweeps. As Einstein once wrote in a letter:

> The fanatical atheists are like slaves who are still feeling the weight of their chains which they have thrown off after hard struggle. They are creatures who—in their grudge against traditional religion as the 'opium of the masses' — cannot hear the music of the spheres.[9]

The time has come to grow out of our teenage sulk, crawl out of the sideboard cupboard and begin thinking for ourselves.

One of my important bits of thinking for myself arose from

my encounter with a steatopygous woman. That's the way she's described in New York's Metropolitan Museum of Art. Steatopygous simply means having a fat backside, but as the US word for that part of the anatomy is so rude in English we'll just have to carry on calling her steatopygous. However, I first became acquainted with this lady on the island of Malta, at Ħaġar Quim.

This prehistoric temple, the world's oldest known man-made structure, stands atop a hill on the south side of the island – its mellow limestone in perfect contrast to the azure blue of the Maltese sky and the nearby Mediterranean. In one of several oval chambers stands a huge stone phallus and in the next, with her full hips, heavy breasts and pregnant belly, the so-called Venus of Malta. Surrounding altars show evidence of prolific animal sacrifice and the whole site is a superb example of an ancient fertility cult. The Venus statue, however, is a replica. As the original had been relocated to the museum in the capital, Valetta, that was where I travelled the following day.

What I saw in Valetta didn't just amaze me but turned my whole notion of religion on its head. There wasn't just one Venus of Malta, but dozens, all in various shapes and sizes in a higgledy-piggledy display. Just in case you're thinking of visiting, I'll mention that the whole place is now tidied up with fewer figurines but all beautifully displayed. My first thought was that these must have been dug up from the local souvenir shop – the place where pilgrims would call and buy their knick-knacks before returning home but then... I looked at the dates of the statuettes and realized that they went back thousands of years.

It took a while for this to sink in.

I'd tended to think of religion as the worship of a male god over the last two thousand years or so. Before that were the Romans and the Ancient Greeks and the Egyptians, but all these gods, I realized, were mere upstarts. People had worshipped the

Venus of Malta for much longer. Why had I never heard of her before?

I returned home, determined to find out more.

I assumed that I'd discovered the centre of a small esoteric cult, peculiar to one small Mediterranean island, but I was wrong. The figure was in fact the focus of a major world religion, - *the* major world religion - extending right across Europe and into southern Russia. I was staggered. I'd studied the Sociology of Religion at college and the name, "Venus" wasn't discussed. When we'd learned something of prehistory at school, the word "goddess" never crossed the teacher's lips. Why had nobody mentioned her before?

The following year I toured Scotland, driving up the western coast and stopping off at several archaeological sites along the way. I didn't find Venus figurines but, looking at prehistory now from a totally different perspective, couldn't help but notice that one chambered cairn after another, consisted of circular apertures covered by large horizontal ovals which showed an amazing similarity to the bits I pull my knickers over every morning. Yet there was no mention of this in the archaeologists' notes. How could they not notice? Had they never seen women's bits? Or had all prehistoric sites been excavated by Victorian gentlemen who never owned up to having seen them in case their wives and their daughters might faint?

When I took a tour of the Creswell caves, near Sheffield, to view their recently-discovered wall paintings, the guide seemed a little embarrassed to mention that the earliest paintings they'd discovered – those towards the far back of the entrance chamber – also appeared to symbolize female genitalia. Must have been some naughty prehistoric children messing about with their charcoal, I was told.

But, I thought, no, no, no... it's the Earth goddess again. You don't see one for forty years, then two hundred turn up at once.

The most famous example is the small statuette given the

name of "Venus" discovered in Willendorf, Austria and dated to approximately 28,000 years of age.[10]

And the latest such figure to be excavated, found in deposits in the Hohle Fels cave in South Germany, was carved in remarkable detail out of mammoth ivory at least 35,000 years ago.[11] This goddess, with her full breasts, broad hips and exaggerated genitalia, can only be a symbol of birth and fertility.

So, Religion is no new-fangled, male-dominated stuff, but goes back to the dawn of time. We may have been taught to think of a male god as Creator, seated in some heavenly workshop, modeling the world as though out of Playdoh and forming us all like a factory line of jelly babies. But a fertility goddess implies not so much a *Creator* as *Creativity*. To give birth is not like stamping out jelly babies but acting as a vessel for new life to pass through. And whereas a creator is remote, looking down and inspecting us, his handiwork, creativity is a force of creative energy which flows through us and inside us.

I have already described creativity as one of the doorways into DreamTime. When we're being at our most creative, we feel as though we're abandoning all sense of who we are and what we want in order to allow our pen or brush to trace over words or pictures that seem mysteriously to exist already. So might that be because, in some previous, unremembered life, the words actually *have* already been written? Have the pictures been already painted and the music played before? Is this elusive muse we encounter one of our Groundhog Day personas who has previously lived the same life? So, when Graham Greene was tapped on the shoulder by the Muse inside the Gents in Piccadilly, and saw the whole of his unwritten novel – the beginning, the middle and the end – was he actually seeing not just the novel he was about to write, but the one he had already written in some previous existence?

Another bit of Groundmut insight occurred on another Spanish Walk. On my first Beehive Walk, reassured by my

Sunflower Guidebook that, *Even after substantial rain the stream shouldn't be particularly deep or difficult, and at times there may be hardly any water at all*[12], I thought, foolishly, that I could do without my boots. There may have been little rain, but that didn't stop the snow melting from the tops of the Sierra Blanca.

I didn't have trekking poles either. Trekking poles were for Big Girls' Blouses. And I thought I'd take the stepping stones in my stride. Being only 5ft 1", however, my stride's a bit short – and as stepping stones are always positioned by giants, I took off my sneakers to paddle.

I didn't paddle far. The river bed was coated with algae and the mossy stones were slippery and the water was up to my knees and I could see I was in for a tumble. Plan B was to make my own stepping stones. I spent a hopeless twenty minutes lobbing rocks from the bank before realizing that – whatever craftsmanship there was to constructing stepping stones – it was lost on me. Mine were all swept away.

I sat down and had a drink and realized that what I needed was a big stick. Or, even better, two big sticks. It didn't take long to find a couple of fallen branches, peel off the twigs and leaves and make myself some trekking poles a girl-guide would've been proud of. With a bit of a giggle, I found myself pole-vaulting from stepping stone to stepping stone and by the time the path re-crossed the stream, I had my new circus act off to a fine art. The path crossed and re-crossed the river again and I never got my socks wet.

As my walk veered up towards the foothills, I was about to leave my sticks by the stream for some other needy traveler, but then... the guidebook mentioned that the end of the walk returned the same way; there weren't so many trees on this side of the river and if anyone else took the sticks, they'd finish up on the wrong side.

Anyway, other travelers would probably be taller and I'd seen nobody else all day so I decided instead to leave my sticks beneath a bush. While I was about it, I'd leave one of my smoothies concealed behind a rock deep in the stream. Then I wouldn't have to carry it over the hills and it would be nice and cool when I got back.

I set off striding past the cork oaks and up the hillside and as I did so, felt strangely reassured. I imagined myself hot and tired, nearing the end of my walk, really fancying a drink and thinking *Oh, what's that peeping out of the river? Could it be a smoothie by any chance?* And *Well, just fancy that... somebody's left two big sticks here.* How nice to think there would be someone watching out for me..

Okay, sad person that I am, I knew it was only me really. But I began to reflect on similar notions people have of being watched over – many would believe, for instance, that their ancestors were watching over them, warning them of danger; many have faith in a special patron saint giving them a helping hand; Socrates and Jung both had their daemons – a strong sense of a guiding spirit – and when I've travelled in India – every taxi, rickshaw, bus and place of work has its own incarnation of the deity, be it Krishna or Hammaman or Ganeesh, the elephant god.

I was reminded of a writing exercise I took part in with the author, Jan Mark, at Lumb Bank near Heptonstall. Jan asked us to each write a list of sentences starting with the words: *I know...* The other fifteen writers, hunched around the huge table, began to scribble furiously. I was at a loss. I couldn't think of anything. I considered writing, *I know this is a table*, before thinking that to a Spaniard, it would be *una mesa* and to a Frenchman, it would look similar to *table* but be pronounced quite differently and anyway, that wasn't *knowing*; it was just a name we give stuff. Then I thought about writing, *I know the sun will rise tomorrow* before realizing that, what I actually meant was that the sun had risen every day so far but of course I had no idea at all what tomorrow would bring and, anyway, it wasn't the sun that rose; it just looked like it. And I thought about writing that *two plus two make four,* before thinking that four was just another way of writing *two plus two.* And then I glanced across the shoulder of Debjani Chatterjee, seated beside me whose neat script claimed: *I know that I am walking on the path that my ancestors have trod.* And I thought that sounded impressive and wondered whether I could copy it but put it in my own words somehow before realizing that, actually, I know nothing at all about my ancestors. I don't have a clue what paths they trod.

The next exercise was a list of sentences starting with the words, *I believe...* If I did badly on the first task, this was ten times worse. Believing in something means that you don't actually know it's true but would like to think it was. Everybody else filled at least two sides of A4. Half the morning had gone and my page contained only two sentences:

I know the world is beautiful
I know that I shall die some day.

For many months afterwards I was haunted by my two meager sentences and the acre of empty space on my accusatory sheets of paper. We tend to identify people by what they believe in, so what kind of person believes in hardly anything at all?

So, to return to the Beehive Walk where I am now a bit further up the hillside, having paused to eat my picnic at a convenient clump of rocks only to be driven away by an infestation of highly-aggressive ants.

These ants roam into my rucksack and scurry inside my sandwiches. They sneak into my sneakers and scuttle inside my socks. As I sprint as fast as I can from their nesting ground, they pinch and peck and nibble. I keep finding them hours later inside my socks and undergarments. I decide that I will write about them in the margin of my Sunflower Guide; I will note in the edges of the page that describes this walk: *Don't sit on the rocks, Linda. Watch out for Killer Ants.* I will write this below the notes saying, *Take trekking poles and waterproof boots.*

I consider this as I walk higher up the hillside. I keep a journal – normally a five-year diary. When I read through entries from the past, I cannot help but write a few words of encouragement now and then to the Linda who has, on occasions, been overcome with anxiety. *You'll be fine, Linda,* I write. *All will be well. Hang on in there!*

So, if we really do have Groundhog Days – if after our earthly death, we actually do – as so many Afterbirders suggest - go through a life-review with the opportunity to select the episodes that we'd like to do better next time – then the process would be a little bit like writing in the margins of a Sunflower book or journal. So... let's just suppose for the sake of argument that there was a Linda in the past who suffered a terrible car crash. Let's say that - chatting on the phone or singing along to her Americana albums – she failed to notice a car overtaking over the brow of a hill. Maybe people were killed; maybe she never walked again. Whatever the outcome, Linda is haunted by the incident for evermore. When she dies her earthly death and has her life review, she notes: *This is something I would like to change next time. I would like to avoid the collision... I would like to ensure that no one dies. I would like to be able to go out walking instead of being in the wheelchair.*

And let us just suppose that – in the life of the Next Linda – she has placed a bookmark. And on the page saved by the bookmark, a note is written into the margins of her life. So, when the Next-Time-Round-Linda lives her life again, she sees the car overtaking over the brow of the hill, before the car sees her. She thinks she sees something about to happen in the future but what she actually sees - as Dr Görtler says, is the incident from her past. Forewarned, she avoids the accident. She thinks for a second, *That was a bit weird,* before driving on and absent-mindedly wondering what she will cook for tea and whether she needs to stop and buy any wine or chocolate.

And let's just suppose that same First Linda had one or two other bits of stuff she'd like to change. A small one was the unseemly business with the myxomatosis-smitten rabbit. She couldn't even look at a rabbit without seeing the poor creature with its weeping eyes. She inserted a Bookmark here as well, so the night before the rabbit incident, the whole unfortunate episode was replayed in a dream. The Next Linda remembered her dream the following day and again, thought it was a vision of the future whereas in fact, it was a replay of her past. Although the rabbit was still killed, this was done quickly and cleanly by the gamekeeper. This Next-Time-Round-Linda went on to inherit a lop-eared white rabbit called Monty. As this same Linda sat writing in her garden, Monty's mad antics reminded her of the Alice in Wonderland rabbit and she began to find that, just as her first book had a quotation about an angel for each and every chapter, this new book produced a whole string of quotations from Alice in Wonderland.

And let us suppose that this same Linda uses most of her Bookmarks for the biggest regret of her life: she became a fervent atheist in her early teens and then went on to pour scorn on anyone who suggested that she might be missing out on life's deeper significance. She raised her eyebrows to the ceiling when anyone related their near-death experience; she scoffed at suggestions of remote healing; she never read books about the latest developments in quantum physics because there was nothing to explain. This life was all there was. If anyone thought differently, they hadn't seen the light; they must have limited intelligence, an extremely limited viewpoint and make very limited company. This Linda filled her life with silly tasks: changing partners, changing places, changing her furniture round, learning the steps of the lobster quadrille and painting the red roses white. Only at the very end of her life - when the lobster quadrille had to stop, did she realize that life had gone by without her ever wondering what it was she came here for. If she could only have her time again, she thought, she would find a spiritual home while she still had strength to wheel her wheel-chair there. So, this Linda took all the rest of her Bookmarks and folded them into origami angels, to scatter in the pathway of the Next-Time-Round-Linda. She took two stout sticks and hid them behind a lamppost on Sheffield's Angel Street and when the Next-Time-Round-Linda stood dithering outside the Quaker Meeting House, picked up the sticks and gave her a good prod, driving her inside.

And when that Next-Time-Round-Linda came downstairs and poured herself a stiff vodka, and spoke to the imaginary angels dancing across the settee and said, *I'm sorry, I don't believe in you...*

The other Linda was the one who whispered loudly in her head: *You think about dying, you think about me...*

Chapter 15

Momento mori: always teatime

"It's always six o'clock now."

A bright idea came into Alice's head.

"Is that the reason so many tea things are put out here?" she asked.

"Yes, that's it," said the Hatter with a sigh: "It's always tea time."

Alice in Wonderland: A Mad Tea-Party

You think about dying; you think about me...

When I walked downstairs to confront my twenty seven angels, this was my garbled, Christmas cracker message. I knew it was a *message* rather than just a common-or-garden thought because it took me so much by surprise and also, because it made no sense. If I'd been *thinking* of a possible answer to my *I'm sorry I don't believe in you...* opening gambit, I'd like to think I would have come up with something a bit more accessible and user-friendly. What was the point of a message that I couldn't understand?

So, that evening, after I'd crept downstairs and poured myself a stiff drink, I took a deep breath and started out by saying, *I'm sorry, I don't actually believe in anything out there...*

And the reply was a kind of silent, implied, *Yes but...* followed by the clear exposition: *You think about dying and you think about me.*

I was shocked. Had I heard it right? Of course I had. If it's a voice inside your head, you don't get static or problems with the graphic equalizer. I just felt disappointed. Sold short. If it really had been the voice of the Great Man Upstairs, he might have told me what to do next, but that was it.

The line went dead.

I pondered on it over the next few days but it didn't get any clearer. Maybe I'd misheard. Like those people standing at the back in the *Life of Brian* who thought they'd heard, *Blessed are the Cheesemakers* instead of *Blessed are the Peacemakers*. I filed the message away like some garbled text sent to the wrong number and got on with the rest of my life.

Enlightenment dripped slowly. The first droplet arrived a few years later.

Nicolas Scorer and his wife, Irene Gay, were elderly stalwarts of our Meeting. I remember hitting the brakes one day as I saw them entwined, teetering across the road with Irene almost blind, leaning on Nicolas's arm and I reflected on the fact that either one of them would find it well-nigh impossible to live without the other.

And so it turned out. I was one of the first to hear the news about Nicolas and offer my condolences. Yet I couldn't help but notice that Irene's face was glowing. When I said, *He was such a wonderful man, Irene…*

… she answered by enthusing, *Yes, yes, and that's why it's so… so* ***wonderful.***

I was shocked. The rapture on Irene's face made my Watership Down moment sound like a funeral dirge. I sought out someone in the meeting connected with pastoral care to voice my concern that the news hadn't sunk in yet and Irene was delirious.

But Janet Hawksworth, to whom I spoke, seemed unconcerned. *Both Nicolas and Irene have always been very spiritual people,* she explained, *and that means living in awareness of the fact that we're going to die. Doesn't it?*

Did it?

I was taken aback but suddenly recalled my Christmas cracker message and began to ponder.

My next droplet of Enlightenment grew out of my obsession

with Americana. This music, otherwise known as alternative country, is a fusion of rock, punk, country and gospel with acts like the Cowboy Junkies, Steve Earle, Gillian Welch, Lucinda Williams, Emmylou Harris and Mary Gauthier. These dirges form the soundtrack to my life, the backdrop to my travels, the playlist for my parties. And friends are either instant converts or they grunt politely. And I understand the problem because I might have cringed at one time. Most of the songs are about death – many of them good, old-fashioned murder ballads, but many rejoicing with heavy bass, sliding fiddles, pounding drums and electric guitars at: *a better home awaiting, in the sky, Lord, in the sky...*

Amongst educated liberals of my generation, religion was always considered "the opium of the people". We despised the credulity of those who sought solace in some "pie-in-the-sky" afterlife rather than strive for reform or even revolution in the here-and-now. Nowhere was this derision stronger than in bewailing those who encouraged America's long-suffering black poor to bear their troubles with fortitude to be *carried home* by *amazing grace* in *sweet chariots, across the River Jordon* where the *family circle would be unbroken* once again. Such a shame they had all the best tunes. It didn't take me long to realize that most of my personal favorites were rocked-up versions of old gospel classics.

But there was something about this attitude that turned my stomach over: the implication that these gullible blacks were like naïve children, in need of our paternal guidance. After reading about Aborigines and Native Americans and DreamTime, I began to question all this. What if the tribal peoples of western Africa also believed that DreamTime was where their ancestors lived and where they would go when they died? What if they brought those beliefs with them to the Americas and related to those aspects of Christianity closest to their own tradition? What if they already knew about the circle of life being unbroken and the Home that was awaiting on the other side of the great river? Maybe we weren't teaching them anything at all.

Maybe they had something to teach us.

Another droplet of Enlightenment arrived whilst I was staying in Krakow. I'd taken a tram to the station but, unable to understand the Polish for "railway station", missed the stop, then tried to catch a tram going back the other way, but not knowing the Polish for "city centre", found myself heading out of town before catching another tram on a long, long track to nowhere. I'd purchased the cheapest "15" ticket, for those travelling for less than fifteen minutes, I thought. But when the ticket inspector got on, I began to wonder if it might have meant under-15s. And anyway, I'd been travelling at least half an hour and not knowing the Polish for anything at all actually, thought it best to disembark before the inspector arrived at my seat. And it looked like the botanical gardens. I followed the straggle of people heading towards some large wrought-iron gates and found myself in Krakow cemetery.

Well, at least the shade was inviting on such a hot day and there was plenty of peace and flowers everywhere, so I set off for a wander.

The cemetery was vast – several square miles, and as I explored the neat pathways, I marveled at the fact that every plot was different. One tomb was constructed like a cave; another had an installation of interwoven branches which would have done Andy Goldsworthy proud. People arrived with plastic carriers from which they produced a plethora of polishing cloths and trowels. They filled water bottles at the pump, before settling down to washing, scrubbing and polishing the slabs of marble, many of which contained laminated photographs. I had a bit of a shock at one plinth when I recognized a familiar face before realizing that the marble had been polished so well, I was gazing at my own reflection.

There were flowers everywhere, giving the impression of a

forest in the springtime and to my amazement, it turned out to be a cracking place to spend a couple of hours. I kept thinking that you couldn't imagine the average Brit spending their Saturdays on their hands and knees, doing all this scrubbing and scouring, weeding and planting, refreshing jars of burning oil and lighting candles. I remembered as a sociology student, learning about the importance of the veneration of the dead, universal in all successful societies i.e. those that have survived and also of course, one of the earliest signs of civilization. If we behave as though someone else's death is of no import, then that means that we don't matter either. As Donne *(the poet, not the aeronautical engineer* says:)

> ...*another manne's death diminishes me because I am involved in mankind.*
> *And therefore never send to know for whom the bell tolls;*
> *it tolls for thee.*[1]

Also in Krakow, I found out about the Camaldolese monks. They live in an impressive monastery on Srebrna Gora (or Silver Mountain) in the southern part of Krakow's Wolski Forest. Part of the Order of Saint Benedict, they live in silent, walled seclusion, share only five meals together a year and meet each other only during prayers. They have the inscription above the entrance: *Momento mori* (Remember you must die). Rumor has it that these monks – with their flowing, white cassocks and long, bushy beards - actually sleep in coffins but this is not the case. However... when monks die, their bodies are placed – not in coffins - but in niches in the crypt and sealed. Each niche is labeled with a tag saying how old the monk was and how long he spent in the hermitage. 80 years later, the niches are opened and the monks take the skulls away to keep with them in their cells.

Assuming they don't keep them to use as plant-pot holders or as a macabre line in reading lamps or ash trays, what would be the point?

We think of the spiritual life as one of good works, prayer and contemplation. So why should it be deepened by keeping the mortal remains of past generations of holy brethren in a row upon the mantelpiece?

The issue is addressed by John Dunne (*the aeronautical engineer*) in The New Immortality:

> Up to about fifty years ago nobody minded admitting that life was a disappointing thing which opened with high hopes and sounding trumpets, moved on to frustration after frustration, and terminated in a disillusioned crawling to the grave. Nobody minded, because everybody supposed that all this was merely the prelude to another life in which they would be promoted to some kind of unimaginable bliss. But, fifty years ago, exponents of popular science began to hammer it into these optimists that the notion of a hereafter in which everything would be put right was utter nonsense. There was, they pointed out, no future life for any of us; and our world, in sober truth, amounted to nothing more than an **execution chamber** – dealing as expeditiously as possible with a continuous procession of new victims. It would be foolish to revile God for this, because there was no God to revile.
>
> That picture, it seems now, was too grim for the human mind to face fairly and squarely. People in general believed it, but they turned their backs to it.[2]

So, as Dunne suggests, if we have no belief in an afterlife, we tend to turn our backs on reminders of mortality. Those who celebrate the Day of the Dead with sugar skulls, visits to the graveyard, with partying and processions are Catholics in Mexico, Brazil, Spain and elsewhere. Those who carry out the weekly or monthly ritual of lighting candles, replenishing the fragrant oil, arranging flowers, and scrubbing and scouring gravestones may simply be going through the motions because that's what all their friends and families do, but in the main are those who don't fear reminders of mortality because they don't think of death as The End. They don't view this world as an execution chamber but a preparation for the afterlife.

So, how does this relate to our spirituality?

Let us just assume that, as at the Mad Hatter's famous tea party, we expect time to stand still. It's always teatime, so we can go round and round the table as often as we like with as much jelly and cake as we can eat; we never need deal with the washing up or the stains on the cloth or the dormouse asleep in the teapot because it will shortly be Time to Change Places.

And if we ignore the fact that life is short and we will die one day, then it doesn't matter what we do. We put up with jobs we hate because we can look forward to our two weeks in the sun, look forward to Christmas, look forward to finding a partner, look forward to getting married, look forward to having children, look forward to them starting school, look forward to the day they leave, look forward to them leaving home, look forward to the day when they get a proper job, look forward to them getting married, look forward to becoming grandparents and then... oops. We can't remember what those two large holes in our pants are for each morning; drivers honk their horns at us when we dither at the crossing; the world is full of new-fangled technology that gets our underwear in a twist; our friends are dead or have forgotten us, the best years of our lives are under the bridge and down the U-bend and we can't remember what it was we came here for in the first place.

This is the horror of the half-life. As described by Herman Melville in Moby Dick: *For as this appalling ocean surrounds the verdant land, so in the soul of man there lies one insular Tahiti, full of peace and joy, but encompassed by all of the horrors of the half-lived life.*[3]

It is not so much that we are terrified of death but terrified that on our deathbed we will come face-to-face with the realization that we've done nothing with our lives apart from shopping, eating, watching TV and faffing about with the computer. Or alternatively that we've filled our lives with tiny, pointless goals like using only the **best** butter as we hear the queen shouting "Off with her head," Or partaking in a lifelong lobster quadrille, changing partners, changing places, changing our minds, changing our tune, going round and round in circles until we fall off the end of the table and someone else takes our plate as we refuse to wake up and take off the lid of the teapot.

The acceptance of life's brevity makes life so much more precious. The knowledge that the party doesn't last for ever means that life becomes more valuable; we relish every taste of cake and cream; we live each second to the full because we are aware in every single moment that we do not last for ever.

So... it's taken many, many years for me to make sense of my Christmas cracker message. When I heard an inner voice that said unmistakably, *You think about dying, you think about me...* it might have been the voice of a steatopygous woman; it might have been the voice of Bohm's implicate order; it might have been the Linda-who-hides-the-big-sticks-and-the-smoothie from some previous existence. It might have been Spider Woman. I don't believe we are born to know and when people tell us that they do know, believe me, they're talking with their fingers crossed behind their backs.

However, I think that nowadays I might make an addition to my list of sentences starting out with *I believe.*

I think that nowadays I would add: *I do believe that death is not The End.*

Chapter 16

The Cheshire Cat: End-of-Life Experience

I wish you wouldn't keep appearing and vanishing so suddenly: you
make one quite giddy!"

"All right," said the Cat; and this time it vanished quite slowly,
beginning with the end of the tail, and ending with the grin, which
remained some time after the rest of it had gone.

Alice in Wonderland: Chapter V1

When I first qualified as a primary schoolteacher, jobs were as
rare as mad hatters' tea parties. The only local position was in a
secondary school – teaching English – and four lessons of music
a week.

As I tried to bluff out my English expertise amongst other
interviewees, I realized that not only were they older and more
experienced than me but none were prepared to teach a single
note of music.

My interview went well. But then came the moment I'd been
dreading as the chairman of the governors leaned forward "…
and the music lessons?"

I did own a guitar. I could play three chords: D; A7; G.
Nothing else. My toes turned upright. Somewhere out of the
ether, I scooped a smile of confidence and pasted it on to my face.
"Oh, yes," I insisted. I took a deep breath. "I can play the guitar
and sing." I ignored the sight of my nose, lengthening out to
meet the board of assembled governors. "And we'll have…" I
dragged out every last ounce of brazen audacity to pipe the
words "… singing lessons."

Back at home the following day, I took down my old guitar
and practised the chords: D… A7… G… D… I practised the

change without looking down at my fingers. I bought an ancient book of so-called popular songs and practised those that went D...A7...G...D – none of them sadly, stuff the kids would have ever heard of. I practised *Skip to my Lou* and *My Grandfather's Clock*. On my first day, I marched into the classroom full of rampaging teenagers, hoisted myself on the edge of the teacher's desk, took a deep breath, played D...A7...G...D... without looking down at my fingers and wailed like a Cheshire cat with its tail caught in a pepper grinder:

Way, hey skip to my Lou
Hey, hey, skip to my Lou...

The class collapsed in hysterics, sidesplitting, stereophonic and totally uncontrollable.

Undeterred, I sang louder. The students hooted. When I asked them to join in and sing, they bellowed and they guffawed.

I feigned deafness as I carried on Skipping to my Lou. When I suggested again that the students might accompany me, they parodied my squawking and invented a load of obscenities about Lou which didn't involve too much skipping.

Lesser mortals would have run home in tears, resigned their job, and hurled their old guitar down the nearest treacle mine, but I had three children, a mortgage and a marriage on the rocks...

I kept on doggedly: *Skip to my Lou, my...*

Some of the more accommodating students began to mouthe the words. I showered them with praise. More followed.

By week two, the hilarity had lessened. The students came to accept the fact that they had a singing teacher who couldn't sing and only pretended to play the guitar. Reassured that their own attempts couldn't possibly be any worse, they began to join the cacophony. By the end of the year, several had ordered guitars. We formed a folk group. We were invited out for gigs. By the end of the following year, the folk group had grown so large, we had to call it a choir. We sang at local festivals. We ditched Lou and all her skipping – and her other unrepeatable stuff – but the song these errant teenagers loved most of all – the one we sang in every lesson was:

> *My Grandfather's clock was too large for the shelf*
> *So it stood ninety years on the floor.*
> *It was taller by far than the old man himself*
> *Though it weighed not a pennyweight more...*

And I'd forgotten all about the song until a few weeks ago when I went to a meeting of the Scientific and Medical Network where Peter and Elizabeth Fenwick, authors of *The Truth in the Light* study of near-death experience, were describing their research into what they call End-of-Life experience. Having collected data from three different studies carried out in nursing homes and hospices in the Netherlands, Ireland and England, the Fenwicks found that 80% of the medical staff had, during the past five years, encountered some kind of inexplicable phenomena surrounding death and those about to die: staff had been aware of light or other visual disturbance around the deathbed; they'd heard about coincidence around the dying person or their relatives and friends; they'd heard about visitations from dead relatives and, somewhat surprisingly, a large amount of evidence concerning stopping clocks.

In their book, "The Art of Dying", the Fenwicks recount the story of the long-case clock (sometimes known as a coffin clock because of its similarity in size) kept in the George Hotel in Piercebridge, North Yorkshire.

In the early years of the nineteenth century, the hotel was run by two brothers named Jenkins. When one of the brothers died, the old clock – which had always kept perfect time – began to go slow. Several clocksmiths tried to mend it, but the old clock continued to lose about an hour every day. Some time later at the ripe old age of ninety, the second brother died. The clock was fully wound and ticking normally, but at his death, it stopped and – in spite of attempts to repair it – never ticked again. It was left standing in the hotel lobby as a tribute to the last brother with its hands pointing to the time at which he died.

In 1875, an American composer by the name of Henry Clay Work (famous for composing *Marching through Georgia*) happened to stay at the hotel. Having been told the story of why a broken clock was still kept in the lobby, Henry was impressed enough to compose a new song:

My grandfather's clock was too large for the shelf
So it stood ninety years on the floor...

...ninety years without slumbering, tick-tock, tick-tock
His life seconds numbering: tick-tock, tick-tock...
But it stopped short, never to go again
When the old man died.

And in honor of this famous clock (*still there in The George, if you're visiting North Yorkshire*), long-case or coffin clocks have been known as "grandfather clocks" ever since.

Much of the Fenwicks' book is concerned with present-day attitudes towards death and dying. Our fears about the end of life, coupled with the physical distance nowadays between many families, results in at least half the UK population dying in hospital, rather than in their own homes.

At other times – in our past, as in other cultures – it was common for people to die in their own beds surrounded by friends and family. One result of the change is that now, in the early years of the twenty-first century, many people have never actually watched anyone die and may feel fearful of being called upon to do so.

What the Fenwicks go on to explain is that this lack of familiarity with death means that many of us are ignorant of the paranormal events – like the sudden stopping of a clock – which often accompany someone taking their last breath.

In this account Peter describes the stopping of several clocks – belonging to the brother of a man who died.

My father died at 3.15am. At about 8.30am I went to see my Uncle Archie, who'd been close to Dad... to tell him about losing Dad and bring him back to the house if he wished. As Uncle Archie opened the door it was clear he was distressed, and as I began to tell him of Dad's passing away he interrupted me and said he already knew... he said no one had telephoned him but told me to look at the clock on the mantelpiece – it was stopped at 3.15, as was indeed his own wristwatch, his bedside clock and all the other clocks in the house. There was even an LED display, I think on a radio, flashing 3.15. I was completely taken aback, but Archie seemed comfortable with the phenomenon and was just concerned at losing someone close.[1]

Clocks are not the only pieces of machinery found by the Fenwicks to stop in sympathy when someone dies. Lucie Green and her uncle were sitting beside her father as he lay in a coma in his hospital bed:

The TV screen went totally blank, the sound went totally and then a nurse came rushing into the room and asked why we had pressed the alarm. At that very moment my father, 58, took his last breath. Nobody had rung the alarm, yet it was ringing in the nurse's office and nobody can explain why the television started malfunctioning. A short while after my father's passing, the TV returned to normal. I later spoke to the nurse about the alarm going off and she said it happened all the time at the point of somebody passing...[2]

These accounts from the Fenwicks provide supporting evidence for many of the areas I've been researching for this book. They point to the suggestion that, as human beings, we may be more than just well-oiled bits of machinery with a well-developed brain; they point to the suggestion of some other kind of dimension, the portal of which appears to open around the time of our death; they also point strongly to an interconnectedness – what Bohm would call the Implicate Order – not only between people who care about each other, but also between people and animals and between some people and the machinery they use.

If I didn't have my own weird relationship with machinery, I would have found the clock-stopping stories implausible. All of us die. Most of us have clocks and watches. We hear nothing at all about the vast majority of people whose clocks don't stop when they die, but every now and then the laws of probability dictate there must be somebody whose clock does stop and then we think of it as some kind of miracle. And yet Uncle Archie's experience, described above, would seem to defy all attempts at rational explanation. And what about Huygens? As described earlier, Huygens discovered synchronicity in clocks. His was not some anecdotal, maybe-it-happens-maybe-it-doesn't, shaggy-dog story, but a repeatable scientific experiment which presaged entrainment applications in various branches of science. We do not know why two pendulum clocks hanging on the same wall should start to tick in unison; we only know they do. And if a clock is sensitive enough to tick in harmony with its twin, might it not be possible for such a clock to tick in harmony with an even more sensitive human being who winds it up and cares for it?

It hardly seems surprising that dogs-who-know-when-their-owners-are-returning-home also know when their owners have just died. This story was told by Michael Finch, whose mother lay in a coma and was dying of cancer in a Macmillan unit. Michael left the hospital to go home and take out the dog:

> I will NEVER forget this as long as I live. At 10.45pm on 12 November 1995 the dog began to howl like a wolf. It was spine chilling. I just knew that this was because Mum had died. For five minutes he howled uncontrollably and then took to his bed. The dog was a King Charles Cavalier, and in his then 12 years had never made such a deep, wild and rasping sound as that. When my father and sister returned about an hour later they confirmed my thoughts, that Mum had died at 10.45pm. [3]

A similar account was received from Ann Liddell who owned a Newfoundland dog:

> At about 4.30am, he started to bark – not his usual sharp warning bark, but howling. I knew instantly that my mother had died, and soon after we got the call from the hospital to confirm this.[4]

One of the most common phenomena reported to the Fenwicks was what they called "coincidence." Someone close to the deceased somehow simply *knew*, in the same way that Uncle Archie *simply knew* his brother had just died. People often reported hearing the voice or feeling the presence of their close friend or relative or, as 76% of deaths occur at night, seeing them in a dream. Again, it would be easy to dismiss this as simply *thinking about* someone. When someone close to us is seriously ill, they're seldom out of our thoughts. We worry about them. We mentally prepare ourselves: *What if they were to leave us? How would we feel?* Many people must be having such thoughts just before they hear the news of someone's death and then take it as a premonition. And yet this feeling, like the elation I experienced when my own mother was dying, is not the same as thought.

And over and over again, people who've no idea that their friend or relative is ill also have such experience. Here the Fenwicks relate a story about General Alfred Fytch who...

...getting out of bed one morning in India saw an old friend, whom he assumed had decided to pay him an unexpected visit. He greeted his friend warmly and sent him to the veranda to order a cup of tea. When he went to join him, the old friend had vanished. Nobody in the house had seen anyone. Two weeks later, he received news that his friend had died 600 miles away at the time he had seen him.[5]

Here is another example sent to the Fenwicks by Jenny Stiles:

My mother died just before Christmas, Sunday 17 December 2006 at 9.10pm. She had suffered a massive stroke six weeks earlier with no chance of recovery. I had been trying to contact my brother in the USA for several months to let him know she had been in a residential care home for 18 months and was rapidly declining. I knew he had moved from Nashville to Washington DC but I had no address or telephone number for him and the search was fruitless. Then out of the blue, four days after our mother died, he called me one evening. He was not surprised to hear she had died, he told me he had seen her walking down the street in Washington the previous Sunday afternoon; the time difference between the UK and USA when he thought he saw her was the time she died, or was "passing over." He described what she had been wearing – it was a cream suit she owned – but my brother had not seen her for nearly ten years and would not have known she had bought that outfit.[6]

When we see a person that we actually know to be dead, we expect to be frightened: we are, after all, actually seeing a ghost.

And yet a remarkable aspect of these end-of-life visitations is that they're described as joyful, comforting and reassuring. Over and over again the Fenwicks were told – even by those who had no previous belief in an afterlife – they felt certain that their friend or relative was finding a way of saying a final Goodbye and in doing so, reassuring them that death is nothing fearful and not in fact The End.

Here's one such comforting visitation:

My father died on 20 April 1989 in the United States, where he lived. I could not go to the funeral because I was nine months pregnant. My son was born on 17 May 1989. Three days later... I was in a private room in a hospital and my son was in his clear cot near my bedside; around 3am my father actually came into my room – I saw him fully. I even remember sitting up in bed, because I did not think he was real, but he was there in my room. I did not think at the time, "Oh, he is dead." He walked over to the cot and looked at my son and smiled. Then we smiled at one another and he nodded his head in approval and left. The next morning I remember his visit vividly. It was a wonderful experience.[7]

The other kind of ghostly visitation is that of deceased relatives appearing at the bedside of the dying. Once again, we might expect the terminally ill to point a trembling finger, drag the bedcovers over their heads and shout the nurse to fetch a bedpan. Quick. But no: they report feeling reassured. Over and over again they hold out their arms and welcome their apparitions and even sit up in bed and reach forward as though hoping to be led away. On some occasions these presences are seen by others in the room – especially children – and include relatives whose death had been kept quiet by well-meaning family members.

Such a case was recorded by Sir William Barrett, a physics

professor at the Royal College of Science in Dublin in the nineteen twenties when his wife, Lady Barrett, an obstetrician, had been called into the operating room to deliver the child of a woman named Doris, dying from a hemorrhage:

Suddenly she looked eagerly towards part of the room, a radiant smile illuminating her whole countenance. "Oh, lovely, lovely," she said. When asked what it was she saw, she replied, "Lovely brightness, wonderful beings." A moment later she exclaimed: "Why, it's Father! Oh, he's so glad I'm coming; he is so glad..."

... and then she added, looking rather puzzled. "He has Vida with him, Vida is with him." [8]

Vida was her sister who had died three weeks earlier but, because of her delicate condition, Doris had not been informed. The incident intrigued Sir William to investigate further and collect similar accounts which he published in 1926 in his book, Deathbed Visions.[8]

So, these are not scary ghosts. When I sat at my mother's bedside, holding her dying hand, she spoke to someone she recognized as though they'd just walked in behind me. She appeared to be greeting an unexpected friend or relative but with no sign of fear. The same was true of Vic, the father of Karl, my ex-partner. For the best part of a year, I visited my next-door neighbor Frank, hospitalized after a heart attack. I worked hard to make his tumbledown house fit for carers to come and look after him; but just as it became ready, the nurse told me that Frank had been talking to his mother and father as though they were there beside him in the room. I suspected with a weighty heart that this meant his days were numbered. He died a week later without returning home.

I am a natural skeptic and realize that the main reason for my attitude towards these end-of-life-events is that they tie in with my own experience. Without this, my response might be much more cynical. And this is the same for us all. We may talk about belief in science or religious faith but at the end of the day, nothing compares with the belief we have in what we've seen with our own eyes.

This fact was illustrated in the debate described earlier between Rupert Sheldrake and Lewis Wolpert at the Royal Society in London. Sheldrake had shown the audience his film of the New York pretty polyphonic parrot describing symbols on the cards his owner was reading in a different room. I'm well aware of how clips of any performing animal bring an audience to life. Most of us enjoy watching animals, especially those doing tricks. But at the end of the debate, Wolpert remained completely unconvinced; his views hadn't changed an iota. And Sheldrake mentioned that while the film was being shown, Wolpert actually looked away – a perfect example of David Bohm's comments that scientists often close their minds to information which might threaten their established ways of thinking:

> ...every time the mind tries to focus on its contradictions, it "jumps" to something else. It simply won't stay with the point... it becomes dead, dull or anaesthetised.[9]

Towards the end of the debate, Wolpert compared belief in telepathy with belief in God:

> **Wolpert:** ...I often think about this in relation to God, if I may be blunt. The odd miracle now and then would help a great deal...
> **Question from the Floor:** A question for Professor Wolpert... I wonder if you'd like to comment on what your thoughts are from what I read - and I'm not sure if this is right - that you were not, in any way, persuaded by depression, until you actually suffered from it yourself. I'm just wondering if you

have an open mind now about depression. You may well...
Professor Lewis Wolpert: Thank you ... I certainly do not
have an open mind. Open minds are very bad ... everything
falls out! So, I don't have an open mind. It may be a stupid
cliché, but on the other hand, too much openness gets you
absolutely nowhere. I mean, I don't have to believe in fairies
and angels and all the nonsense other people ... or astrology
or telepathy. In relation to depression, I said I didn't
understand depression. It's not that I didn't believe in it. I
knew that people got depressed. My own father got very
depressed, but I didn't understand what it was about. Yes, I
think if I actually experienced repeatedly, a telepathic
experience where somebody could actually transmit to me,
something really extraordinary, I would have to rethink my
position, yes, certainly...[10]

Most of us would sympathise. In order to believe in telepathy or
the existence of God, Wolpert says he needs personal experience.
In his own words: *The odd miracle now and then would be a great
help...*

But this is not what we expect from scientists. When
experiments show that quantum particles fired through a slit can
turn into waves – or not – it's a fact that takes some believing. But
scientists don't keep on saying year after year: *Sounds like a load of
humbug; I'll believe that when I see it for myself!* They accept that
none of us can experience everything in the world and every now
and then we have to learn from the experience of others. OK, so
they're more likely to believe the evidence of other scientists
who've published their results in peer-assessed journals, because
that's how ideas in science develop. But for ideas to develop,
people first have to consider that there's something worth
investigating.

Research on human perception has demonstrated that we
often act as though we're completely blind to the unexpected.

Studies by DJ Simons from Harvard University show 46% of observers failing to register a larger-than-life gorilla appearing for several seconds in the midst of a basketball game: when observers are preoccupied with other tasks, they tend to see what they expect to see - a prospect in which a gorilla has no place. [11]

I'm reminded of a story about Captain Cooke and his explorations in the South Pacific. The story goes that those South Pacific Islanders had no concept and therefore no expectations of tall ships appearing over the horizon and therefore, for them, these tall ships did not exist. We might assume that their ability to see something depended on other members of their tightly-knit community being able to see it too and having a word or concept to describe it. The story may be apocryphal, for how can anyone know what the islanders saw and what they didn't?

But I fear that like the South-Sea Islanders, scientists are also part of a tightly-knit community, relying on peer endorsement to give them courage to speak out. In a similar way, Peter Fenwick describes the scientists who ridiculed Benjamin Franklin's invention of the lightning conductor and those who laughed at Stevenson's plans to run a locomotive on the Liverpool-Manchester railway. He quotes from A.R. Wallace, one of the leading evolutionary thinkers of the nineteenth century:

The first great lesson in the enquiry into these obscure fields of knowledge (is) never to accept the disbelief of great men or their accusations of imposture or of imbecility as of any weight when opposed to the repeated observation of facts by other men, admittedly sane and honest.[12]

Chapter 17

Conclusion

"Fan her head!" the Red Queen anxiously interrupted.
"She'll be feverish after so much thinking."
Alice through the Looking Glass, Chapter Nine.

When I began this book I called it Groping in the Dark. That's what I thought I was doing, fumbling my way down a rabbit hole, exploring the unknown.

I expected a labyrinth. I expected to wander round a maze and when I reached the chapter called Conclusion, come crawling out again. I expected to be a bit wiser. But I didn't, in all honesty, expect the rabbit hole to lead anywhere. I wasn't expecting to come up with anything new, and when the Groundmut theory leaped out at me like a white rabbit out of a Mad Hatter's top hat, you could have knocked me down with a feather duster.

There's not enough space in one book to do this theory justice. I've described, for instance, doorways into DreamTime but there are plenty more such portals waiting to be explored. Countless authors have described the spiritual benefits of taking mind-altering drugs. I did consider this, purely you understand, in the interests of academic research. However, I know how easily I'm distracted and, had I taken such a path, fear the page you're looking at now would be an empty piece of paper. Or an illustration of a magic mushroom and a pixie with an illegal grin on its face sitting cross-legged on the top.

So, this is far from a comprehensive illustration on the lid of the box of your jigsaw; it's not the Eiffel Tower. But it's a suggestion worth pursuing by those who have the resources. For the first time in our history, we do actually have the wherewithal to investigate the unexplained: international co-operation is available with a few clicks of a mouse; computer technology means that working out probability curves is also just as simple. Some would question whether we have the cash but somehow or other we find billions to spend on research into cosmetic surgery and for the development of military hardware.

And funding bodies will only spend money on projects if we tell them that this is what we want.

So, why don't we? Why is there such a taboo? Why such a veil of secrecy spread across everything connected with The Effect?

Those who've experienced these phenomena describe them as the most important events of their lives; they don't want to hear them ridiculed. Yet once such people have the courage to speak out in public, the floodgates open. Priestley almost sank up to his neck in accounts of precognitive dreams and when Peter and Elizabeth Fenwick talked about their research on the Richard and Judy TV show, they were inundated with emails from viewers, many bemoaning that they'd never before felt able to share their experience for fear of what others might think. A quote from one of their respondents, Ali:

> I have not been able to talk about what happened, or rather what I witnessed, on the night my great-aunt, Odette, passed away... I wanted to talk and talk about it, but not many people in my world are prepared or willing to listen... One particular response I received from a family member was, "That's not right, that doesn't happen"... to completely deny my "experience" I found very hard to accept.[1]

Once I knew this book was going somewhere, once I felt convinced that my Groundmuts had legs, I overcame my reluctance to respond to the question: *What are you writing about?* and began to discuss The Effect - often with total strangers. It didn't take long to realize that many of those I spoke to – especially those who'd known bereavement – also had their stories.

You might cynically imagine that these people were attention-seeking or eager to impress but if so, you'd be wrong; our conversations frequently followed the same path: I'd be rabbitting away, chatting about my research; they'd ask a few questions, then go quiet. They'd look away pensively. They'd appear about to speak then change their minds. They'd wait for a pause in my chatter-boxing before offering very quietly, *Actually, a strange thing happened to me once...*

And I would always have to prompt them: *Are you going to tell me about it?* Or some such. They would need coaxing before disclosing any more.

They'd begin their story. Hesitantly. Their voice would have a different texture; this is important. They would look away from me – that's important as well – because they would be seeing someone else in their mind and hearing someone else and would relay the conversation exactly as it happened because, generally speaking, they would finish by saying that they had never spoken to anyone else about the incident before. The other important factor is that, whilst telling me – man, woman, young or old – they would always have tears in their eyes. As I mentioned before, The Effect, is accompanied by changes in our demeanor. Maybe you can sense this just by reading. These people were not showing off, nor wanting to impress but sharing something precious. I've not included any of their stories because they were offered in confidence. I have however invited Liz to tell this story about her daughter, Hayley. I've known Liz for eighteen years and she has the same surname as me through having the good judgment and taste to marry my ex-husband

Hayley was rushed into Chesterfield Royal Hospital with a suspected acute neurological disorder, was there thirty-six hours and even after a brain scan was still undiagnosed. The results of the scan were sent to Sheffield Hallamshire Hospital who immediately diagnosed a burst brain abscess and directed that Hayley be sent immediately there for an emergency operation. Hayley was unconscious at this stage but seemed to respond only to me. They warned me that they didn't think she would make it. I wasn't allowed to go in the emergency ambulance with her because of all of the equipment needed so I had to drive there on my own quickly to be able to meet her there.

It was on this journey that, amid copious tears, I remember hitting the steering wheel with my palms and saying aloud: 'No. I cannot live without her. Listen to me. I cannot live without her. She can't die, she's got so much to live for.'...And I guess this became a rant throughout the journey as I felt desperate and cross. I realized later that I was talking to whatever higher power there is and, in particular, to my mother's "God" She was extremely high church and when her first husband had cancer she told me that, before he'd died, 'God' had asked her one day if she could cope on her own and she'd reluctantly said she could if she had to... I clearly wasn't intending to be so compliant.

Once Hayley was home and recovering all her faculties, (She had lost her speech initially, 25% of her skull, her short term memory and usage of her left side at this point) she started to say something about what she'd thought she'd heard during the period when she was unconscious but then stopped herself because she felt silly. I asked her to continue and she went on to say that she remembered feeling very tired, so sick of fighting and of the intense pain that she just wanted to give in and let it all go away... But she became aware of me being a bit cross, hitting something and telling her that I couldn't manage without her and so she'd tried to carry on.

You can imagine when Hayley knew about the car incident it all fell into place.[2]

John Dunne, writing in 1938, describes people's disillusionment at a loss of belief in an afterlife. He talks about: *a more evil undercurrent, a definitely malicious contempt for all human life.* He goes on to say that Man:

> ...is sensible enough to realize that a life which is to be poisoned at every instant by the knowledge that it is a mere scurrying to extinction is a life which cannot be worth anyone's preserving. He is consistent enough to perceive that the termination of all human existence in a general holocaust would be a happening of no great moment. As for the notion that such a catastrophe might spell disappointment to some selfish deity – that strikes him as nonsense which, if it were true, would be a matter for hilarity rather than for lamentation.[3]

I find these words, written just before the outbreak of the second world war and the greatest holocaust in human history, most poignant. But was the Holocaust really kindled by people's lack of belief in an afterlife? Were we really more likely to commit genocide in this and subsequent wars because we no longer believed that acts of murder would jeopardize our immortal souls? Much of the blame for war has been laid at the door of religion yet during our secular century, we've seen two world wars, an unspeakable holocaust, the deliberate bombing of civilians in Guernica; Dresden, Hiroshima and Nagasaki, the killing fields of Cambodia, genocide committed by Stalin, Mao's Great Famine, genocide in Rwanda, ethnic cleansing and further genocide in Bosnia... just to name but a few.

What Dunne envisaged with his theory of serial time was a way of reclaiming life's value. He was proposing what he called, "a new immortality," redeeming the concept of eternal life for atheists and agnostics: we no longer needed religion to provide us with eternity, he claimed; we could live our lives again and again but each time seeing further and understanding more.

A similar voice was that of Victor Frankl.

During his incarceration in Auschwitz, Frankl realized that the most important factor keeping prisoners alive was whether or not they had anything to live for. Those who lived were those who were loved, who had wives and children or parents still alive. Or thought they did. Likewise, those with strong religious faith or who had a sense of vocation. Time and time again, those who lived were those who, like Frankl himself, were able to see themselves fulfilled sometime in the future. As he quotes from Nietzsche: "He who has a *why* to live for can bear almost any *how*."

As a doctor, Frankl helped his fellow prisoners survive the worst horrors of the camp, but after his release, as a practising psychotherapist, he found his patients had enough food, they had warm and comfortable homes, they had employment... and yet many suffered from depression and anxiety, many suffered minor ailments with no apparent cause; many harbored thoughts of suicide; many complained of what he called "Sunday neurosis", coping as the hectic week rushed by, but then overcome with anxiety when they finally woke to a long and empty day.

All this was due, Frankl deduced, to what he called "an existential vacuum" – a life devoid of meaning. People were disillusioned with politics and religion. Although they pursued other quests – earning more money or making their homes more comfortable – they seemed to be papering over what they feared at their hearts to be an aching void. As Frankl says: *Not a few cases of suicide can be traced back to this... Such widespread phenomena as depression, aggression and addiction are not understandable unless we recognize the existential vacuum underlying them.*[4]

At the start of Groundhog Day, Phil Conners is just such a miserable, complaining character, pouring scorn on the inhabitants of Punxsutawney and their simple pleasures. As Phil says to a fellow drinker in the bar:

Phil: What would you do if you were stuck in one place and every day was exactly the same and nothing that you did mattered..?
Fellow drinker: Sums it up for me.[5]

The advice Victor Frankl gave to his patients was this:

Live as if you were living already for the second time and as if you had acted the first time as wrongly as you are about to act now![6]

A bit of a mouthful for a maxim: a bit too long to write across your T-shirt or have printed on your favorite mug. But it's also the advice from Dr Görtler, who told his fellow residents in their hotel on the Yorkshire moors: *You can return to the old, dark circle of existence, dying endless deaths or you can break the spell and swing out into new life...*[7]

When I've suggested that Dreamtime is where we come from and where our souls return, most people have to take this simply on trust. For those surviving the trauma of near-death experience however, their attitude towards what happens when we die is totally transformed.

In studies carried out by Elizabeth and Peter Fenwick, 72% of the 350 people sampled felt changed by their experience. These changes included becoming more spiritual, a "better person" or more socially conscious but by far the most common change was their attitude towards death. Over and over again, people expressed their conviction that death no longer held any fear. As one such Afterbirder reported:

I have never really feared death since. It opens up marvelous possibilities! If this life were all we had, I should think it most illogical and rather a poor deal for many. As it is, my experience suggests there may be something much more meaningful hereafter. I hope so.[8]

The notion that part of us lives on after death has been present in almost every other known society. As Peter and Elizabeth Fenwick explain:

These beliefs appear in some form or another in virtually every culture throughout recorded history, and there are indications that even in prehistory the dead may have been buried with some sense of expectation. Indeed, so universal is the assumption that something **does** happen next that the reductionist scientific culture of the West is almost alone in its unshakable belief in the finality of death.[9]

In most other cultures there's an assumption that who we are as individuals extends further than the limits of our body. Just as was common in western culture in the past, people talk about the concept of a Soul. This, like Bohm's implicate order, is what is assumed to connect us invisibly to one another and also to whatever exists Out There. Faust sold his soul for the secrets of alchemy and so he could make love to the most beautiful woman in the world; Robert Johnson sold his at the crossroads so he could play the world's meanest finger-picking guitar. But in our contemporary western society it seems we've taken ours to the pawnshop and forgotten to pick up the ticket; or allowed someone to sneak into our rooms at night and scarper off with ours, leaving in its place nothing more than Dunne's "execution chamber" together with Frankl's nationwide stress and depression.

However, there are moments when an amputee may feel an occasional twitching from a limb that isn't there. A man without legs can watch someone dance and find his lacking limbs stepping out to join them. It's called a Phantom Limb. And it's my heartfelt belief that, although scientists, academics and intellectuals might insist till the cows come home that our souls no longer exist, we still sometimes feel them twitching. We sense them twitch when we fall in love and feel overwhelmed by a power greater than ourselves; we feel them tremble when we hold our child for the very first time, or when we're completely knocked out by beauty – mountains, oceans or the sight of our favourite footballer banana-ing the ball. Our souls tap their feet in unison as we play our favorite music and stop dead in their tracks when we hear that someone's died.

Our souls may be gathering dust in some Lost-and-Found somewhere; they may be seated on a high shelf in the pawn shop waiting for us to fumble through our pockets for the missing ticket. But I am convinced that these ethereal bits of us are indestructible. I am well aware that the conclusion of this book is hardly the place for me to start describing how we might reclaim our souls, begin to nurture them and lead a more spiritual life, but if I do have chance to write another book, then this will be its theme. I will call it *Feeling the Effect.*

Scientists, as mentioned before, shy away from mention of a soul because of its associations with religion, the assumption being in our secular times that religion and science don't mix.

This phenomenon is relatively new. Plato was a religious man who also understood science; so was Charles Darwin. Most of the world's great scientists have seen their role as illuminating the wonders of God, rather than denying His existence.

Priestley would not have called himself religious but an experience which changed his life was a vision of what he called "the stream of life", described in *Rain upon Godshill*. a collection of autobiographical essays published in 1938.

I dreamt I was standing at the top of a very high tower, alone, looking down upon myriads of birds all flying in one direction; every kind of bird was there, all the birds in the world. It was a noble sight, this vast aerial river of birds. But now in some mysterious fashion the gear was changed, and time speeded up, so that I saw generations of birds, watched them break their shells, flutter into life, weaken, falter, and die. Wings grew only to crumble; bodies were sleek and then, in a flash, bled and shriveled; and death struck everywhere at every second. What was the use of all this blind struggle towards life, this eager trying of wings, all this gigantic meaningless biological effort? As I stared down, seeming to see every creature's ignoble little history almost at a glance, I felt sick at heart. It would be better if not one of them, not one of us all, had been born, if the struggle ceased for ever. I stood on my tower alone, desperately unhappy. But now the gear was changed again and time went faster still, and it was rushing by at such a rate, that the birds could not show any movement but were like an enormous plain sown with feathers. But along this plain, flickering through the bodies themselves, there now passed a sort of white flame, trembling, dancing, then hurrying on; and as soon as I saw it I knew that this flame was life itself, the very quintessence of being; and then it came to me, in a rocket-burst of ecstasy, that nothing mattered, nothing could ever matter, because nothing else was real but this quivering and hurrying lambency of being. Birds, men, or creatures not yet shaped and colored, all were of no account except so far as this flame of life travelled through them. It left nothing to mourn over behind it; what I had thought was tragedy was mere emptiness or a shadow show; for now all real feeling was caught and purified and danced on ecstatically with the white flame of life. I had never felt before such deep happiness as I knew at the end of my dream of the tower and the birds... [10]

This sense of ecstasy is similar to that described in much near-death experience in that it has no rational explanation. Why should a vision of millions of dead birds produce a sense of ecstasy? Yet this feeling of intense bliss is characteristic of a doorway opening into DreamTime; and of course, the notion of "following your bliss" is an important part of the Buddhist pathway to Enlightenment.

What Priestley discovered in his vision was the ability to *pull back* and see from a wider perspective. The death of a bird is a sad event and to think of the number of birds dying in the whole world is distressing. But to pull back several stages and see instead, a feathered plain, with life dancing through, is not just a beautiful diorama, but a field of hope and glory similar to Jung's description of looking down from a mountain summit; it resonates with Frankl's vision of himself speaking in a warm and comfortable lecture hall at a time when the horrors of the concentration camp were reduced into memory. And it has similarities with the vista of the Snake Pass from the plane coming in to land in Manchester.

If Priestley had lived more recently, he would have become familiar with Chaos Theory, the Butterfly Effect and fractal geometry. Scientists have found, for instance, that the behavior of a large crowd of people (such as those leaving a stadium) has a strong resemblance to a shoal of fish or a flock of birds; people are only conscious of themselves; they don't see the whole pattern, but if they could, they would see themselves actually moving together as though they were one unit. Many of these patterns are only visible through a wide-lens camera or through computer simulations. When examined in close-up, there is no pattern, just random chaos and disorder; it's only when we zoom out and see the larger picture that the motifs begin to surface.

Darwin envisaged a similar pattern. When we observe a few generations of any living organism, there's no hint of it changing and adapting; however, if we pull back and take a long-term view over thousands of generations, a pattern starts to emerge. We see this most clearly in organisms with a very short reproductive cycle. Some of my research students have been observing the speed with which bacteria become immune to antibiotics. The students leave a few bacteria in dishes in the lab and when they return next morning, find millions. A dose of antibiotics appears to wipe them out, but always there are rare mutants who, through some stroke of resilience, cling on to life. They may be only one in a million, but it takes no time at all for them to grow and reproduce, passing their unique defense system on to future generations.

Darwin had this ability to pull back and see this pattern. What he saw, like Priestley's vision, was the whole of creation reaching upwards and outwards – he saw creatures stagger from the sea, first-footing their faltering steps upon dry land; he saw land-bound creatures struggling to fly, lifting their feet and fluttering with all the restlessness of zugunruhe. He saw the whole diorama of the deaths of millions and millions of creatures, but also witnessed the flame of life, flickering through, quickening and lambent. He saw life's longing for itself and called it Evolution.

Priestly regarded his Godshill vision as an illustration of serial time. We may mourn the death of each single creature but recognize that this upward-and-outward movement, this sense of coming-back-better-next-time can only take place because our timespan is so short. Death is not a failure but a reaching out, a step up. A time when we're able to see, as my dear Friend, David Brayshaw described in such lapidary words, the great river of life from which, as individual drops we have become separated, but to which we will return.

For me, this reaching outward and upward is what I understand as living the spiritual life; if pushed, I'd describe it as God. I see evolution as one of the many facets of God and certainly not a demonstration that no god exists.

There are many traditionalists who wouldn't want to water

down divinity with concepts such as creativity, goddesses, Groundhog Days, evolution, DreamTime and multiple-universe theory. My personal concept of the divine includes everything that has us reaching above and beyond ourselves: synchronicity and string theory, DreamTime and dark matter, Groundhog Days, Gardens of Forking Paths, entanglement and evolution. All of this involves living with what Priestley calls "will and imagi- nation" and having the courage to think about what happens when we die. As Priestley expresses The Effect:

To die is not to close our eyes when we come to the end of our Time One: it is to choose to live in too few dimensions. [11]

There is another important aspect of Groundmut theory which I've been afraid to mention for fear of sounding facile, but here goes:.

My own experience has convinced me of the personal power of prayer. I believe it has on occasion been possible for me to change the course of events by what Dr Görtler called, *Feeling, imagination and will.* By what I've come to call "accessing the control centre." Many of you will have experienced similar life- changing, transcendental moments. Some of you - and my heart goes out to you if you're still reading this regardless - will have seen my words blur into a blood-red soup of rage. *Not that old garbage.* You will have felt this most especially if you have tried the so-called power of prayer in your darkest hour and found it simply hasn't worked.

You may also want to point out that this so-called power hasn't worked for plenty of other people too. It might have failed someone you know. And for one of the most demonstrable examples of this failure, we have only to look to those tragic families herded on to the trains that would deliver them to the most diabolical places of incarceration ever devised. Were most of them not righteous, godly people? Wouldn't they all have offered - not just a casual, flick-of-the-wrist *well, wouldn't it be more convenient if...* but would have prayed earnestly every hour and minute of their journey into hell. Were there not priests and rabbis in their midst who would have led them? And would those with children not have prayed that, at the very least, if they were not to survive, then the lives of the children might be spared?

The last thing I want to do is in any way belittle such terrible suffering. The last thing I want is to offer trite and facile solutions to the greatest dilemma faced by human existence and especially by anyone of faith.

However...

Yesterday evening I attended a lecture at Sheffield Showroom organised by Café Scientifique. The first thing the speaker, Dr Tony Padilla from Nottingham University, said was:

What is Heaven and what is Hell but examples of parallel worlds...?

If there really is a world in which Schrödinger's cat, with his life hanging in the balance of a decaying phial of poison, can wake from his long and peaceful sleep and live on, then there has to be another world in which the box is opened and he lies motionless inside. If Multiple Universe Theory has any real implication, this is it: when there is an actual choice to be made then the results of our decisions stand together side by side, whether that is as simple as the two sides of a flipped coin or as daunting as a state of Heaven and a state of Hell.

And if this is the case, then when someone cries for help for themselves or for those they hold most dear, there is a universe which wraps its arms around them and carries them to safety.

We do not always live inside that universe.

We also have to live with the decayed phial, the motionless cat and a world in which we are all too aware of the depths to which we can be driven by our fear. And people who have suffered have suffered just as much and nothing we can say or do will make that any easier.

In conclusion I simply want to highlight the need to devote more time and resources to exploring the concepts covered in this book. The days of Dunne lounging in his armchair in his gentleman's club in Mayfair, drowsily dreaming up experiments to explain why Time, as he described it, "got mixed up" are dead and gone. Research projects are dreamed up by gigantic corporations and by government departments and they cost millions. They don't ask questions about what's happened to the human soul or about what happens when we die. But on the other hand, we never tell them that is what we want to know.

Our neglect of this is a crying shame. What is the international cost of dealing with the effects of Frankl's "existential vacuum"? How many millions do we spend worldwide on antidepressants? How much on the results of alcohol and drug abuse and other measures of slow suicide? How many work hours do we lose through depression and through stress?

My other major conclusion is that we can learn from those who are dying. Over and over again they have tried to share with us their realization that there is more to life than this dark cave in which we sit and name the shadows. When it's time to leave the cave, they report seeing a light - no ordinary back-door to the rabbit hole but a light that is all-encompassing, loving, enfolding, beautiful and compassionate. They speak of it as though it is alive.

It seems important to remember that we have not been born to sit and name the shadows. We have been put here to look after the place, do what we can for each other and explore. Searching for the light is one of the ways that we explore.

All of us can seek the light. We do it when we see ourselves standing on a hilltop gazing back at our journey; we do it when we fall in love; we do it when we sink ourselves in silence; we do it when we share the last few moments of the life of somebody we love. We don't need to be shown the way because, like other living things, we have a homing device to guide us.

We call it The Effect.

Bibliography

Adams D: Hitchhikers guide to the galaxy: Pan Books: London 1979. Adapted from series first broadcast on BBC radio.

Almond D: The savage: Walker books, 2008

Appleyard B: How to live forever or die trying: Simon & Schuster 2007

Atwater PMH: I died three times: Starving Artists Workshop 1998 p.22

AtwaterPMH: , Vital Signs, June 1981[1]

Bailey, Lee W. & Yates, Jenny: The Near-Death Experience: A Reader: Routledge, 1996

Barrett, Sir William: Deathbed visions: Rider and Co, 1926

Beardsworth T: A Sense of Presence: Religious Experience Research Unit, Oxford 1977

Birkhead T: The wisdom of birds: Bloomsbury 2008

Bohm D: Wholeness and the implicate order: Routledge: London 1980

Bohm, D. On Creativity, Routledge: 1996

Borges JL 1899-1986 Collected fictions; translated by Andrew Hurley:London: Allen Lane, 1999

Borges J L:Collected Fictions, Penguin 1999., translated by Maria Kodama

Brottman M: Hollywood Hex, Creation Books, 1999.

Brottman M: Phantoms of the Clinic: From Thought-Transference to Projective Identification London: Karnac Books, 2011.

Burnell J B: Broken for Life: Swarthmoor Lecture, pub by Quaker Home Service, 1989

Cameron J: The Artists Way: Penguin 2002

Davies PCW & Brown J: Superstrings: Cambridge University Press,, 1988

Dick PK VALIS: Gollanz 1981

Dunne JW: Experiment with time, Faber: 1927

Dunne, JW. The New Immortality, Faber & Faber, 1938

Dunne JW, Intrusions: Faber, 1955

Edney R, Lesmoir-Gordon N & Rood Introducing Fractal Geometry: Icon Books 2006

W: Elkin AP: The Australian Aborigines:Angus & Robertson Sydney, 1974.

Emerson RW: Complete Essays & Other Writings: Random House NY 1940

Fenwick E & Fenwick P: The Truth in the Light: Headline, 1995

Fenwick P & E: The art of dying: Continuum 2008: p. 160

Frankl V. Man's search for meaning, Beacon Press, 1959

Fox M & Sheldrake R: Natural grace: Bloomsbury 1996

Gregory C: Native Science: Natural laws of interdependence Clear Light Publishers Santa Fe, New Mexico 2000

Gribbin J: In search of Schrodingers Cat: Corgi Books 1984

Gribbin J & M: The science of Philip Pullman's His Dark Materials: Hodder 2003

Grof and Halifax, The human encounter with death NY, 1977

Gurney E, Myers F W & Podmore F: Phantasms of the living, Adamant Media Corporation: Elibron Classics 2007 (facsimile of Trubner & Co, London 1886)

Gleick J: Chaos: Vintage 1998

Halpern P & Wesson P: Brave new universe: Joseph Henry Press, Washington DC 2006

Hawking S & Penrose R: The nature of space and time: Princeton University Press 1996

Hawking S: The universe in a nutshell: Bantam Spectra 2001

Jeans J. The mysterious universe: Harmondsworth: Penguin: 1937

Jung CG: Synchronicity: an acausal connecting principle (Volume 8); Bollingen Foundation, New York NY trans Hull RFC: 1960

Jung CG: Memories, dreams, reflections, Collins and Routledge & Kegan Paul:1961

Jones R: The luminous trail, 1947

Kaku M: Hyperspace: OUP 1994

Kaku M & Trainer J: Beyond Einstein: Bantam Books, 1987.

Kübler-Ross E: On life after death: 2008, Celestial Arts, Berkely California.

Kübler-Ross E: Death the final stage of growth Spectrum, Prentice-Hall Inc New Jersey 1975

Lockwood M: The labyrinth of time, OUP, 2005

Maury A. Sleep and dreams: Paris: Didier:1865

McTaggart L: The field: Harper Collins 2001

McTaggart L: The intention experiment, Harper Collins 2007

Meier CA: Atom and archetype: Letters of Pauli and Jung: Princeton University Press, New Jersey, 2001.

Melville H: Moby Dick: Bentley London 1851

Noyes R Jr & Kletti R Notizen über den Tod durch Absturz tr in The experience of dying from falls: Farmingdale, NY, 1980.

Osis and Haroldsson, At the hour of death, Hastingshouse/ Daytrips Publications: NY 1977.

Ouellette J: Black bodies & quantum cats: Penguin USA 2005

Ouspensky PD: A new model of the universe: Knopf NY1931

Ouspensky PD: The fourth way: Knopf NY 1957

Panati C: Supersenses: Jonathan Cape 1974.

Parnis S: What happens when we die: Hay House 2005

Peake A: Is there life after death? Chartwell Books, 2006.

Peake A: The daemon Arcturus London 2008

Pfister O: Shock thoughts and fantasies in extreme mortal danger, 1981,

Peat D: Blackfoot physics Fourth Estate Ltd. London: 1995

Plato: The Republic

Priestley J.B: I Have been here before, 1937, The Plays of J.B. Priestley, volumes 1-3, 1948-59, William Heinemann Ltd.

Priestley JB: Man and time: Aldous Books Ltd 1964

Pullman P: His dark materials: Scholastic 1995

De Quincy T: Confessions of an English opium eater, Macmillan,

1956

Radin D: The conscious universe HarperOne NY 1997

Roach M: Spook, W.W. Norton & Company, 2006

Ring, Kenneth and Cooper, Sharon: Mindsight: Center for Consciousness Studies, Institute of Transpersonal Psychology, Palo Alto: 1999

Sabom M B. Recollections of death: A medical investigation, Harper Collins: New York, 1982

Sabom MB: Light and death: Zondervan 1998

Samanta-Laughton M: Punk science: O Books 2006

Sheldrake R: The Presence of the past: morphic resonance and the habits of nature, Collins, 1988

Talbot M: Mysticism and the new physics, Routledge & Kegen Paul 1981

Talbot M: The holographic universe, Grafton Books 1991

Tiller W: Conscious acts of creation – the emergence of a new physics: Quality books inc

Robert Herhold, "Kubler-Ross and Life after Death: Against Raising Hope of Raising the Dead: Contra Moody and Kübler-Ross, p.65 Lancet 2001; 358: 2039-45

, Lommel. [2]

"Notizen über den Tod durch Absturz tr Russell Noyes, Jr & Roy Kletti in, "The Experience of Dying from Falls." Farmingdale, NY, 1980.

Schoken und Shockphantasien bei höchster Todesgefahr, tr Roy Kletti and Russell Noyes Jr in "Mental States in Mortal Danger,

R.C.A.Hunter, American Journal of Psychiatry, 1967

Oldfield C & J: Landscapes of Andalucia and the Costa del Sol: Sunflower books: London 1999

Scot R: The Discoverie of Witchcraft facsimile of 1584 edition: London: Elliot Stock, 1886.

Sheldrake R: Dogs that know that their owners are coming home: Random House: 1999

Sheldrake R: The presence of the past: London : Collins, 1988

Sturrock J Paper tigers : the ideal fictions of Jorge Luis Borges: Oxford: Clarendon Press 1977

Thoreau H D: Walden: Life in the Woods: 1854

Wallace A R: On miracles and modern spiritualism, 1874

Whitrow GJ: The Nature of Time: Thames & Hudson, 1972

Wyschogrod E ed: The Phenomenon of Death: NY Harper & Row Inc 1973

Zaleski C: Otherworld Journeys: Accounts of near-death experience in Medieval and modern times, Oxford University Press, 1987

References

Chapter 1

1. Luke 4: King James Bible
2. Batt M: Bright Eyes 1978
3. Cha KY, Wirth DP, Lobio RA Does Prayer Influence the Success of in-vitrio fertilisation-embryo-transfer? *J. Reprod Med* September 2001
4. Lorenz E: Meeting of the American Association for the Advancement of Science in Washington, D.C.: Predictability: does the flap of a butterfly's wings in Brazil set off a tornado in Texas? 1972
5. Plato: The Republic, Book V11 516b-c; trans. Paul Shorey

Chapter 2

1. Jung CG: Synchronicity: *An acausal connecting principle* (Volume 8); Bollingen Foundation, New York NY trans Hull RFC: 1960
2. Cameron J: The artists way: Penguin, 2002
3. Isiah 40: 31 King James Bible
4. Hawking S: The universe in a nutshell: Bantam Spectra 2001

Chapter 3

1. Cohen L: Anthem: The Future: Sony music inc Canada: 1992
2. Kübler-Ross E: On Death and Dying in The Phenomenon of Death: editor Wyschogrod E, NY Harper & Row Inc 1973
3. Loewi O: An autobiographic sketch, perspectives in biology and medicine: Vol IV:1 1960:17.
4. Michio K: Hyperspace, Oxford University Press, 1994

Chapter 4

1. Grosso M: The archetype of death and enlightenment in the near-death experience in Bailey Lee W, Yates J, editors: The

near-death experience: a reader: Routledge, 1996

2. Kubler-Ross, E. On life after death: Celestial Arts: 1991 p.5

3. Sabom, Recollections of Death: Harper Collins *p.83, 1982*

4. Sabom, Light and death: Zondervan: 1998

5. Fenwick, P & E, The truth in the light, Headline, 1995

6. Ibid

7. Atwater, PMH: Vital signs, June 1981 in Zaleski C: Otherworld journeys: OUP, 1987

8. Greyson & Bush: Distressing near-death experiences, in Near-death experience: a reader, Bailey & Yates, Routledge, 1996

9. Zaleski C: Otherworld journeys: OUP, 1987

10. Osis & Haroldsson, At the hour of death, Hastingshouse/ Daytrips Publications 1997 28-30

11. Kubler-Ross E: Foreword to Grof and Halifax, *The Human Encounter with Death, p.v11, NY, 1977*

12. Kubler-Ross E: On life after death: Celestial Arts: 1991, p.7

13. Ring K & Cooper S: Mindsight: William James Center for Consciousness Studies, Institute of Transpersonal Psychology, Palo Alto: 1999

14. Kubler-Ross E:On life after death: Celestial Arts: 1991, p.6

15. Ibid p.9

16. Fenwick, P & E, The truth in the light, Headline, 1995 p.117

17. Ibid p.115

18. Jung CG: Memories, dreams, reflections, Collins and Routledge & Kegan Paul, 1961, p.326

19. Fundacio Gala-Salvador Dali, Figueras, Catalonia

20. Museum of Religious Art, Glasgow, Scotland

21. Radin D: The conscious universe HarperOne NY 1997

22. Zaleski C: Otherworld journeys, OUP 1987, p. 177

23. Herhold RM: Kubler-Ross and life after death: one does not need Easter if the soul is immortal: Christian Century 93 1976(14):364-365

24. Vicchio, SJ. Against raising hope of raising the dead: contra

Moody and Kubler-Ross. Essence: 1979: 3(2):51-67

25. Van Lommel P: Lancet 2001; **358**: 2039-45

26 Fenwick P & E: The art of dying: Continuum 2008: p. 160

27 Noyes R Jr & Kletti R Notizen über den Tod durch Absturz tr in The experience of dying from falls: Farmingdale, NY, 1980.

28 Kletti R & Noyes R J Schoken und Shockphantasien bei höchster Todesgefahr, tr in Mental states in mortal danger: Issues in the study of ageing, dying and death: v5 n1 p5-20 1981

29 Hunter RCA American Journal of Psychiatry, 1967

30 Kubler-Ross E On life after death, Celestial Arts: 1991: p.2

Chapter 5

1. www.hep.shef.ac.uk/research/dm/**boulby**/info.php

2. Sample I: Has dark matter finally been detected? The Guardian: 13 Dec 2009

3   Elkin AP : The Australian Aborigines:Angus & Robertson Sydney, 1974.Also, see dreamhawk.com

Chapter 6

1. Graham Greene, letters to Catherine Walston, 30 September, 1947

2. Jung CG: Memories, dreams, reflections, Collins and Routledge & Kegan Paul, 1961, p.8

3. Amis M: The Guardian: Book Club: January 2010.

4. Almond D: The savage: Walker books, 2008

5. Keaney Brian: personal email

6. Brottman M: Hollywood hex, Creation Books, 1999.

7. Rooney A: personal email

8. Fox M & Sheldrake R: Natural grace: Bloomsbury 1996

9. Quaker meetings in Fuengirola: contact: zvi@gotadsl.co.uk

Chapter 7

1. Jung CG: Memories, dreams, reflections, Collins Routledge & Kegan Paul 1961 p.207
2. Lockwood M: The labyrinth of time: Oxford University Press: 2005 p.54
3. Jeans, Sir J. 1937: The Mysterious Universe: Harmondsworth: Penguin, p. 145
4. Priestley JB Man and time: Aldus Books Ltd 1964
5. Ibid: p.253
6. Ibid: p242
7. p.242
8. p.245
9. p.204

Chapter 8

1. Scot R: The Discoverie of Witchcraft facsimile of 1584 edition: London: Elliot Stock, 1886.
2. Jung CG , Memories, dreams, reflections, Collins Routledge & Kegan Paul 1961
3. Sheldrake, R. Royal Society of Arts, London, 15 Jan 2004
4. Priestley JB Man and time: Aldus books Ltd 1964 p.268
5. www.prestoncityparish.com
6. Dunne J: An Experiment with Time: London, Faber
7. Cohen L: Anthem
8. Dunne: Ibid
9. Priestley: Ibid
10. Scot R ibid

Chapter 9

1. Maury, A. Sleep and Dreams: Paris: Didier, 1865: p.133-4
2. Priestley JB Ibid: p.120
3. Kruska D: Effects of domestication on brain structure and behaviour in mammals, Human Evolution, volume 3, number 6, December 1988, p.473-485

4. Sheldrake, Royal Society lecture, 15 Jan 2004
5. Dunne: ibid
6. Dunne, An Experiment with Time, p.98
7. Ibid
8. ibid
9. Oldfield C & J: Landscapes of Andalucia and the Costa del Sol: Sunflower books: London 1999
10. Thoreau H D: Walden: Life in the Woods: 1854

Chapter 10
1. Peoc'h: R Psychokinetic Action of Young Chicks on the Path of An Illuminated Source: Journal of scientific exploration: 1995 Vol. 9, No. 2, pp. 223-229
2. Talbot M: The holographic universe, Harper Collins, 1996: p.124
3. Meier CA: Atom and Archetype: Letters of Pauli and Jung: 1932-58, Princeton University Press, New Jersey, 2001.
4. Talbot ibid p.149
5. Sheldrake R: Dogs that know that their owners are coming home: Random House: 1999:
6. Sheldrake, R. Royal Society of Arts, London, 15 Jan 2004
7. *Sheldrake R:* The presence of the past: morphic resonance and the habits of nature
8. Talbot M: The holographic universe, Harper Collins, 1996:
9. Bohm D: Wholeness and the implicate order: Routledge: London 1980
10. Little Bear, L: Foreword in Native Science: Natural Laws of Interdependence Gregory C: Clear Light Publishers Santa Fe, New Mexico 2000 pp 10-11
11. Close F Guardian 24 Sept 2011

Chapter Eleven
1. McTaggart L: The Intention Experiment, Harper Collins 2007
2. Jung CG , Memories, dreams, reflections, Collins Routledge

& Kegan Paul 1961, p.333-4
3. Jones R: The luminous trail, 1947, pp163-164
4. Brottman M: Phantoms of the Clinic: Karnac, London 2011 p.106
5. ibid p.113
6. Jung CG , Memories, dreams, reflections, Collins Routledge & Kegan Paul 1961
7. Priestley JB Man and time: Aldus books Ltd 1964 p.39
8. Birkhead T: The wisdom of birds: Bloomsbury 2008
9. Anon: *Trate du Rossignol (A Treatise on the Nightingale)* 1707 in Birkhead T ibid
10. Rumi: The Tavern
11. Priestley JB: I have been here before, 1937: first produced at the Royalty Theatre, London: 22 Sept 1937. The plays of JB Priestley: Heinemann Ltd 1948

Chapter Twelve
1. Adams D: Hitchhikers guide to the galaxy: Pan books: London 1979. Adapted from series first broadcast on BBC radio
2. Talbot M: Mysticism and the new physics
3. BBC4: Parallel Worlds; parallel lives: filmed and directed by Lockwood L: BBC Scotland, 20073
4. Borges: The Library of Babel: collected fictions, Penguin 1998.

Chapter Thirteen
1. Rubin D: Columbia pictures 1993
2. The Garden of Forking Paths, Borges, Collected Fictions, Emece Editores, Buenos Aires and Penguin, 1998 p.125
3. ibid
4. Dick P VALIS: Gollanz 1981p.210
5. Zaleski C Otherworld journeys, OUP, p.11
6. Priestley JB Man and time

7. Ecclesiastes, ch.1, verse 9, 15: King James Bible:

8. Faulkner, RO (ed) Ancient Egyptian Book of the Dead, p.29-31, British Museum, 1985

9. De Quincy T: Confessions of an English opium eater: Macdonald, 1956

10. Hulin, M, Sur La Chute En Montagne quoted in Peake A Is there life after death? Chartwell Books, 2006, P.341

11. Pfister O: Shock thoughts and fantasies in extreme mortal danger, 1981

12. Atwater PMH: I died three times: Starving Artists Workshop 1998 p.22

13. Priestley JB: Man and Time ibid

14. Priestley JB: I have been here before, 1937: first produced at the Royalty Theatre, London: 22 Sept 1937. The plays of JB Priestley: Heinemann Ltd 1948

15. Rhine LE: American Journal of Parapsychology:Psychic Powers: 17,18

16. Recollections of Abraham Lincoln, Lamon: Chicago, 1895

17. Cox W in Steiger B: ESP: Your Sixth Sense, Award Books, New York 1966

18. www.visitmalta.com

19. ibid

20. LorenzLorenz E: meeting of the American Association for the Advancement of Science in Washington, D.C.: Predictability: does the flap of a butterfly's wings in Brazil set off a tornado in Texas? 1972

21. Lockwood: The labyrinth of time, OUP 2005 p.373

22. Hameroff, Kaszniak & Scott (1998: 647) Time and Consciousness: Overview (1998b), 645-7 270

Chapter Fourteen

1. Priestley JB: Act 3: I have been here before, 1937: first produced at the Royalty Theatre, London: 22 Sept 1937. The plays of JB Priestley: Heinemann Ltd 1948

2. Bohm, D. On Creativity, Routledge, p.79
3. Frankl, V. Man's Search for Meaning, Beacon Press, 1959, p.95.
4. Frankl, V. Man's Search for Meaning, p 94-95
5. McTaggart L: The field
6. Ibid
7. David Bohm: On Creativity: p,26
8. Bohm, p.20
9. Isaacson, Walter, Einstein and Faith, Time Magazine, 2007
10. Conard NJ: Origins of the Female Image, Nature: 14 May, 2009.
11. Conard NJ: A female figurine from the basal Aurignacian of Hohle Fels Cave in southwestern Germany, Nature: 14 May, 2009
12. Oldfield C & J: Sunflower Books, 1999: Andalucia and the Costa del Sol, Walk 16: The Beehive Walk

Chapter Fifteen

1. Donne J: No manne is an Island
2. Dunne J: The new immortality, Faber & Faber: 1938.
3. Melville H: Moby Dick: Bentley London 1851

Chapter Sixteen

1. Fenwick P & E: The art of dying: "David": p.135, Continuum, 2008
2. Ibid p. 132
3. Ibid p.142
4. Ibid p.141-2
5. Gurney E, Myers F W & Podmore F: Phantasms of the Living, Adamant Media Corporation ([1886]2005) quoted in Fenwick & Fenwick 2008.
6. Ibid p. 122-3
7. Ibid:
8. Barrett, Sir William: Deathbed visions: Rider and Co, 1926

9. Bohm D On creativity ibid: p.26
10. Sheldrake R & Wolpert L: Royal Society of Arts, London 15 Jan 2004
11. Gorillas in our midst: sustained inattentional blindness for dynamic events: Perception, 1999, vol 28, pp 1059-1074 Simons D, Chabris C, Harvard University
12. Wallace A R: On miracles and modern spiritualism, 1874

Chapter Seventeen
1. Fenwick & Fenwick ibid P.159
2. Hoy Liz 2011
3. Dunne, The New Immortality, p.14
4. Frankl V. Man's Search for meaning, p.131-2
5. Groundhog Day; ibid
6. Frankl V, Man's search for meaning, p.175
7. Priestley JB: I have been here before
8. Fenwick & Fenwick ibid
9. Fenwick & Fenwick: The art of dying p.1-2
10. Priestley JB: Rain upon Godshill, Heinemann 1939
11. Priestly: Man and Time p.351-3

BOOKS

O is a symbol of the world, of oneness and unity. In different cultures it also means the "eye," symbolizing knowledge and insight. We aim to publish books that are accessible, constructive and that challenge accepted opinion, both that of academia and the "moral majority."

Our books are available in all good English language bookstores worldwide. If you don't see the book on the shelves ask the bookstore to order it for you, quoting the ISBN number and title. Alternatively you can order online (all major online retail sites carry our titles) or contact the distributor in the relevant country, listed on the copyright page.

See our website **www.o-books.net** for a full list of over 500 titles, growing by 100 a year.

And tune in to myspiritradio.com for our book review radio show, hosted by June-Elleni Laine, where you can listen to the authors discussing their books.

MySpiritRadio